Preserving the Saudi Monarchy

Samuel E. Willner

Preserving the Saudi Monarchy

Political Pragmatism in Saudi Arabia, c.1973–1979

Samuel E. Willner
University of Haifa
Haifa, Israel

ISBN 978-3-031-30005-9   ISBN 978-3-031-30006-6   (eBook)
https://doi.org/10.1007/978-3-031-30006-6

© The Editor(s) (if applicable) and The Author(s), under exclusive licence to Springer Nature Switzerland AG 2023

This work is subject to copyright. All rights are solely and exclusively licensed by the Publisher, whether the whole or part of the material is concerned, specifically the rights of translation, reprinting, reuse of illustrations, recitation, broadcasting, reproduction on microfilms or in any other physical way, and transmission or information storage and retrieval, electronic adaptation, computer software, or by similar or dissimilar methodology now known or hereafter developed.

The use of general descriptive names, registered names, trademarks, service marks, etc. in this publication does not imply, even in the absence of a specific statement, that such names are exempt from the relevant protective laws and regulations and therefore free for general use. The publisher, the authors, and the editors are safe to assume that the advice and information in this book are believed to be true and accurate at the date of publication. Neither the publisher nor the authors or the editors give a warranty, expressed or implied, with respect to the material contained herein or for any errors or omissions that may have been made. The publisher remains neutral with regard to jurisdictional claims in published maps and institutional affiliations.

This Palgrave Macmillan imprint is published by the registered company Springer Nature Switzerland AG.

The registered company address is: Gewerbestrasse 11, 6330 Cham, Switzerland

For attaining wisdom and discipline;
for understanding words of insight;
for acquiring a disciplined and prudent life,
doing what is right and just and fair;
for giving prudence to the simple,
knowledge and discretion to the young –
let the wise listen and add to their learning,
and let the discerning get guidance –
for understanding proverbs and parables, the sayings, and riddles of
the wise.
The fear of the Lord is the beginning of knowledge,
but fools despise wisdom and discipline.
Proverbs 1:2-7

To my dear friend and mentor
Ambassador Avi Granot

PREFACE

For nearly one hundred years of preserving their monarchy, the Saudi royals have followed the principles of tribal tradition in their everyday decision-making. Habitually, these decision-making processes are very secretive, and highly personal. For the most part, the Saudi monarchy prepares important foreign and domestic policy issues through unofficial and less formal mechanisms. While Saudi foreign policy is often driven by pragmatism, its primary objective is to serve the aim of preserving the Saudi monarchy.

Due to many socioeconomic and national security-related challenges that the Saudi kingdom will likely face soon, it is expected that its government will have to implement unprecedented policy adaptations. Therefore, understanding Saudi decision-making is more important today than perhaps ever before. However, due to the fundamental characteristics of the enigmatic Saudi communications, it is nearly impossible to gain access to its inner sanctum. Traditionally, those who have held positions near the key Saudi royals have not leaked sensitive information unless such information was purposefully leaked. For this reason, and based on the above-mentioned limitations, I have decided to focus on the period of 1973–1979.

By concentrating on an earlier period of Saudi history, I have been able to capture many previously unpublished and only recently declassified records about the secretive maneuvering of the Saudi monarchy, which are very relevant for an analyst, or an academic scholar, who is tasked to decipher Saudi communications, as well as for the political world and the media in general. Given the ocean of misinformation and disinformation that is readily available, the fact of the matter is quite often not as it first appears. In fact, many of the described events are so thrilling that they could become an inspiration for a best-selling spy novel or a Hollywood thriller. I wish that you enjoy reading this book as much as I have writing it.

Haifa, Israel   Samuel E. Willner

Acknowledgments

During more than five years devoted to the research, analysis, and writing of the dissertation on which this book is based, I have been blessed to benefit from the support and assistance of several individuals. First, I would like to express my great appreciation and thankfulness to my PhD supervisors Prof. Soli Shahvar, Dr. Eran Segal, and Prof. Gabriel Ben-Dor. Second, I wish to thank Prof. Alexander Bligh, Prof. Amatzia Baram, Prof. Shaul Chorev, Dr. Shosh Ben-Ari, and Ambassador Avi Granot. Third, I am thankful to many other friends and colleagues who have challenged and inspired me, and who have helped me to refine my analytical skills. Fourth, I want to thank the Department of Middle Eastern and Islamic Studies, the Ezri Center for Iran and Gulf States Research, the Chaikin Chair for Geostrategy, and the University of Haifa for providing financial scholarship and excellent facilities for my research. Finally, I want to thank my dear wife and best friend Michelle.

CONTENTS

1 Introduction   1

Part I   The Foundations of Political Leadership in Saudi
Arabia   7

2 Tribal Decision-Making: From Traditional to Modern
Context   9

3 Central Characteristics of Saudi Foreign Policy   21

Conclusion of Part I The Foundations of Political Leadership
in Saudi Arabia   31

Part II   The 1973 Arab–Israeli War and the Arab Oil Embargo   33

4 Emerging Pan-Arabism and the Politicization of Arab Oil   35

5 Conflicting Interests and King Faysal's Decision to
Support Egypt's War Efforts   53

Conclusion of Part II The 1973 Arab–Israeli War and the
Arab Oil Embargo   71

Part III   The End of the Oil Embargo and the Murder of
King Faysal (1973–1976)   73

6   Towards the End of the Oil Embargo   75

7   Threats of a New Oil Embargo   95

8   The Murder of King Faysal   103

9   The Top-Secret Saudi Plan to Use the USSR to Pressure
the United States   125

Conclusion of Part III The End of the Oil Embargo and the
Murder of King Faysal (1973–1976)   135

Part IV   The Survival of the Saudi Monarchy During the
Carter Administration (1977–1981)   139

10   Saudi Concerns of the Marxist and Arab Revolutionary
Threats (1977–1978)   141

11   The 1978–1979 Islamic Revolution in Iran   149

12   Inspired by the Islamic Revolution: Rebellions, Uprisings,
and Coup Attempts   165

13   Saudi, CIA Messages to President Carter: A US Policy
Change Toward the Saudis Is Necessary   187

Conclusion of Part IV The Survival of the Saudi Monarchy
During the Carter Administration (1977–1981)   203

14 Final Conclusions	207
Appendix	215
Selected Bibliography	221
Index	235

ABBREVIATIONS

AMFAF	Archives of the Ministry of Foreign Affairs, Finland
ARAMCO	Arabian-American Oil Company
AWACS	Airborne Early Warning and Control
BPD, MBPD	barrels per day, million barrels per day
BSO	Black September Organization [*Munazzamat Aylul al-Aswad*]
CIA	US Central Intelligence Agency
CBS	Columbia Broadcasting System
CRS	Congressional Research Service
DOD	US Department of Defense
FCO	UK Foreign and Commonwealth Office
FBIS	Foreign Broadcasting Information System (as part of the CIA Directorate of Science and Technology)
FRUS	Foreign Relations of the United States
IEA	International Energy Agency
IMF	International Monetary Fund
IRI	Islamic Republic of Iran
KGB	USSR Committee for State Security [*Komitet Gosudarstvennoy Bezopasnosti*]
KSA	Kingdom of Saudi Arabia
MED	Middle East Department
MEED	Middle East Economic Digest
MEES	Middle East Economic Survey
MEJ	Middle East Journal
MENA	Middle East and North Africa

xviii ABBREVIATIONS

MFASA	Ministry for Foreign Affairs of Saudi Arabia
MFAF	Ministry for Foreign Affairs of Finland (archives)
MI6	Secret Intelligence Service (United Kingdom)
MOD	UK Ministry of Defence
NATO	North Atlantic Treaty Organization
NENA	Near East and North Africa Department
OAPEC	Organization for the Arab Petroleum Exporting Countries
OPEC	Organization for the Petroleum Exporting Countries
OSS	Office of Strategic Services (predecessor of the CIA)
QNA	Qatar News Agency
PDPA	People's Democratic Party of Afghanistan
PDRY	People's Democratic Republic of Yemen (South Yemen)
PFLO	Popular Front for the Liberation of Oman
PFLP	Popular Front for the Liberation of Palestine
PIW	Petroleum Intelligence Weekly
PLO	Palestinian Liberation Organization
RAF	UK Royal Air Force
SAMA	Saudi Arabian Monetary Authority (Saudi Arabian Monetary Agency)
SAS	UK Special Air Services, (a special forces unit in the British Army)
SPA	Saudi Press Agency
UAE	United Arab Emirates
US	United States of America
USSR	Union of Soviet Socialist Republics (Soviet Union)
YAR	Yemen Arab Republic (North Yemen)
YAR	Yemen Arab Republic (North Yemen)

List of Names

Abd al-Karim, Tayeh	Iraqi Minister of Petroleum (1974–1982)
Abd al-Quddus, Ihsan	Chairman of the Board, Cairo newspaper *Al-Ahram* (1974–unknown)
Adams, James	Assistant Under-Secretary for Foreign and Commonwealth Affairs (Public Departments), FCO, London (1980–1982)
Adelman, Morris	American energy economist (b. 1917–d. 2014)
Adham, Kamal	Director, Saudi General Intelligence Directorate (1965–1979)

ABBREVIATIONS xix

Akins, James	Ambassador, US Embassy, Jeddah (1973–1975), Director, Office of Fuels and Energy, US Dept. of State (1968–1973)
Ali, Anwar	Governor, Saudi Arabian Monetary Authority (1958–1974)
Ali-Riza	Affiliation unknown (commenting the Mecca rebellion 1979)
Ameen, Mike	President, Mobil Middle East Development Corp, Beirut, Lebanon and London, UK (1975–1988), Vice President of Government Relations, Aramco, Washington, D.C. (1972–1975), Chief Representative, Aramco, Riyadh (1953–1972), FBI Special Agent (1951–1953), Officer, US Marines (1942–1951)
Armitage, Henry St. John	Counselor, British Embassy, Jeddah (early 1970s)
Asad, Hafiz al-	President of Syria (r. 1971–2000)
Asad, Rifat al-	Commander, Syria's Defense Companies (1971–1984), brother of Hafiz al-Asad
Azimi, Riza	Iranian War Minister (1969–1978)
Aziz, Tariq	Deputy Prime Minister of Iraq (1979–2003), Iraqi Minister of Information (1974–1977)
Bakhtiyar, Shapur	Prime Minister of Iran (1979)
Bakr, Ahmad Hasan al-	President of Iraq (1968–1979)
Bani-Sadr, Abu al-Hasan	President of Iran (1980-1981)
Baring, Rowland	Ambassador, British Embassy, Washington (1971–1974)
Beaumont, David	Staff Member, MED, FCO, London (late 1970s)
Begbie, R.M.	Colonel, Defence Attaché, British Embassy, Jeddah (unknown years)
Blomsted, Henrik	Embassy of Finland, Addis Ababa (1965–1969)
Boissard, Mike G.	UK Ministry of Defence, London (unknown years)
Brezhnev, Leonid	General Secretary, Communist Party, Soviet Union (1964–1982)
Brzezinski, Zbigniew	President Carter's National Security Advisor (1977–1981)

xx ABBREVIATIONS

Bumedien, Hawwari	President of Algeria (1976–1978), Chairman, Algerian Revolutionary Council (1965–1976)
Burrows	HM Treasury, London
Bush, George H. W.	Vice President of the United States of America (1981–1989), Director, Central Intelligence Agency (1976–1977), Chairman, Republican National Committee (1973–1974)
Campbell, Alan	Deputy Under-Secretary of State, FCO, London (1972–1975)
Carrington, Peter	British Secretary of State for Defence (1970–1974)
Carter, Hodding III	Spokesman, US Department of State (1977–1981)
Carter, Jimmy	President of the United States of America (1977–1981)
Chapra, Umer,	Economic Advisor, SAMA (1965–1999)
Clark, Terence J.	Staff Member, MED, FCO, London (unknown–1976)
Close, Raymond	CIA Station Chief in Jeddah (in the 1970s, exact years unknown)
Cooper, Charles A.	Staff Member, US National Security Council (1973–1974)
Craig, James	Ambassador, British Embassy, Jeddah (1979–1984), Councilor, British Embassy, Damascus (1976–1979), Councilor, British Embassy, Jeddah (1967–1970)
Davies, Emrys	Staff Member, Financial Relations Department, FCO, London (unknown–1976)
Daud, Muhammad	President of Afghanistan (r. 1973–1978)
Din, Muhammad Salah al-	Editor of the Saudi daily newspaper *Al-Madinah* (unknown years)
Duri, Izzat Ibrahim al-	Deputy Chairman, Iraq's Revolutionary Command Council (1979–2003)
Edgley, Peter	Government Official, Overseas Department, Bank of England, London (late 1970s)
Egerton, Stephen	Staff Member, Arabian Department, FCO, London (unknown–1972)

Eid, Guy	*Charge d'Affaires*, Belgian Embassy, Khartoum, Sudan (unknown–1973)
Eilts, Hermann	Ambassador, US Embassy, Cairo (1974–1979)
Ellingworth, Richard	Head of Oil Department, FCO, London (1969–1971)
Ford, Gerald	President of the United States of America (1974–1977)
Fortescue, Adrian	Staff, British Embassy, Washington (early 1980s)
Fretwell, John	Minister, British Embassy, Washington (1980–1982)
Fulbright, J. William	US Senator (Democrat, Arkansas) (1945–1974)
Gharazi, Muhammad	Iranian Minister of Petroleum (1981–1985)
Giscard d'Estaing, Valery	President of France (1974–1981)
Gray, John	Councilor, British Embassy, Jeddah (1980–1982)
Haig, Alexander	US Secretary of State (1981–1982)
Hannay, David	Head of Energy, Science and Space Department, FCO, London (1977–1979)
Hart, Parker T.	Vice President, Bechtel Corporation (1973–1990), US Ambassador to Saudi Arabia (1961–1965)
Hashimi, Faysal ibn Ghazi al-Faysal al-Husayn ibn Ali al- (aka. Faysal II)	King of Iraq (r. 1939–1958)
Hashimi, Husayn ibn Ali (aka. Sharif Husayn) al-	King of Hejaz (r.1916–1924) and the Emir of Mecca

xxii ABBREVIATIONS

Hashimi, Husayn ibn Talal ibn Abd Allah al-Husayn ibn Ali al-	King of Jordan (r. 1952–1999)
Helaissi, Abd al-Rahman al-	Ambassador, Embassy of Saudi Arabia, London (unknown years)
Helenius, Veli	Minister, Ministry of Foreign Affairs, Helsinki (1964–1967)
Herdman, Mark	Diplomat, British Embassy, Jeddah (mid-1970s)
Hilal, Ezz al-Din	Minister of Petroleum, Egypt (1973–1984)
Hollaway, Tim	Counselor, British Embassy, Jeddah (late 1970s and early 1980s)
Horan, Hume A.	Deputy Head of Mission, US Embassy, Jeddah (1972–1977)
Hunt, Rex M.	Staff Member, MED, FCO, London (unknown-1974)
Husayn, Saddam	President of Iraq (r. 1979–2003), Vice President of Iraq (1968–1979)
Ibn Khaldun, Abu Zayd Abd al-Rahman ibn Muhammad	Fourteenth-century Arab historian (b. 1332–d. 1406)
Ignotus, Miles	Alleged penname of Secretary of State Henry Kissinger (in 1975)
Ingman, Martti	Minister, Ministry for Foreign Affairs, Helsinki (unknown years)
Ives	Group Captain, Defense Attaché, British Embassy, Jeddah (mid-1970s)
Jakobson, Max	Finland's Ambassador to the UN (1965–1971)
Jiluwi, Abd al-Muhsin ibn Abd Allah al-	Governor of the Eastern Province (1967–1985)
Karjalainen, Ahti	Minister of Foreign Affairs, Helsinki, Finland (1972–1975)

ABBREVIATIONS xxiii

Kay, Jolyon C.	Counselor, British Embassy, Jeddah (1974–1977)
Kealy, Robin A.	Staff Member, MED, FCO, London (unknown-1977)
Kekkonen, Urho	President of Finland (1956–1982)
Kennedy, Robert F.	US Senator (Democrat, New York) (1965–1968)
Khomeini, Ruhollah	Supreme Leader of the Islamic Republic of Iran (1979–1989)
Kimche, David	Director General, Israel Ministry of Foreign Affairs (1980–1987), Deputy Director of Mossad (unknown-1979)
Kimche, Jon	British journalist, brother of David Kimche (b. 1909–d. 1994)
Kissinger, Henry	US Secretary of State (1973–1977), National Security Advisor to President Nixon (1969–1975)
Klee, M.P. de-	Colonel, Defense Attaché, British Embassy (late 1970s)
Lamb, Robin D.	Diplomat, British Embassy, Jeddah (late 1970s)
Lassila, Carolus	Ambassador, Finnish Embassy, Jeddah, and Beirut (1971–1977)
Layden, Anthony M.	Staff Member, MED, FCO, London (late 1970s)
Lees, Brian E.	Colonel, Defence Attaché, British Embassy, Jeddah (1975–1979)
Levy, Walter	American energy economist, Oil Analyst, OSS (1943– around 1945)
Lindsay, Robert (aka. Lord Balniel)	British Minister of State for Foreign Affairs (1972–1974)
MacRae, Christopher	Counselor, British Embassy, Baghdad (early 1970s)
Mahmud, Ahmad Muhammad	Foreign Affairs Editor of *Al-Madinah*, Jeddah (unknown years)
Malhuq, Abd Allah al-	Ambassador, Saudi Embassy, Khartoum, Sudan (c. 1970s)

xxiv ABBREVIATIONS

Mansur, Abdul Kasim	Alleged penname used by the Saudi royal family, *The Armed Forces Journal* (1980)
Mansuri, Abd al-Rahman al-	Legal Advisor, Saudi Ministry of Foreign Affairs (unknown years)
Masud, Muhammad Ibrahim	Deputy Minister, Saudi Ministry of Foreign Affairs (unknown years)
Mawardi, Abu al-Hasan Ali ibn Muhammad ibn Habib al-	An eleventh-century imam and philosopher (972–1058)
McGregor, Robert	Staff Member, Arabian Department, FCO, London (early 1970s)
McMahon, Christopher	Executive Director, Bank of England, London (1970–1980)
Meek, I.	First Secretary Economic, Economic and Commercial Department, British High Commission, Lagos (early 1970s)
Merrick, Roger	Deputy Director of Arabian Peninsula Affairs, US Department of State (unknown years)
Miers, David	Head, MED, FCO (1979–1983)
Moberly, John C.	Assistant Under-Secretary, Middle East Affairs, FCO, London (1979–1982)
Moore, George	*Charge d'Affaires*, US Embassy, Khartoum, Sudan (1972–1973)
Morris, Willie	Ambassador, British Embassy, Jeddah (1968–1972)
Muir, Richard	Staff, British Embassy, Washington (late-1970s)
Munro, Alan	Head, East African Department, FCO (1977–1978), Head, MED, FCO, London (1979)
Musaddiq, Muhammad	Prime Minister of Iran (r. 1951–1953)
Nasir, Jamal Abd al-	Chairman of the Revolutionary Command Council (1954–1956), President of Egypt (r. 1956–1970)
Nixon, Richard	President of the United States (1969–1974)
Noel, Cleo	Ambassador, US Embassy, Khartoum, Sudan (1972–1973)

ABBREVIATIONS   xxv

Numan, Ahmad Muhammad	Special Advisor to the President of YAR (years unknown)
Oberwetter, James C.	Ambassador, US Embassy, Riyadh (2003–2007)
Pahlavi, Muhammad Riza Shah	King of Iran (r. 1941–1979)
Pakenham, Henry	Staff Member, FCO, London (early 1980s)
Pakenham, Michael	Minister, British Embassy, Washington (1978–1983)
Pérez, Carlos Andres	President of Venezuela (1974–1979, 1989–1993)
Peretz, David	Government Official, H.M. Treasury, London (late 1970s, early 1980s)
Pharaon, Rashad	Personal Advisor to King Faysal and King Abd al-Aziz (1943–1975)
Phillips, Alan	Private Secretary to the Secretary of State, FCO, London (mid-1970s)
Pinch, N.	Government Official, U.K. Department of Trade and Industry, London (early 1970s)
Qadhafi, Muammar	Leader of Libya (1969–2011)
Quandt, William	Member, US National Security Council (1972–1974, 1977–1979)
Qazimi, Abd al-Mutalib al-	Kuwaiti Minister of Petroleum (1975–1978)
Rabin, Yitzhak	Prime Minister of Israel (1974–1977)
Radcliffe, James C.	Staff Member, MED, FCO, London (mid-1970s)
Reagan, Ronald	President of the United States of America (1981–1989)
Rothnie, Alan K.	Ambassador, British Embassy, Jeddah (1972–1976)
Roosevelt, Kermit	CIA agent (1943–1958), head of Operation AJAX TP (1953 coup in Iran)
Rousel, Peter	Chairman of the Republican National Council Committee (1973–1974)
Rumaih	Ambassador, Saudi Embassy, Abu Dhabi (c. 1970s)
Rösiö, Bengt	Ambassador, Swedish Embassy, Jeddah (1974–1977)

Sadat, Anwar al-	President of Egypt (1970–1981)
Said, Qabus ibn Said Al	Sultan of Oman (r. 1970–2020)
Sanussi, Muhammad Idris ibn Muhammad al-Mahdi al-	King of Libya (r. 1951–1969)
Saqqaf, Umar	Saudi Minister of State for Foreign Affairs (1968–1974)
Saud, Abd al-Aziz (aka. Ibn Saud) Al	King, and founder of the Kingdom of Saudi Arabia (r. 1932–1953)
Saud, Abd Allah ibn Abd al-Aziz Al	King of Saudi Arabia (r. 2005–2015), Deputy Prime Minister (1982–2005), Second Deputy Prime Minister (1975–1982), Commander, Saudi National Guard (1962–2010)
Saud, Abd al-Muhsin ibn Abd Allah al-Jiluwi Al	Governor of the Eastern Province (1967–1985)
Saud, Abd al-Muhsin ibn Abd al-Aziz Al	Governor of Medina (1965–1985)
Saud, Fahd ibn Abd al-Aziz Al	King of Saudi Arabia (r. 1982–2005), Deputy Prime Minister (1975–1982), Second Deputy Prime Minister (1967 1975), Minister of Interior (1962–1975)
Saud, Faysal ibn Abd al-Aziz Al	King of Saudi Arabia (r. 1964–1975)
Saud, Faysal al-Musaid ibn Abd al-Aziz Al	King Faysal's assassin (b. 1944–d. 1975)
Saud, Khalid ibn Abd al-Aziz Al	King of Saudi Arabia (r. 1975–1982), Deputy Prime Minister (1964–1975)

Saud, Mansur ibn Abd al-Aziz Al	Saudi Defense Minister (1943–1951)
Saud, Muhammad ibn Abd al-Aziz Al	Full-brother of Khalid ibn Abd al-Aziz (b. 1910–d. 1988)
Saud, Nayif ibn Abd al-Aziz Al	Minister of Interior (1975–2012), Deputy Minister of Interior (1970–1975)
Saud, Nasir ibn Abd al-Aziz Al	Governor of Riyadh (1938–1951)
Saud, Saud ibn Abd al-Aziz Al	King of Saudi Arabia (r. 1953–1964)
Saud, Saud al-Faysal ibn Abd al-Aziz Al	Minister of Foreign Affairs (1975–2015), Deputy Minister of Petroleum (1971–1975)
Saud, Sultan ibn Abd al-Aziz Al	Saudi Minister of Defense (1963–2011)
Saud, Turki al-Faysal ibn Abd al-Aziz Al	Director, Saudi General Intelligence Directorate (1979–2001)
Saunders, Harold H.	US Assistant Secretary of State for intelligence and Research (1975–1978), US National Security Council Staff (1973–1975)
Schlesinger, James R.	US Secretary of Energy (1977–1979), US Secretary of Defense (1973–1975), Director of Central Intelligence (1973)
Scowcroft, Brent	President Ford's Deputy Assistant for National Security Affairs (1975–1977)
Segar, Christopher	Staff Member, MED, FCO, London (late 1970s)
Selassie, Haile	Emperor of Ethiopia (r. 1916–1974)
Shaibani	Advisor to Prince Abd Allah ibn Abd al-Aziz Al Saud (in 1960s and 1970s)

xxviii ABBREVIATIONS

Sharon, Andre	Analyst, Drexel, Burnham, Lambert Inc, New York (around 1978–1979)
Shawwaf, Ziyad	Ambassador, Embassy of Saudi Arabia to Sweden and Finland (unknown years), Head, Western Department, Saudi Ministry of Foreign Affairs (unknown years)
Shura, Ismail	Director of Arab Affairs, Saudi Ministry of Foreign Affairs (c. 1970s)
Sick, Gary	Member, US National Security Council Staff for MENA (1976–1981)
Sirhan, Bishara Sirhan	Murderer of US Senator Robert F. Kennedy (b. 1944)
Sisco, Joseph	Under Secretary of State for Political Affairs (1974–1976), Assistant Secretary of State for Near Eastern and South Asian Affairs (1969–1974)
Sorsa, Kalevi	Minister of Foreign Affairs of Finland (1972, 1975–1976), Prime Minister of Finland (1972–1975, 1977–1979)
Stalin, Joseph	General Secretary, Communist Party, Soviet Union (1922–1952)
Sudayri, Turki al-	Editor-in-Chief, Saudi newspaper *Al-Riyadh* (1974–2015)
Tatham, David E.	Staff Member, MED, FCO, London (unknown–1981)
Thatcher, Margaret	British Prime Minister (1979–1990)
Thacher, Nicolas	Ambassador, US Embassy, Jeddah (1970–1973)
Thunayan, Iffat al-	Queen, the influential, last wife of King Faysal ibn Abd al-Aziz (b. 1916–d. 2000)
Tomkys, Roger	Head, Near East and North Africa Department, FCO (1977–1980)
Tötterman, Richard	Secretary of State, Ministry of Foreign Affairs, Helsinki (1970–1975)
Tunnell, Hugh	Staff Member Oil Department, FCO, London (early 1970s)
Turki, Abd al-Aziz al-	Affiliation unknown (security of Saudi oil installations)

Udeh, Muhammad Daud	Leader of *Al-Fatah*, and the Black September Organization (unknown years)
Uthaymin, Abd Allah al-	Saudi historian (b. 1936–d. 2016)
Uusivirta, Pentti	Counselor, Embassy of Finland, Washington
Walker, Harold	Counselor, British Embassy, Jeddah (1973–1975)
West, John C.	Ambassador, US Embassy, Jeddah (1977–1981)
Wilton, John	Ambassador, British Embassy, Jeddah (1976–1979)
Winchester, Ian S.	Counselor, British Embassy, Jeddah (1970–1972)
Wittmer, Bill	President, Tennessee Gas Pipeline Company (unknown years)
Wolfowitz, Paul	Director, Policy Planning Staff, Dept. of State (1981–1982)
Wright, Patrick	Head, MED, FCO, London (1972–1974)
Yamani, Ahmad Zaki	Saudi Minister of Petroleum (1962–1986)
Yamani, Muhammad Abdu	Saudi Minister of Information (1975–1982)
Yassa, Fuad	Representative of *Al-Fatah*, Khartoum, Sudan (unknown-1973)
Zumwalt, Elmo Russell	Admiral, Chief of Naval Operations, US Navy (1970–1974)

List of Charts

Chart A.1	Oil Prices (1970–1985), money of the day	218
Chart A.2	Crude oil production in Saudi Arabia (1970–1985)	218
Chart A.3	Crude oil exports from Saudi Arabia (1970–1980)	219
Chart A.4	Oil revenues of Saudi Arabia (1960–1980), money of the day	219
Chart A.5	Gold prices (1975–1985)	220

LIST OF TABLES

Table A.1	The chronology from 1967 to 1981	215
Table A.2	The sons of Abd al Aziz ibn Abd al-Rahman (ca. 1880–1953)	217
Table A.3	The most important branches of the sons of Al Saud	217
Table A.4	The Saudi kings and heir apparents	217

CHAPTER 1

Introduction

The Kingdom of Saudi Arabia is the world's largest exporter of petroleum, and its ruling family Al Saud is the richest and most influential monarchy on the globe. Following the end of the Second World War (1939–1945) and the start of the Cold War (1946–1989), Saudi Arabia emerged as a strategic partner to the Western economic powers due to its significant petroleum reserves, considerable oil export capacity, and political stability. Over the past half a century, oil wealth and financial power have been principal foreign policy tools for the kingdom. Mainly due to Saudi Arabia's decades-long strategic role in the oil markets, but also because of its compelling financial power, the political maneuvering of the Saudi monarchy has been studied from many contrasting angles and by people coming from different disciplines. Despite the wide-ranging academic and professional interest expressed in Saudi Arabia, its monarchy has often been perceived as an enigma and that its decision-making has been described as unpredictable. In *Preserving the Saudi Monarchy*, I will point out that such a perception is erroneous. One of the primary reasons why such a misperception prevails is because Saudi decision-making process is usually very secretive, personal, and quiet, and because of this it has been difficult for outside observers to analyze it.

The Kingdom of Saudi Arabia is a dynastic, absolute monarchy of which political leadership is fundamentally based on desert tribal [*badawī*] culture, values, and tradition. Principally, this is what makes the Saudi system distinguishably different to other political systems. Therefore, because of

© The Author(s), under exclusive license to Springer Nature Switzerland AG 2023
S. E. Willner, *Preserving the Saudi Monarchy*,
https://doi.org/10.1007/978-3-031-30006-6_1

Al Saud's *badawī* roots, its decision-making is based on tribal group cohesion [*'asabīyah*]. Moreover, I argue that since the Saudi monarchy operates according to such fundamental principles of *'asabīyah*, a Saudi king is not supposed to rule as an authoritarian leader. Although the Saudi king is the final arbiter of decision-making, he is expected to make all important decisions by shaping family consensus through consultation. Furthermore, I argue that instead of pursuing ideological purity, the royal family has been highly pragmatic when it has formulated foreign and domestic policy, and that the survival of the monarchy always went beyond the survival of individual members of the royal family.

OVERCOMING THE METHODOLOGICAL CHALLENGES

This study explores the behind-the-scenes workings of the Saudi monarchy. Moreover, it mirrors the foundations of tribal culture and endeavors to portray the fundamental characteristics of the enigmatic Saudi royal family. In any analytical work, however, it is essential to ask the right questions. The basic questions that any individual, who desires to understand any specific event in history, needs to answer are what happened; where it happened; when and how it happened; what the motivating forces behind it were; and how are the facts of the matter connected. In terms of the analytical process, it is also useful to ask oneself, what is the source of information; for what reason the information or disinformation was released; did I get my assessment right; and could there possibly be alternative explanations? However, the challenge in the case of Saudi Arabia is that "very few westerners really understand the Saudi mentality," which is what journalist and writer Thomas Lippman has observed.[1]

A principal explanation to why the Saudis have often been misunderstood is the fact that the royal family is very secretive, and that the monarchy's most important decisions are commonly formulated in private by senior Saudi royals. What further complicates the analysis of the Saudi royal family is the matter that the political discourse in the kingdom is usually filled with fiercely conspiratorial interpretations of events, and that both friendly and hostile actors repeatedly "muddy the waters" with

---

[1] Thomas Lippman, *Inside the Mirage: America's Fragile Partnership with Saudi Arabia*, Boulder, CO: Westview Press, 2004, 3; Amatzia Baram, *Saddam Husayn and Islam, 1968–2003: Ba'thi Iraq from Secularism to Faith*, Washington, D.C.: Woodrow Wilson Center Press, 2014, 11.

misinformation and disinformation.[2] In fact, William Quandt, a former member of the US National Security Council (1972–1974 and 1977–1979), has rightfully argued that the veil of secrecy is rarely lifted on the inner workings of the royal family. Furthermore, he has described that "those who try to penetrate the inner sanctum are viewed as enemies and those who talk too freely are seen as unfriendly, if not dangerous."[3] Interestingly, such remarks are very much in line with an ancient Bedouin proverb, which says that "a gossiper is neither pleasant nor pleased" [*al-inqaylī mā yinḥalī wa-la yiriḍī*].[4]

Under these above-mentioned circumstances, it is quite challenging to make meaningful conclusions about how the monarchy operates behind the scenes without having either an inside source within the senior ranks of the royal family (something that is very rare to obtain) or without consulting thousands upon thousands of pages of declassified diplomatic communications, commentaries, press reports, and academic research—some of which is poor quality and some of which is excellent quality. Indeed, many previously published works about the oil-rich desert kingdom fail to explain the survival of the Saudi monarchy through the prism of tribal decision-making.

In studying the royal family, one must exercise due caution regarding sources, given the ocean of misinformation and disinformation that is readily available. Most of the information that has been accessible for this study is based—on the one hand—on open sources, such as newspapers, and—on the other hand—on restricted and confidential, declassified diplomatic communications and intelligence reports compiled by foreign diplomats serving in Saudi Arabia and neighboring countries. Although the information which such reports provide is often incomplete, and although their assessment is occasionally incorrect, they usually contain useful pieces of information. Moreover, it is particularly important to interpret various indirect messages and clues, and furthermore, to read between the lines and use many minuscule pieces of information to understand what is happening within this secretive monarchy.

---

[2] Gary Samore, *Royal Family Politics in Saudi Arabia*, 1953–1982, Unpublished PhD dissertation, Harvard University, 1984, v; Quandt, *Saudi Arabia in the 1980s*, 107.

[3] William Quandt, *Saudi Arabia in the 1980s: Foreign Policy, Security and Oil*, Washington, D.C.: The Brookings Institution, 1981, 107.

[4] Clinton Bailey, *A Culture of Desert Survival: Bedouin Proverbs from Sinai and the Negev*, New Haven, CT: Yale University Press, 2004, 392.

NOTE ON TRANSLITERATION

The transliteration system from Arabic to Roman alphabets in this book is that used in the *International Journal of Middle East Studies* (*IJMES*).

OVERVIEW OF THE BOOK

The purpose of this book is to provide new perspective to the study of Saudi Arabia and its monarchy—its political leadership and decisions. Moreover, *Preserving the Saudi Monarchy* analyzes how that decision-making evolved before, during, and after the Arab-Israeli War of 1973, and the subsequent Arab oil embargo that followed; the run-up to and aftermath of the 1975 murder of King Faysal; discussions over the oil and financial weapons; and Saudi responses to the Carter presidency in the United States. Through the prism of tribal decision-making, this book sheds new light on several important political events, which have shaped the political leadership in Saudi Arabia. This book is divided into four parts.

Part I: The Foundations of Political Leadership in Saudi Arabia (Chaps. 2–3) Saudi Arabia is a dynastic monarchy of which political leadership is based on tribal-familial traditions. Essentially, its decision-making functions in a comparable manner as the other tribal-based states, where the royal family led by the king makes all important decisions concerning its national interests. The royal family's foremost interest is to preserve the Saudi monarchy. In fact, its survival has been so important an objective that often in utter secrecy the royal family has been very pragmatic in pursuing policies that would ensure such an outcome. In Chaps. 2 and 3, I will introduce the tribal-familial foundations of Saudi decision-making upon which its foreign policy is based.

Part II: The 1973 Arab-Israeli War and the Arab Oil Embargo (Chaps. 4–5) In formulating its foreign policy around the events of the 1973 Arab-Israeli War, the Saudi monarchy demonstrated great sensitivity to the risks posed by the radical Arab governments (Chap. 4). To make their contribution to the Arab battle against Israel, the Saudis acted in two major ways. The first was the generous Saudi financial assistance to Egypt of which original purpose had been to get Egypt to withdraw from the war in Yemen. The second—and more controversial based on some of the central and pragmatic characteristics of Saudi policymaking, was King Faysal's October 1973 decision to use the 'oil weapon,' and to join the Arab oil embargo against the United States. This was a major turning point in the history of the Saudi monarchy.

Being drawn into the war against Israel was not in the interests of the Saudi government. While King Faysal had advocated for supporting Egypt and joining the Arab oil embargo, the royal family messaged Israel through the US Central Intelligence Agency (CIA) that the Saudi military forces were under strict instructions not to become involved in the fighting (Chap. 5). To understand the circumstances under which Saudi Arabia had joined the Arab oil embargo, one would have to examine the upsurge of political Arabism in the 1950s, and furthermore, its contribution to the significant rise of anti-Saudi activity in the early 1970s (Chap. 4). Although the long-term aim of the radical regimes was probably to overthrow the Saudi royal family and replace it with a radical Arab republic, their more immediate objective was to change the course of Saudi Arabia's pro-Western foreign policy, and more specifically, to alter its conservative oil policy.

Part III: The End of the Arab Oil Embargo and the Murder of King Faysal (1974–1976) (Chaps. 6–9)
King Faysal decided to terminate the oil embargo in mid-March 1974—five months after it had been imposed. Before the embargo was over, however, the oil prices had quadrupled from the pre-embargo levels and consequently, the world economies were seriously struggling because of high fuel prices. Due to the high economic stress, and the fear of the oil embargo's increasingly negative impact on the political stability of several US strategic allies, the Nixon Administration (1969–1974) decided to apply pressure, and adopted psychological warfare campaign against the Saudi monarchy (Chap. 6). As the records indicate, the American psychological warfare made King Faysal nervous and worried, but it did not make him change his position. Rather, the US pressure seems to have made him more stubborn to pursue his policy and reluctant to terminate the embargo (Chap. 7). Moreover, some of the circumstantial evidence points out that Faysal's inability to understand the importance of the Saudi-US relationship in the aftermath of the oil embargo turned him into a major liability to some of the senior princes (Chap. 8). The chain of events, which led into the assassination of King Faysal in March 1975, was a major turning

point in Saudi policymaking. Although their relationship with the United States improved following Faysal's death, the Saudis were not satisfied about the level of military assistance that the United States was willing to provide. To improve the situation, the Saudis decided to put pressure on the United States and launched a secretive disinformation campaign to make it look as if the monarchy was in a process of establishing relations with Moscow (Chap. 9). The challenge, of course, was how to convince the United States that the Saudis were making a radical change into their earlier anti-Communist policy.

Part IV: The Survival of the Saudi Monarchy during the Carter Administration (1977–1981) (Chaps. 10–13)
President Jimmy Carter's term (1977–1981) in the White House was not an easy period for Saudi Arabia. While the political turmoil in Iran was paving a way for the revolution in that country, the Saudis encountered increasing radical Arab activity against their monarchy (Chap. 10). Meanwhile, the political events of Iran's Islamic Revolution (1978–1979), which led to major disruptions in the Iranian oil exports, and which created chaos in the oil markets, were a major trigger for global financial instability. Despite Saudi Arabia's attempts to stabilize the oil markets by increasing its own oil exports, the oil prices kept going up under tense circumstances. The revolution in Iran brought to power a Shi'i theocratic regime that was heavily anti-American and anti-Saudi (Chap. 11). Following the geopolitical instability, the revolution in Iran further encouraged radical activity in Saudi Arabia and in the surrounding region (Chap. 12). On several occasions, the Saudis communicated that the United States should do more to ensure the survival of the Saudi monarchy (Chap. 13). Although the Saudis had made several attempts to appeal to President Carter so that he would change his foreign policy approach, the Saudis must have realized that no matter how hard they would try to convince the US President, he would still not do enough to secure the Saudi interests.

PART I

The Foundations of Political Leadership in Saudi Arabia

The Kingdom of Saudi Arabia is a dynastic monarchy wherein political leadership is based on tribal traditions. Principally, the Saudi decision-making functions in a similar manner as the other tribal-based states, where the royal family led by the king makes decisions concerning the national interests. The royal family's foremost interest is to preserve the Saudi monarchy. However, Saudi decision-making processes have traditionally been very secretive. In fact, secrecy has provided the royal family more flexibility to maneuver about the unseen and to take advantage of the opportunities that may arise in the political realm. Interestingly, as it seems, pragmatism is a key characteristic of foreign affairs in Saudi Arabia. In the next two chapters, I will introduce the tribal-familial foundations of the Saudi political system upon which its foreign policy is based on.

CHAPTER 2

Tribal Decision-Making: From Traditional to Modern Context

SURVIVAL IN THE TRADITIONAL TRIBAL CONTEXT

Like many of the powerful Arabian families, the Al Saud has its historic and cultural background in the desert life [*badāwa*]. Traditionally, the desert provided its people—the *badawī*—a wide scope for movement and a zone of defenses against outside enemies. More specifically, a *badawī* is a person who lives in the desert, but who is not necessarily a tribal Bedouin. For these tribes, life in the desert was commonly tough, and thereupon often only the strong and shrewd survived. Accordingly, in his renowned work *Muqaddimah*, the fourteenth-century Arab historian Ibn Khaldun characterized the traditional *badawī* life as *mustaūḥish*, which derives from the words: 'lonely,' 'oppressed,' and 'deserted.' The word *mustaūḥish* can also mean 'wild' and 'savage.'[1] Due to these underlying challenging living conditions, the strife to survive was an important factor when the *badawī* tribes made decisions.

The main feature of tribal social structure is that it is based on kinship. In a traditional tribal system, family [*ahl*] is the anchor of everyday life.

---

[1] Ibn Khaldun was one of the most prominent historians of the Islamic world. He belonged to a clan of South Arabian origin, and it is believed that his family had immigrated to Spain in the eighth century, during the early years of the Muslim conquest of Spain. Ibn Khaldun, *The Muqaddimah: An Introduction to History*, transl. Franz Rosenthal, vol. 1–2, London: Routledge & Kegan Paul, 1958, vol. 1, xxix–lxvii.

© The Author(s), under exclusive license to Springer Nature Switzerland AG 2023
S. E. Willner, *Preserving the Saudi Monarchy*,
https://doi.org/10.1007/978-3-031-30006-6_2

9

10 S. E. WILLNER

After the family come the extended family [*hayy*][2] and the tribe [*'ashīrah, qabīlah,* or *jūl*].[3] Tribal relationships were necessary for personal survival because tribes protected their individual members. This concept of survival is described in an old Bedouin proverb, which indicates that "a man without a kin group is like a dress without sleeves" [*al-wāḥad bilā khamsa zay thaūb bilā irdān*]. As Clinton Bailey explains, this proverb is a metaphor of a person who is insufficiently covered—meaning that without the protection of his family he is more vulnerable to various threats.[4] Furthermore, on a tribal level, smaller tribes formed alliances [*ḥilf*] with stronger tribes so that they could defend themselves better against more significant adversaries. Naturally, the closer the relationship between the various members of the tribe, the more firm is the loyalty an individual tribesman feels for his fellows. Such hierarchy of loyalties is expressed in a classical statement of tribal solidarity, which says that: "I and my brother will fight my cousin; but I and my cousin will fight the stranger" [*ānā w-ākhūwī 'āl ibn 'ammī, w-ānā w-ibn 'ammī 'āl al-gharīb*]. In other words, despite everyday-life competition between brothers, they often united in times of conflicts against more distant relatives and common enemies.[5]

---

[2] The Arabic word *hayy* refers to 'living being,' 'organism,' 'tribe,' and 'tribal community.' Hans Wehr, *A Dictionary of Modern Written Arabic*, ed. Milton Cowan, London: George Allen and Unwin, 1966.

[3] The Arabic word *qabīlah* refers to 'tribe,' while *'ashīrah* refers to 'clan' or 'closest relatives.' The Arabic word *jūl* means 'people,' 'nation,' or 'tribe.' Wehr, *A Dictionary of Modern Written Arabic*.

[4] In this proverb, the Arabic word *khamsa* refers to the most important group of a Bedouin, which is his paternal clan. "A *khamsa* consists of all the people within five generations: the generation of the youngest male member of the group and all the men in the generation of his father, grandfather, and great grandfather. In other words, the *khamsa* comprises all the living descendants of the youngest person's great-great grandfather, who singly constitutes its fifth generation." See: Bailey, *A Culture of Desert Survival*, 122–123.

[5] Andrea B. Rugh, *The Political Culture of Leadership in the United Arab Emirates*, New York, NY: Palgrave Macmillan, 2007, 19, 111; Bailey, *A Culture of Desert Survival*, 159. In addition to establishing unity between tribes, a Saudi king would also need luck [*ḥaẓ*] to be successful. The word *ḥaẓ* literally means 'fate' or 'destiny,' which seems to point out that tribesmen expected their leader to have not only prosperity but also good fortune. Abd Allah al-Salih al-Uthaymin, "Success of King Abdul Aziz in Unifying the Country," in *A History of the Arabian Peninsula*, ed. Fahd al-Semmari, transl. Salma K. Jayyusi, London: I.B. Tauris, 2010, 74, 191; David Holden and Richard Johns, *The House of Saud*, London: Sidgwick & Jackson, 1981, 15; Peter Hobday, *Saudi Arabia Today: An Introduction to the Richest Oil Power*, New York, NY: St. Martin's Press, 1978, 22.

2 TRIBAL DECISION-MAKING: FROM TRADITIONAL TO MODERN CONTEXT   11

Preserving honor [*sharaf*] has been paramount in *badawī* tribal relations. In such a cultural context where tribal loyalties [*wafā'*][6] have played a major role in individual tribal member's survival, being a person of honor and respect [*'izza*] has often been a matter of life and death. In this regard, an old Bedouin proverb says that "neglect your wealth, but not your honor" [*hīn iflūsak walā tahīn namūsak*], which means that honorable behavior in tribal relations is much more important than one's wealth.[7] Such principle derives from the fundamental perception that without personal honor—there would be no tribal protection, and without protection and security—there would be no survival. If a tribe's member has no respect, it would translate into him having no personal security: "as a bird without wings cannot fly, so a man without kinsmen knows no respect" [*tīr bila jinhān mā jidrik al-hūm, ū-rājlin bila raba'qilīl al-maqām*]. This metaphor means that a tribal group would ultimately protect only those members who were honorable.[8]

In addition to retaining personal honor through nobility and honesty [*amānah*],[9] one would also need to show courage [*shajā'ah*], bravery, and hospitality [*karāmah*] to defend one's honor. Furthermore, another proverb puts it well by revealing that "everyone is trusted by his reputation for trust" [*al-kul amāntahu widā'tahu*], which means that one would need to establish trust before being trusted. Therefore, based on Bailey's explanation of this proverb, one can conclude that a member of the Saudi royal family would always need to be conscious that his image is part of his deterrence, and thus it is vital to his personal security and survival.[10] Moreover, the concept of good reputation is also described in the following Bedouin proverb, which says that "a man is like a china cup, once

---

[6] The root of the word *wafā'* (fulfillment, faithfulness, fidelity, loyalty) comes from the verb *wafā*, which means 'to be perfect' or 'to be complete.' Wehr, *A Dictionary of Modern Written Arabic*.

[7] Bailey, *A Culture of Desert Survival*, 45. Furthermore, as Sandra Mackey indicates, the concept of honor is the most difficult aspect of the Saudi mindset for a Westerner to comprehend. See: Sandra Mackey, *The Saudis: Inside the Desert Kingdom*, Boston, MA: Houghton Mifflin Company, 1987, 117.

[8] Bailey, *A Culture of Desert survival*, 123.

[9] The root of the word 'honesty' [*amānah*] is *amuna*, which literally means 'to be faithful' or 'to feel safe.' The word *amn* means 'security' and 'protection.' Furthermore, the word *amān* means 'security.' Wehr, *A Dictionary of Modern Written Arabic*.

[10] Bailey, *A Culture of Desert survival*, 226, 397.

12   S. E. WILLNER

cracked, is useless" [*ar-rājil zay finjāl ṣīnī—in anthalam khirib*]. In other words, if one's reputation is once defiled, it cannot be restored.[11]

THE CONCEPT OF SHAPING CONSENSUS THROUGH CONSULTATION AND OTHER CENTRAL CHARACTERISTICS OF SAUDI POLICYMAKING

The political leadership in the Saudi monarchy is organized around tribal traditions. In such a political system, king is the most powerful and most important decision-maker, and who—according to the tribal tradition, is not supposed to rule as a dictatorial leader. Instead, he is expected to formulate Saudi policies together with the senior members of the royal family. In reflecting such a concept, Crown Prince Fahd explained in 1982 that a king who did not resort to the concept of consensus deviated from his authority and was suffering from arrogance.[12]

While being the head of the royal family—and thus also the head of the state, the Saudi king is the final arbiter of decision-making. In doing so, he must shape consensus [*ijmā'*] through consultation [*shūrā*] with senior members of the monarchy. In other words, an unwritten rule of such a decision-making system is that the king should always consult its senior members before making any major decisions. In Saudi Arabia, the most important decisions are usually made by a limited circle of senior members of the royal family—namely, the *ahl al-'aqd w-al-hal* ('the people who summon and find solutions' or 'those who bind and loosen'). According to the customary practice, this has included series of unofficial and official consultations between various senior members of the family in the presence of relevant non-royal advisors.

The concept of having consultations is described in a traditional Bedouin proverb, which says that "it is better to destroy with people's consent than to build on one's own initiative" [*takhrab bi-rei al-jamī'a walā ta'mar bi-rei wāḥad*].[13] Moreover, another proverb indicates that "there is no gain in a kin group whose rights get lost among themselves"

---

[11] Ibid. 23.

[12] Crown Prince Fahd made his remarks to Saudi domestic television and the Kuwaiti newspaper *As-Siyasah*. The interview was published jointly by the Saudi newspapers *Ukaz* and *Al-Jazirah*, March 29, 1982. *Foreign Broadcasting Information System (FBIS) Daily Report: Middle East & Africa*, March 30, 1982, C6-C9.

[13] Bailey, *A Culture of Desert Survival*, 190.

2 TRIBAL DECISION-MAKING: FROM TRADITIONAL TO MODERN CONTEXT   13

[*lā khair fī qūm yidaīya'al-ḥaq mā baynuhum*].[14] The first proverb indicates that members of the tribe insist on having consultations even if there is a possibility that the outcome of the consultation is not what they want. The second proverb illustrates that internal conflicts are harmful and could lead to the collapse of the monarchy. Therefore, in such a political system, tribal solidarity, or group cohesion [*'aṣabīyah*],[15] has always played a vital role.

To reduce the potential risks involved in political maneuvering, and furthermore, the risk of its enemies being able to use the possible disunity against it, the Saudi monarchy prefers to operate privately. It makes decisions collegially with due regard for the unofficial rank of each participant involved in the decision-making process. Based on such a practice, the Saudi royal family has used the cover of collegial responsibility to shield its members from the risks that controversial decisions could cause. According to such a practice, the authority of the Saudi government, or alternatively the name of the king, was invoked and the role of the individual members of the royal family was downplayed to minimize their exposure to outside pressure, and thus to shield these people in question. By doing so, individual princes were able to shun the responsibility and claim that they had limited ability to negotiate beyond what the royal family had already decided. As a diplomatic correspondence indicates, such a decision-making strategy has occurred when a particular decision has required utmost discreetness and when it had implications for relationships among the senior levels of the Saudi monarchy. This decision-making approach implies that the Saudis preferred to prepare coordinated position in advance following discussions about the possible implications of its decisions.[16] Principally, the Saudi political culture does not encourage open debate of strategically important decisions.

Part of being an arbiter of decision-making, and the head of the state, a Saudi king is the final decision-maker in the monarchy. This means that the king has the right to veto decisions and go against the consensus of the

---

[14] Bailey, *A Culture of Desert Survival*, 128.

[15] The grammatical root of the Arabic word *'aṣabīyah* derives from the word *'aṣaba* which means 'to bind up,' 'to tie,' while *i'itaṣaba* means 'to form a league' or 'to team up.' The word *'aṣabīyah* can also refer to 'fanaticism' or 'bigotry,' but also to 'national consciousness' and 'team spirit.' Wehr, *A Dictionary of Modern Written Arabic*.

[16] "US-Saudi Relations" (confidential report), David Myers (MED, FCO, London) to Craig, February 12, 1982, no. 11, *FCO 8/4772*.

14   S. E. WILLNER

family. However, if the king is unable to make decisions or if he fails in decision-making, it will weaken his position and open opportunities for his rivals to challenge him. Similarly, if the king makes decisions without first consulting the royal family, he is more likely to risk the interests of the Saudi monarchy. Therefore, in certain circumstances—where the king repeatedly decides against the interests of the senior members of the monarchy, and such that would threaten its survival—the senior members of the royal family may overrule the king, limit his authority, and, in extreme cases, even depose him.[17] As such, a successful Saudi king would have to know how to operate in tribal politics. In other words, it has been necessary that an adroit king leads Saudi Arabia.

Nevertheless, the absence of a strong and shrewd leader could lead into a situation where tough decisions are postponed until there is less uncertainty about the decision-making options.[18] Naturally, this should not exclude the possibility of deciding not to do something. Moreover, a decision not to decide, is also a decision. The literature presents few reasons for the above-mentioned approach. First, Nadav Safran has argued, that in situations which have involved a choice between equally risky short-term or long-term options, the Saudi monarchy has intentionally refrained from a decision to play time.[19] Second, according to Sandra Mackey, such an approach is a consequence of preserving honor and pride. Therefore one reason why the royal family would postpone its decision (which also relates to the first point) would be because of the possibility that it might be wrong.[20] Additionally, decisions cannot be made under pressure, asserts Quandt, and continues saying that "yes and no answers are avoided if at all possible, but infinite variations of 'maybe' are available."[21] Finally, because of the prevailing secrecy in decision-making, political discourse in Saudi Arabia is often filled with wildly conspiratorial interpretations of events. This is a process, which tends to lead into many rumors and conspiratorial thinking. As a foreign observer, William Quandt acknowledges that "[in

---

[17] Mordechai Abir, *Saudi Arabia: Government, Society and the Gulf Crisis*, London: Routledge, 1993, 7.

[18] "US/Saudi Relations" (confidential report), Muir to David E. Tatham (MED, FCO, London), February 9, 1979, no. 9, *FCO 8/3420*.

[19] Nadav Safran, *Saudi Arabia: The Ceaseless Quest for Security*, Cambridge, MA: The Belknap Press of Harvard University Press, 1985, 455.

[20] Mackey, *The Saudis*, 117.

[21] Quandt, *Saudi Arabia in the 1980s*, 150; Mackey, *The Saudis*, 120.

2 TRIBAL DECISION-MAKING: FROM TRADITIONAL TO MODERN CONTEXT   15

Saudi Arabia] lack of evidence is never a conclusive reason for rejecting an interpretation."[22]

Although Alexander Bligh has duly argued that Saudi's political interests are not always clearly defined in public, and that the monarchy determines its national goals on an ad hoc basis, such statement might not be completely accurate.[23] Throughout the existence of the Saudi monarchy, there has been a substantial gap between the royal family's political rhetoric and action.[24] In fact, it is very possible that because there has often been disparity between Saudi foreign policy interests and the publicly manifested justification for such actions, it could appear as if its political interests were not clearly defined.[25]

ROYAL SUCCESSION AND THE LEGITIMACY TO LEAD THE SAUDI MONARCHY

The royal succession is an essential part of leadership and decision-making processes in the Arab monarchies. Similarly, the succession process is central to Saudi decision-making because it reflects how the inner dynamics work in the royal family. It is central as it might indicate who pulls the strings and who is respected and powerful inside the royal family. It can also indicate who is qualified and who is disqualified to rule. In addition, it might reveal who prefers instead to influence from the shadows. Fortunately, assessing royal succession in Saudi Arabia and the princely rivalries in the monarchy reveals valuable insights of the inner workings of its political system.[26]

---

[22] Quandt, *Saudi Arabia in the 1980s*, 107, 108–109. See also: Steffen Hertog, *Princes, Brokers and Bureaucrats: Oil and the State in Saudi Arabia*, Ithaca, NY: Cornell University Press, 2010, 30; and Alexander Bligh, "Changes in the Domestic-Foreign Policies Relationship in the Saudi Context in the Wake of the Change of the Guard," *The Journal of the Middle East and Africa* 9, 2018, 93–116.

[23] Bligh, *From Prince to King*, 2.

[24] Barry Rubin, *Revolution until Victory: The Politics and History of the PLO*, Cambridge, MA: Harvard University Press, 1994, 114.

[25] This could also be an explanation to an observation discussed by Holden. As he has argued, with a play on the word *majlis* some Saudis call their leadership's decision-making "the *ma'aleesh* system, roughly translatable as the 'never mind system' [...in which there are] men who appear to have no intention of ever reaching a decision about anything." David Holden, "A Family Affair," *New York Times*, July 6, 1975, 151.

[26] Bligh, *Prince to King*, 5.

16   S. E. WILLNER

The Saudi royal succession has its roots in the pre-Islamic tribal norms, where the leadership was passed from one generation to next within a particular family. In a tribal society there are two main rules for succession: seniority and primogeniture. In such a political system the succession was not necessarily passed from father to son, but, rather, the principle of seniority was flexible. As such, the main principle of Saudi royal succession has been that 'the eldest able' among the royal family should rule the kingdom—depending on which of these eldest male relatives was seen to possess the qualities of shrewdness, good fortune, in addition to having exceptional skills in arbitration and the ability to shape consensus through consultation.[27] Furthermore, the legitimacy for a member of the monarchy to claim candidacy in becoming the heir apparent depends on various factors, including his tribal origin, seniority, maternal descent, the number of full-brothers, prestige, personality, personal preferences, and leadership qualities—all according to tribal tradition. In addition to these above-listed factors, an important criterion for membership in the royal family's ruling class is its members' capacity to participate in policy formulation and decision-making. While seniority helped in the succession process, it did not guarantee political prominence.[28] A Saudi leader needed to be strong. Under the leadership of a weak leader, the kingdom could end up in collapse.

Little is known about the tribal-familial conflicts that occasionally emerge within the Saudi monarchy, and between the Saudi royals. Such familial divisions can have a variety of origins. However, misguided policies, which endanger the survival of the monarchy, are no-doubt the gravest concern for the royal family. Since the establishment of the modern Saudi kingdom in 1932, at least two major succession crises have taken place. The first one is a well-documented political crisis, which primarily

[27] See: Sarah Yizraeli, *The Remaking of Saudi Arabia: The Struggle between King Sa'ud and Crown Prince Faysal, 1953–1962*, Tel Aviv: The Moshe Dayan Center for Middle Eastern and African Studies, 1997, 32; Samore, *Royal Family Politics in Saudi Arabia*, 84; Michael Herb, *All in the Family: Absolutism, Revolution, and Democracy in the Middle Eastern Monarchies*, Albany, NY: State University of New York Press, 1999, 28; Joseph A. Kechichian, *Succession in Saudi Arabia*, New York, NY: Palgrave, 2001, 10; Christine Moss Helms, *The Cohesion of Saudi Arabia: Evolution of Saudi Arabia*, Baltimore, MD: The Johns Hopkins University, 1981, 57; Bligh, *Prince to King*, 8.

[28] Joseph A. Kechichian, *Power and Succession in Arab Monarchies: A Reference Guide*, Boulder, CO: Lynne Rienner Publishers, 2008, 246; Bligh, *Prince to King*, 89, 103; Abir, *Government*, 7, 9.

evolved around King Saud's (r. 1953–1964) mismanagement of government funds, and which nearly bankrupted the Saudi monarchy.[29] The second one is a less known succession crisis that surfaced following King Faysal's controversial decision to join the October 1973 oil embargo, and that culminated into Faysal's assassination in March 1975.[30] This second succession crisis will be analyzed in detail in the coming chapters. Going back to King Saud's reign, one should point out that the king had not only led with his misguided policies, but he had also concentrated power to his sons and to his branch of the family (Banu Khalid). Such policies were not in the interests of the other influential members of the royal family. Eventually the family had had enough, and led by Crown Prince Faysal, the senior royals reached a consensus to abdicate King Saud. As the records seem to point out, the common denominator, which led into King Saud's abdication, on the one hand, and King Faysal's assassination, on the other hand, is that both Saud and Faysal had failed to protect the principal interests of the monarchy, and thus they had lost their support within the senior ranks of the royal family.

Based on the principles of tribal tradition, the king's authority has revolved around the support of the vast Al Saud family, which represents a variety of interests and opinions, and which consists of several branches of the monarchy (power groups). The most important branches of the royal family include: Al al-Shaikh (King Faysal), Sudayri (Fahd, Sultan, Musaid, Abd al-Rahman, Nayif, Turki, and Ahmad), Shammar (Abd Allah), and Jalwi (Muhammad and Khalid). The members of the Saudi monarchy can be divided into three circles based on their proximity to the center of power. In the 1970s and 1980s, the innermost circle consisted of probably less than a dozen senior royal princes who could be described as key decision-makers, and who altogether made all the important decisions on foreign and domestic affairs. In addition to their position in policy formulation, these senior princes also served as the final arbiters in matters of family politics. The second circle comprised of about two hundred influential princes from the Abd al-Rahman (1850–1928) and the Abd al-Aziz (aka. the Ibn Saud, ca. 1880–1953) branches of the royal family and the

---

[29] See, for instance: Bligh, *From Prince to King*.

[30] Indeed, the 1973 oil embargo was not the first embargo that the Saudis had participated. In fact, the Arab oil producers had attempted to use the oil embargo already in 1956 and 1967. In response to the Arab-Israeli wars at the time, they had declared an oil embargo against the countries that they claimed had been supporting Israel. The issue of politicization of Arab oil will be discussed in Chap. 4.

18   S. E. WILLNER

descendants of the *Araif*.[31] The third circle included the remaining several thousand royal princes, who enjoy wealth and status, but who have no significant political power.[32]

The authority of each senior prince was essentially based on the influence of his power group, namely, the importance of his mother's tribe in relation to the Al Saud. In contrast, in August 1982 Kamal Adham, the former Head of the Saudi General Intelligence Directorate [*Ri'āsat al-Istiḫbārāt al-ʿĀmah*] (1965–1979),[33] explained that there has been an unwritten convention according to which "the sons of slave girls could not succeed to the very top positions. A prince needs the backing of a noble family: he must have *akhwāl*, maternal uncles."[34] Thus, those royal princes whose mothers were from prominent families (e.g., Jiluwi, Sudayri, and Shammar) displayed stronger political credentials.[35] That being said, the prospective ruler's family background has played a decisive role in the recent succession processes. For the sake of prolonging the Saudi monarchy, these senior princes were, primarily, expected to promote the shared interests of the royal family, while at the same time considering the preferences and priorities of his tribal power group. This could include, for instance, promoting close family members to positions of power. Despite occasional disagreements and power battles, the Saudi monarchy's long

---

[31] Faysal ibn Turki (r. 1834–1837; 1843–1865) had four sons: Abd Allah (r. 1865–1871; 1871–1873; 1876–1889), Saud (r. 1871; 1873–1875), Muhammad, and Abd al-Rahman ((b. 1850) head of the family from 1975 until 1902, and imam until his death in 1928). The "*Araif*" branch of the royal family includes the descendants of Abd al-Rahman's brother, Saud ibn Faysal. This branch of Abd al-Aziz's cousins had allegedly turned against the Al Saud after they had been captured in a battle in 1904 by the tribe of Rashid. However, to avoid family dissention, they were later pardoned and allowed to return to Riyadh. *Araif* is a Bedouin term for camels lost and recaptured. Thus, the family branch was called *araif*. The other two sons of Faysal ibn Turki, Abd Allah and Muhammad, had no children. Alexander Bligh, *From Prince to King: Royal Succession in the House of Saud in the Twentieth Century*, New York, NY: New York University Press, 1984, 105–114; Samore; *Royal Family Politics*, 38. See also: Appendix A.

[32] Bligh, *From Prince to King*, 98–99. Similarly, in 1975 Holden argued that "probably not more than 100 princes are genuinely influential and perhaps only 30 could be called key men." David Holden, "A Family Affair," *New York Times*, July 6, 1975, 151.

[33] Kamal Adham was also a former Advisor to King Faysal and King Abd al-Aziz. He was also a close confidant to several of the senior princes.

[34] *Akhwāl* is the plural of *khāl*, which means a 'maternal uncle'; see: "Succession," August 9, 1982; Wehr, *A Dictionary of Modern Written Arabic*.

[35] Kechichian, *Power and Succession*, 247. However, it is useful to note that very little research exists on the influence of maternal decent on succession in Saudi Arabia.

survival could indicate that pragmatism and unity within the royal family was still far more important than the self-interest of these individual family members or any power group.[36] Finally, although all these above-discussed criteria are important for a prospective leader, being an adroit decision-maker is possibly the most decisive factor for a royal prince, who desires to claim leadership in Saudi Arabia.

---

[36] In the 1960s, domestic unrest, coup attempts, and princely rivalries had seriously threatened Al Saud's monarchy. Therefore, in October 1967, as a response to such threats, King Faysal introduced the concept of having a deputy crown prince by appointing Prince Fahd as the Second Deputy Prime Minister and as a second in line to the throne after Deputy Prime Minister Khalid. By making such an appointment, it is possible that King Faysal wanted to balance between the Sudayri-branch of the family and the rest of the royal family. However, such a practice, where a leader would name two or more successors and prescribe the order of the succession, was based on a theoretical non-binding model of Islamic succession that was developed by al-Mawardi (972–1058)—an eleventh-century imam and philosopher, who resided in Baghdad. See: Bligh, *From Prince to King*, 8–9, 86–87. See also: Kechichian, *Power and Succession*, 4; Nabil Mouline, "Pouvoir et Transition Générationnelle En Arabie Saoudite," *Critique Internationale*, 46, 2010: 125–146.

CHAPTER 3

Central Characteristics of Saudi Foreign Policy

The main objective of Saudi foreign policy is to steer the kingdom's foreign relations with other states. Saudi Arabia's foreign policy is established on its strategic interests, which are paramount to preserving its monarchy. Based on the principles of *badawī* tribal-familial decision-making, the senior members of the royal family formulate Saudi foreign policy privately through high-level decision-making processes and with little public discussion or explanation. For the most part, its foreign policy is carefully crafted and articulated through unofficial and less formal mechanisms (i.e., consultations between senior members of the family). While the foreign policy is solely in the hands of the royal family, it is supported by various ministries and government institutions. Behind the veil of secrecy, Saudi foreign affairs are based on clear objectives.

Generally, Saudi decision-making operates in a similar fashion as the other tribal-based states, where the leading tribe makes decisions concerning the national interests. In foreign policy, the Saudi king is the ultimate decision-maker, although he is still bound to the unwritten principles of tribal-familial norms. Therefore, the king's role is to shape the consensus *vis-à-vis* the kingdom's foreign policy through consulting various power groups within the royal family. These power groups, namely, the different branches of the royal family and princely coalitions (or alliances), can represent diverse domestic considerations, but also varying foreign policy aspirations. However, unity in decision-making has been a fundamental factor in maintaining the Saudi monarchy. Yet, if the royal family is split

© The Author(s), under exclusive license to Springer Nature Switzerland AG 2023
S. E. Willner, *Preserving the Saudi Monarchy*, https://doi.org/10.1007/978-3-031-30006-6_3

21

22 S. E. WILLNER

about a major foreign policy issue, the king would make the ultimate decision. It is also possible that in certain cases the position of the king could contradict the interests of the other senior members of the monarchy. However, political pragmatism was so important for the royal family that major deviation from such an integral principle could have fatal consequences for the ruler.

Saudi Arabia's foreign policy serves its primarily objective, that is, to preserve the Saudi monarchy. To that end, its foreign policy is commonly pragmatic, characterized with calculated risk-taking. Traditionally, the Saudis have preferred not to engage in risky situations, if possible, and in general, the royal family seems to be risk aversive. However, the monarchy has taken calculated risks if its survival was at stake, and if such decisions were beneficial. Carolus Lassila, the Ambassador of Finland to Saudi Arabia (1971–1977), has described the calculative nature of Saudi decision-making in his diplomatic communications. His analysis indicates that in Saudi Arabia most of the major decisions are based on *raison d'état* and that the monarchy is usually careful when it formulates decisions. He explains that Saudi decision-making processes are unemotional and even manipulative. Therefore, being a shrewd, manipulative, and even dangerous leader was essential because the ruler's skills in personal relations often had life or death consequences for himself and the royal family. Thus, due to the need to survive in an environment characterized by many challenging domestic and foreign policy issues, the Saudi decision-making has overtime evolved "and it has become unemotional and calculative." Lassila notes that it would be foolish to characterize Saudi politics and policies as "primitive; and [one] that would be based on imagination and improvisation." He goes even further by describing that on many occasions the Saudi position is "carefully planned."[1] As he puts it, primitive and old-fashioned characteristics of decision-making are side effects or that they might even be 'clear bluff'—smoke and mirrors.

---

[1] "Pieniä huomioita huomaamattomasta suurvallasta" [Observations about an unnoticed superpower] (secret report), Lassila to Ahti Karjalainen (Minister of Foreign Affairs, Helsinki), July 1, 1973, J-50/18, *Saudi Arabia, AMFAF*. See also: Karen Elliott House, *On Saudi Arabia: Its People, Past, Religion, Fault Lines – and Future*, New York, NY: Vintage Books, 2013, 13.

SILENT FOREIGN POLICY

The concept of silence in Saudi Arabia's foreign policy reflects two fundamental approaches in its decision-making. First, it reflects the decision-maker's desire to play it safe and clear him from taking responsibility for bad decisions. Second, it reflects the decision-maker's preference for highly personalized behind-the-scenes foreign relations. Based on this underlying concept of silence, Saudi foreign policy is best described with the Arabic words *ṣamt* and *ṣāmit*. The word *ṣamt* (and *ṣumūt*) refers to 'silence' while *ṣamata* means 'doing something quietly,' 'to be silent,' or 'to be taciturn.' In terms of not taking responsibility for bad or just risky decisions, Royal Advisor Rashad Pharaon's following remarks indicate that King Faysal often used such an approach. The exact date of the discussion is not recorded but according to the British diplomatic communications, Pharaon, who served as an advisor to King Faysal, had once told Willie Morris, the British Ambassador to Saudi Arabia (1968–1972) that his greatest difficulty when King Faysal returned his submissions without comment was to decide whether this signified approval, a closing of the matter or the need to submit a different argument to get approval for a case.[2] In accordance with this common practice of shunning responsibility, Faysal's conduct also highlights that he was the ultimate decision-maker in the royal family, and because of this, he did not have to demonstrate others that the power was in his hands. Correspondingly, in Saudi decision-making the concept of *ṣāmit* refers to a situation where silence indicates approval. Therefore, depending on the context of the matter, this means that if a person does not say anything, it usually implies his consent.[3] Moreover, due to the nature of Saudi decision-making, it has been necessary that the royal advisors and emissaries know how to read and interpret the messages they receive from the king and the senior princes. Misjudgment could have fatal consequences.

In Saudi foreign policy, silence has also translated into highly personalized foreign relations, the use of indirect channels of communications, and the preference of establishing informal agreements over formal signed documents. This is because the royal family has valued flexibility and reduced political risk that is often involved if such sensitive information is

---

[2] "Nature of Saudi Policies" (confidential report), Walker to J. Robert Young (Staff Member, MED, FCO, London), May 25, 1974, no. 15, *FCO 8/2332*.

[3] See, for instance, King Faysal's reaction when Minister of Petroleum Yamani presented him Washington's request to supply oil to the US Navy (December 1973) (see chapter X).

24   S. E. WILLNER

leaked to the press.[4] In order to maintain secrecy, and in order to preserve face and avoid unintentional leaks of sensitive information, the royal family has used trusted and loyal middlemen to mediate (*wasṭa* means 'between,' 'middle,' 'intermediary,' while *wisāṭa* means mediation) important negotiations with various parties or states.[5] Furthermore, in terms of communicating with foreign governments, the Saudis have often been indirect when they present important messages, while repeatedly downplaying the most depressing foreign policy issues. In this book, I have frequently analyzed the Saudi communications with its important partner United States. One can conclude from these diplomatic communications that when the royal family had an urgent message to convey to Washington, it usually started with the normal diplomatic channels via the US Embassy in Jeddah. However, if the royal family felt that its message did not reach Washington through official diplomatic channels or if it felt dissatisfied about Washington's response to its strategic interests, the royal family was apt to try indirect channels of communication. These channels included using the representatives of the Saudi Aramco. In fact, Aramco was a powerful oil company. It had significant commercial interests, and it had high-level government contacts in Washington. In addition to using such an indirect channel via Aramco, the Saudis also communicated to Washington through friendly foreign governments, including the British government and King Husayn of Jordan. However, if these attempts also

[4] "US-Saudi Relations" (confidential report), David Myers (MED, FCO, London) to Craig, February 12, 1982, no. 11, *FCO 8/4772*; Bligh, *Prince to King*, 2.

[5] For instance, following the improved relations with Egypt and to manage the threat posed by Iraq, the Saudis approached President Sadat to mediate between Syria and Saudi Arabia. What seem to have not been commonly known at the time is that the Saudis were utilizing their relatively close family relations with the al-Assad. Interestingly, Prince Abd Allah's sister-in-law was married to Rifat al-Assad, the brother of Syrian President Hafiz al-Asad, who rose to power through a military coup in November 1970. At the time, Rifat al-Asad served as the Commander of the Defense Companies [*Sarāya al-Difāʿ*] (1971–1984), which was a highly trained paramilitary force whose main task was to defend the Asad regime and the capital Damascus from internal and external threats. In Damascus, consequently, Prince Abd Allah earned a nickname 'Syria's Prince,' perhaps because of this important family connection. The British Embassy in Jeddah attempted to figure out why Abd Allah had such a special role but ended up concluding that "it was difficult to know on what the reputation was based, but Abd Allāh was usually chosen to entertain leading Syrian and had been to Damascus before with messages from the King." "Saudi Foreign Policy" (restricted document), John Gray (Staff Member, British Embassy, Jeddah) to FCO (London), December 2, 1980, no. 175, *FCO 8/3746*; Robert Baer, *Sleeping with the Devil: How Washington Sold Our Soul for Saudi Crude*, New York, NY: Three Rivers Press, 2004, 104–105.

3 CENTRAL CHARACTERISTICS OF SAUDI FOREIGN POLICY 25

failed, the royal family resorted to using local and international press.[6] As it seems, the Saudis have frequently used the press to convey indirect messages to various governments.

EMISSARIES REPRESENTING THE ROYAL FAMILY AND ITS INTERESTS

The non-royal advisors have played a vital role in the process of formulating foreign policy in Saudi Arabia. Although all the important decisions are made solely by the Saudi royal family, several trusted non-royal advisors and ministers have participated in the decision-making process and advised the inner circle of Saudi royals. For a non-royal advisor to remain in his position, he needed to, first, understand (and communicate to the real decision-makers) that his position was only to advise and not to make decisions. Second, he needed to possess the ability to listen carefully to the king's mood. Third, understand what the royal family's interests were and how the king desired to pursue them. Namely, these advisors needed to have an exceptional knowledge of the royal family and its strategic interests. Fourth, the non-royal advisors needed to correctly interpret the king's often indirect and sometimes cryptic messages. Finally, and perhaps most importantly, the advisers needed to be loyal and discreet. Accordingly, the importance of having trustworthy allies and advisors is described in an old Bedouin proverb, which implies that "companions make sure each other arrives" [*rafīq yivaṣṣil rafīq*].[7] In other words, due to the challenging geopolitical circumstances, it was essential that the loyalty of the royal family advisors was beyond doubt.

Given the secretive nature of Saudi policymaking, only the most reliable and loyal advisors were allowed to participate in the foreign policy formulation process, and at times, asked to represent the monarchy in negotiations with foreign governments. Many of these emissaries were powerful men and influential Saudi politicians. However, most of the issues, upon which they had authority to negotiate, had already been formulated in

---

[6] As recalled by Roger Merrick, the Deputy Director of Arabian Peninsula Affairs at the US Department of State. See: "US/Saudi Arabia: Article from the September Edition of the *Armed Forces Journal*" (confidential report), Adrian Fortescue (British Embassy, Washington) to Michael Pakenham (Minister, British Embassy, Washington), September 17, 1980, *FCO 8/3744.*

[7] Bailey, *A Culture of Desert Survival,* 170.

26 S. E. WILLNER

advance by the royal family. Accordingly, when the royal family wanted to negotiate with Washington concerning defense or security-related issues, it dispatched senior advisors to represent Riyadh. The royal family provided guidelines and a framework upon which the Saudi emissary needed to negotiate. In certain instances, the emissaries improvised based on the predetermined framework, and based on their knowledge of the king's mindset. For instance, during King Faysal's reign, Minister of Petroleum Ahmad Zaki Yamani (1962–1986) was one of the king's most distinguished emissaries. Faysal trusted Yamani because he was very loyal to him and because he knew Yamani would not go against him. This could also explain what is discussed in the later chapters, that some of the senior princes were complaining about Yamani, possibly because of his loyalty to King Faysal but possibly also because Yamani's statements reflected Faysal's position. Nevertheless, Yamani represented the royal family and negotiated with the foreign governments according to those guidelines that the king had assigned to him.[8]

SAUDI FOREIGN POLICY IS ESTABLISHED ON DEFENSIVE POSTURE

The foreign policy of Saudi Arabia is based on cautious dealings with foreign powers. Therefore, to survive, the royal family has calculated that it is better to avoid publicly declared alliances with those states that could alienate it from other states. It has also avoided being forced into one camp in the divided Arab world. However, since its foundation, Saudi Arabia has been a pro-Western monarchy, and its perception of the West was set apart from the revolutionary Arab regimes of Baghdad (Iraq), Tripoli (Libya), Damascus (Syria), and Aden (South Yemen). Contrary to those revolutionary regimes, Saudi foreign policy has been free of deeply rooted anti-Western sentiments. In fact, the unification of the Saudi kingdom in the 1920s and 1930s and its subsequent independence in 1932 was achieved because of an alliance with Britain, not of a struggle against it. Thus, the absence of anti-Western legacy made it easier for the Saudi

---

[8] See, for instance: Dawisha, "Internal Values and External Threats: The Making of Saudi Foreign Policy": 129; Mason, *Foreign Policy in Iran and Saudi Arabia*; Patrick, *Saudi Arabian Foreign Policy*; Quandt, *Saudi Arabia in the 1980s*; and Rieger, *Saudi Arabian Foreign Relations*. For further reading, see, for instance: Jeffrey Robinson. *Yamani: The Inside Story*, New York, NY: The Atlantic Monthly Press, 1989.

3 CENTRAL CHARACTERISTICS OF SAUDI FOREIGN POLICY   27

monarchy to establish diplomatic relations with the Western powers. Similarly, the Saudi partnership with the United States was based on pragmatic calculations—predominantly because the United States was a major arms supplier. Another important reason for the Saudi-US partnership was that the Soviet Union was aligned with the radical Arab regimes who wanted the Saudi monarchy deposed. For this reason, Saudi Arabia's political alliances *vis-à-vis* the Soviet camp were limited as Moscow supported Marxist revolutionary movements in accordance with its interests in the Cold War-conflict.[9]

Due to the presence of the Soviet-backed revolutionary Arab governments in the neighboring states, the Saudis perceived that the surrounding region accommodated many hostile adversaries who attempted to undermine their monarchical rule. Consequently, the Saudi foreign policy has been established on defensive posture. Most importantly, the Saudis have not been interested in unnecessary, costly conflicts. This preference of being cautious of being too much involved in other people's affairs is described in the following Bedouin proverb, which indicates that "glancing about breeds trouble" [*shaffit naẓar yuḥṣul minha ḍarār*].[10] Furthermore, the royal family has avoided risky foreign policy ventures in case they would fail and cause great embarrassment, and hence endanger the survival of the monarchy. For this reason, the Saudis have tried to avoid direct conflict with other states.

Fundamentally, preserving the Saudi monarchy has always come first and the ideological preferences second. According to Prince Turki al-Sudayri, the editor-in-chief of the daily Saudi newspaper *Al-Riyadh*,[11] the royal family has favored for quiet, behind-the-scene politics and diplomacy, which he says is "played like chess where you anticipate your

---

[9] See, for instance: Jacob Goldberg, *The Foreign Policy of Saudi Arabia: The Formative Years, 1902-1918,* Cambridge, MA: Harvard University Press, 1986, 183–184; Mason, *Foreign Policy in Iran and Saudi Arabia*; Patrick, *Saudi Arabian Foreign Policy*; Quandt, *Saudi Arabia in the 1980s*; Rieger, *Saudi Arabian Foreign Relations*; Dawisha, "Internal Values and External Threats: The Making of Saudi Foreign Policy," 129; 'Abd Allah al-Kabbah, *Al-sīyāsah al-khārijīah al-Sa'ūdīyyah* [The Foreign Policy of Saudi Arabia], Riyadh: Al-Farazdaq Commercial Press, 1986; J.E. Peterson, *Saudi Arabia and the Illusion of Security,* New York, NY: Oxford University Press, 2002, 30, 34; and Gulshan Dietl, "Foreign Policy of Saudi Arabia: Internal and External Contexts." *India Quarterly*, 4, 3–4, (1985): 363–375.

[10] Bailey, *A Culture of Desert Survival*, 391.

[11] See: Said Aburish, *The Rise, Corruption and Coming Fall of the House of Saud*, New York, NY: St. Martin's Press, 1996, 218.

28   S. E. WILLNER

opponent's next move."[12] Interestingly, Turki al-Sudayri's chess remarks indicate that the royal family tends to reflect carefully about its coming foreign policy moves, and furthermore, about what could be the other states' reaction to its policymaking. Moreover, Saudi foreign policymaking is fundamentally based on having a long-term perspective instead of attempting to achieve immediate gain. This, in turn, is in line with an old Bedouin proverb, which says that "patience can destroy mountains" [*ṭūlt al-bāl bit-hidd jibāl*]. As Bailey puts it, the power of patience can solve problems, "even those that may appear as formidable as a mountain."[13] Such a logic of operation indicates that Saudi actions in relation to its adversaries have been rooted in a cold calculation of its political, economic, and strategic strengths and weaknesses.[14]

Regardless of how carefully the Saudis deliberate their foreign policy, there is always an element of surprise that can impede their decision-making. This perplexing factor can derive from the possibility of misjudgment and mistakes in the decision-making. For this reason, I argue based on the findings of this book that, primarily, the royal family has been traumatized by the fear that they could lose the grip of their people, and by the threat of revolutions, which could threaten and overthrow the royal family, as had happened when the monarchies were overthrown in Egypt (1952), Iraq (1958), Yemen (1962), Libya (1969), and Iran (1979). Only secondarily, the Saudis have perceived that their kingdom could become an object of foreign military invasions.[15] Given these historic circumstances and strategic issues, the Saudis have been consistent about their deeply rooted anxieties, which have determined their opposition to any plans that aimed to consolidate Arab countries into a larger unity.

Most importantly, the Saudis have calculated that they would not be able to dominate the Arab world due to several strategic challenges—

---

[12] Based on a the British Embassy's discussions with Turki al-Sudayri on December 7, 1981; see: "Saudi Foreign Policy: Arab/Israel" (confidential memo), Richard J.S. Muir (British Embassy, Jeddah) to Christopher M.J. Segar (MED, FCO, London), no. 142, *FCO 8/4209*; "Annual Review for 1977" (confidential report), John Wilton (Ambassador, British Embassy, Jeddah) to David Owen (Secretary of State for Foreign and Commonwealth Affairs, FCO, London), January 4, 1978, *FCO 8/3256*.

[13] Bailey, *A Culture of Desert Survival*, 231.

[14] See, for instance: Robert Mason, *Foreign Policy in Iran and Saudi Arabia*, London: I.B. Tauris, 2015, 82.

[15] For instance, the Egyptian involvement in the Yemen Civil War during 1962–1967, the 1978–1979 Islamic Revolution in Iran, and the ongoing civil war in Yemen (since 2014).

predominantly, however, due to insufficient military strength. Instead, at the time, such political unions were—and would have been—dominated by the traditional centers of the Arab world, namely Cairo, Baghdad, and Damascus. Subsequently, the Saudis had recognized that the circumstances of Arab unity would represent a direct challenge to their monarchy, and moreover, it would eradicate their independence altogether and submit the Saudi monarchy to the authority of other Arab states. Therefore, within the framework of its pragmatic foreign policy approach, the aim of Saudi foreign policy was not to contemplate visions that could overstep the territorial limits of the Kingdom of Saudi Arabia.[16]

[16] Goldberg, *The Foreign Policy of Saudi Arabia*, 178–184.

Conclusion of Part I The Foundations of Political Leadership in Saudi Arabia

CONCLUSIONS

Behind its veil of secrecy, the Saudi monarchy appears to be highly pragmatic, which is in part due to its deeply rooted tribal thinking in which prolonging the survival of its monarchy, and relying to the protection of the family, on the one hand, and the tribal loyalties, on the other hand, have played such a critical role. This, in turn, points out that the Saudis have compromised when political pragmatism was needed to preserve the monarchy. As the coming chapters will indicate, such pragmatism is a noticeable part of Saudi foreign affairs.

First, and perhaps most importantly, the Saudis always put their own interests at first and therefore the survival of their monarchy is far more important than ideological motives. Second, Saudi decision-making processes appear to be calculative, and even manipulative. While the Saudi royal family operates in secrecy, and while its thinking appears to be highly conspiratorial, its decision-makers are remarkably capable of taking advantage of similar mindset of its foreign counterparts.

Third, while preserving the honor of its decision-makers plays a significant role in the Saudi mindset, such principle did not rule out calculated risk-taking whenever it was necessary. While it seems to be true that the Saudis usually avoids risks—more interestingly, it appears to be that the royal family was willing to take substantial risks if it had calculated such decision was worthwhile taking.

Fourth, the Saudis make decisions based on the principle of consultation and consensus. Although the Saudi king is the most powerful decision-maker within the royal family, the role of the family, and the need of compromise, is essential in the decision-making process where key policies are formulated. Naturally, the king is the final arbiter of decision-making, but he should not be an authoritarian leader. Although the king has a veto over the family consensus, however, in cases of a significant conflict between the king and the key members of the royal family, the family has taken the lead from the king by initiating a succession process (which usually starts well before a new leader takes over from the old king). In other words, a Saudi leader cannot make decisions as an absolute monarch but, rather, he always needs to consider the interests of the monarchy.

Finally, a decision not to do something is also a decision. Although a foreign observer might think that Saudi political interests are not always clearly defined, Saudi logic of operation reveals that the kingdom's foreign policy is much more organized than what is considered by the Westerners.

PART II

The 1973 Arab–Israeli War and the Arab Oil Embargo

In the process of formulating its foreign policy around the events of the 1973 Arab–Israeli War, the Saudi royal family showed great sensitivity to the risks posed by the radical Arab states situated around its borders. Therefore, to make their contribution to the Arab battle against Israel, the Saudis acted in two major ways. The first was the generous Saudi financial assistance to Egypt, the original purpose of which had been to get Egypt to withdraw its forces from the 1960s Yemen War, and thus, to stop threatening the kingdom. The second, and more controversial in terms of the pragmatic Saudi foreign policy, was King Faysal's decision to use the 'oil weapon' [*silāḥ al-nafṭ*], and to join the Arab oil embargo against the United States in October 1973. This decision was a major turning point for the Saudis. Although it had been made in the name of the Saudi government, however, the royal family had been divided about the issue of joining the oil embargo.

Being drawn into a war against Israel was not in the interests of the Saudi monarchy. While King Faysal had advocated for supporting Egypt and joining the Arab oil embargo, the royal family messaged Israel through the US Central Intelligence Agency (CIA) that the Saudi military forces were under strict instructions not to become involved in the fighting. To understand the circumstances under which Saudi Arabia had joined the Arab oil embargo, one would first need to investigate the upsurge of political Arabism in the 1950s, and furthermore, its contribution to the significant rise in anti-Saudi activity in the early 1970s. By targeting the Saudi kingdom, the radical regimes were primarily motivated by their hegemonic self-interests. Although their long-term aim was probably to overthrow the Saudi monarchy and replace it with a radical Arab republic, their more immediate objective was to change the course of Saudi Arabia's pro-Western foreign policy, and more specifically, to alter its conservative oil policy.

CHAPTER 4

Emerging Pan-Arabism and the Politicization of Arab Oil

ABD AL-NASIR'S PAN-ARABISM

The foreign policy interests of the radical Arab governments have conflicted with the pragmatic Saudi foreign policy. Since the late 1950s, several revolutionary Arab governments had repeatedly sponsored subversive activity against the Western-oriented Saudi monarchy. These included the governments in Cairo (Egypt), Baghdad (Iraq), Tripoli (Libya), Damascus (Syria), and Aden (the Marxist People's Democratic Republic of Yemen (PDRY), also known as South Yemen).[1] The radicalization of these Arab regimes was inspired by the emergence of pan-Arab ideology[2] following Lieutenant-Colonel Jamal Abd al-Nasir's military coup against the Egyptian monarchy in July 1952 and his election to the presidency in June 1956.[3] Abd al-Nasir served as the president of Egypt until his death in September 1970. The secular and socialist pan-Arab ideology promoted by Abd al-Nasir was an inspiration in the struggle against the Arab

---

[1] These five Arab regimes were all involved in sponsoring subversion against Saudi Arabia, although not at the same time and intensity.

[2] Historically, pan-Arabism is said to have started around the end of the First World War (1914–1918) and was at first primarily aimed against the Ottoman Empire.

[3] Abd al-Nasir led Egypt from 1954 until 1970. He served as the chairman of the Revolutionary Command Council (November 1954 until June 1956) and as the president (June 1956 until September 1970).

© The Author(s), under exclusive license to Springer Nature Switzerland AG 2023
S. E. Willner, *Preserving the Saudi Monarchy*, https://doi.org/10.1007/978-3-031-30006-6_4

35

36 S. E. WILLNER

monarchies. Because of such a radical political enterprise, Saudi Arabia became one of the principal targets of their revolutionary ideology and activity.[4]

Inspired by Abd al-Nasir's pan-Arabism and republicanism, several Arab monarchies in the Middle East and North Africa were overthrown by the revolutionary forces. In July 1958, King Faysal II of Iraq (r. 1939–1958) was overthrown and executed along with the rest of the royal family; in September 1962, the royal family of the Imamate of Yemen were overthrown and replaced by the Yemen Arab Republic (YAR) (also known as North Yemen); and in September 1969, King Idris[5] of Libya (r. 1951–1969) was deposed. In addition to the above mentioned, the revolutionary forces also targeted King Husayn of Jordan (r. 1952–1999) numerous times, but he managed to evade these assassination attempts.

During Abd al-Nasir's time in power, Egypt was a leading sponsor of revolutionary activity against the Arab monarchies. To pursue Arab unity and Egyptian hegemony, Abd al-Nasir interfered in the political affairs of other Arab states. Based on his political aspirations, it was essential that the Western-oriented Arab monarchies would be eliminated for his pan-Arab and republican ideology to be successful. Following the collapse of the short-lived (1958–1961) United Arab Republic (UAR)[6]—the union between Egypt and Syria—Egypt started to eye on Yemen. After the overthrow of Yemen's royalist regime in 1962,[7] Egypt began to support the

---

[4] For instance, several coup attempts took place in Saudi Arabia in the late 1960s, which were mainly organized by young army and air force officers. These revolutionaries also included many Saudi intellectuals and even royal princes.

[5] The Kingdom of Libya was ruled by Muhammad Idris ibn Muhammad al-Mahdi al-Sanussi.

[6] The years that followed Syrian independence in 1946 were characterized with considerable upheaval and several coups. For the Syrians, joining Egypt in the UAR in February 1958 was mainly an attempt to overcome the possible communist threat of taking over the power following the continued chaos in the country. The Egyptian-dominated union lasted until September 1961 when a *coup d'état* took place in Syria and, consequently, the UAR was terminated.

[7] UAR had been in confederation with the Mutawakkilite Kingdom of Yemen (North Yemen) during 1958–1961, which was called United Arab States (UAS).

revolutionary forces that were fighting against the Saudi-backed royalists in North Yemen.[8]

For Egypt, the war in Yemen provided an avenue to exercise its influence in the Arabian Peninsula. Through supporting the new republican government in North Yemen, Abd al-Nasir wanted to put pressure on the traditional regimes in the Peninsula.[9] In fact, he had calculated that by sending the Egyptian military he would be able to quickly establish a bridgehead in Arabia, and from where he could take over the Saudi kingdom.[10] The Saudis were concerned about the Egyptian involvement in the Arabian Peninsula, because during the 1950s and 1960s the Saudi revolutionaries had been inspired by the pan-Arab ideology.[11] In addition, Abd al-Nasir' pan-Arabism helped to stir an armed revolt in the Omani province of Dhofar, which shared a border with South Yemen.[12]

Abd al-Nasir's anti-Saudi activity continued until 1967 when Egyptian military suffered a devastating defeat in the June Arab-Israeli War (also known as the Six-Day War). Because of the military defeat, Abd al-Nasir's position in the Arab world weakened. Consequently, the Saudis took advantage of the changed situation. On the one hand, Egypt needed to

[8] Mordechai Abir, *Oil, Power and Politics: Conflict in Arabia, the Red Sea and the Gulf*, London: Frank Cass and Company, 1974, 35–36. For further reading, see: Joseph, P. Lorenz, *Egypt and the Arabs: Foreign Policy and the Search for National Identity*, Boulder, CO: Westview Press, 1990.

[9] Abir, *Oil, Power and Politics*, 35. See also: Saeed Badeeb, *The Saudi-Egyptian Conflict over North Yemen, 1962-1970*, Boulder, CO: Westview Press, 1986.

[10] Furthermore, to achieve these objectives in the Arabian Peninsula, he had tried to take advantage of the severe disputes that had shadowed the royal family. These disagreements had escalated considerably after King Saud had concentrated power to his branch of the royal family, and after he had seriously mismanaged Saudi Arabia's finances. The financial mismanagement had increased the public debt, and consequently, the kingdom was heading toward government bankruptcy. See, for instance: Gerald De Gaury, *Faisal: King of Saudi Arabia*, London: Arthur Barker Limited, 1967, 90.

[11] F. Gregory Gause, *Saudi-Yemeni Relations: Domestic Structures and Foreign Influence*, New York, NY: Columbia University Press, 1990, 59; Abir, *Oil, Power and Politics*, 54.

[12] In fact, the rebellion in Dhofar started already in 1962 but it began to obtain more revolutionary characteristics following the June 1967 Arab-Israeli War and the withdrawal of the British forces from Aden in November of the same year. South Yemen (PDRY), which was ruled by a radical government under the leadership of the National Liberation Front—a Marxist paramilitary organization—began to support the rebellion in Dhofar. In 1976, after years of fighting, the revolt was finally put down with the help of Iranian and Jordanian military and British special forces. See: David C. Arkless, *The Secret War: Dhofar, 1971-1972*, London: W. Kimber, 1988; Tony Jeapes, *SAS: Operation Oman*, London: W. Kimber, 1980; John Townsend, *Oman: The Making of the Modern State*, London: Croom Helms, 1977.

refocus its military efforts, and therefore it decided to revise its hostile policy toward Saudi Arabia and the other Arab monarchies. On the other hand, the humiliating outcome of the Arab-Israeli War provided Saudi Arabia an opportunity to buy Egypt out from the war in Yemen. Therefore, in return for Egyptian military withdrawal (which took place in December 1967), the Saudis provided Egypt with hundreds of millions of dollars. These funds were meant to support Egyptian economy following the closure of the Suez Canal—and furthermore, to rebuild its army so that it could confront Israel in a future military conflict.[13] Although the Saudi-Egyptian relations improved following the evacuation of the Egyptian forces, and after Egypt had seized supporting the republican forces in North Yemen, the political relations between the two countries improved in a meaningful way only after the death of Abd al-Nasir in September 1970.[14] When Anwar al-Sadat became the President of Egypt (r. 1970–1981), Egypt was no longer considered radical in the Arab world. While the relations between Saudi Arabia and Egypt got better, the epicenter of the pan-Arab revolutionary activity moved gradually from Cairo elsewhere, namely to Tripoli (Libya), Baghdad (Iraq), and Damascus (Syria). According to Mordechai Abir, Damascus became the epicenter for the activities of the Saudi Communists, and it sponsored anti-Saudi radio broadcasts and newspaper commentaries, while Baghdad hosted Saudi Ba'athists and gave shelter and support to other small leftist Saudi groups.[15]

THE POLITICIZATION OF ARAB OIL

The politicization of Arab oil has its roots in 1951 when the Arab League [*Al-Jāmi'ah al-'Arabīyyah*] established a committee of Arab oil experts, and in 1954 a permanent office was created to deal with its members'

---

[13] Furthermore, the Egyptian forces suffered heavy losses due to the difficult terrain and the guerrilla war waged by the royalist forces against its troops. As such, the war in the Yemen came close to bankrupting Egypt because of the high financial cost of the war. Gause assesses the Saudi-Yemeni relations and the Egyptian involvement in the war in his following work: F. Gregory Gause, *Saudi-Yemeni Relations: Domestic Structures and Foreign Influence*, New York, NY: Columbia University Press, 1990.

[14] See: "King Faisal: Oh, Wealth and Power," *Time Magazine*, April 7, 1975, 14, 24; Abir, *Oil, Power and Politics*, 36; Henry Kissinger, *The White House Years*, Boston, MA: Little, Brown & Company, 1979, 1276–1289.

[15] Mordechai Abir, *Saudi Arabia in the Oil Era: Regime and Elites; Conflict and Collaboration*, London: Croom Helm, 1988, 112, 127; and Mordechai Abir, *Saudi Arabia: Government, Society and the Gulf Crisis*, London: Routledge, 1993, 54.

issues around petroleum. Furthermore, in September 1960, the Organization for Petroleum Exporting Countries (OPEC) was established,[16] while some seven years later, in January 1968, the Organization of the Arab Oil Exporting Countries (OAPEC) [*Munazzamat al-Aqtār al-'Arabīyyah al-Muṣaddirah lil-Nafṭ*] was founded. These two oil producer organizations were instrumental in the process of shifting the control of oil production, the nationalization of petroleum production facilities, and increasing the oil prices following the 1973 oil embargo. In terms of the Arab oil politics, OAPEC's founding members—the monarchies of Saudi Arabia, Libya, and Kuwait—had originally intended the organization to be politically conservative. However, OAPEC's political discourse took a dramatic turn in September 1969 when Colonel Muammar Qadhafi seized the power in Libya after his military coup against King Idris.

While being the youngest Arab leader at the time when he came to power, President Qadhafi (r. 1969–2011) felt that his political future was in constant doubt. Therefore, in promoting *Nasserism*, the new leadership in Libya sought reassurance and endorsement through bold pan-Arab foreign policy ventures. Like Ba'athist Iraq,[17] the Libyan leader Qadhafi promoted Arab socialism and unity between Arab states, while his political aspirations were extended to oil and the OAPEC. Therefore, in accordance with Qadhafi's political aspirations, the Libyan regime pressured OAPEC to modify its objectives and to accept more radical member states.

---

[16] OPEC was established with the principal aim of unifying its member countries' petroleum policies. OPEC, *Official Resolutions and Press Releases, 1960-1980*, Oxford: Pergamon Press, 1980. For more on OPEC and the politics of oil, see, for instance: Mohammed E. Ahrari, *OPEC: The Failing Giant*, Lexington, KY: The University Press of Kentucky, 1986; Nathan, J. Citino, *From Arab Nationalism to OPEC: Eisenhower, King Saud, and the Making of U.S.-Saudi Relations*, Bloomington, IN: Indiana University Press, 2002; Ali D. Johany, *The Myth of the OPEC Cartel: The Role of Saudi Arabia*, New York, NY: John Wiley, 1982; Ragaei, El Mallakh, ed. *OPEC: Twenty Years and Beyond*, Boulder, CO: Westview Press, 1982; Dankwart A. Rustow and John F. Mugno. *OPEC: Success and Prospects*, London: Martin Robertson & Company, 1976; Dankwart A. Rustow, *Oil and Turmoil: America Faces OPEC and the Middle East*, New York, NY: Norton, 1982.

[17] Following the pro-Nasserist 1958 "Free Officers" coup that overthrew King Faysal II, Iraq's foreign policy became more pan-Arab. Several coups came and went until one year after the June 1967 Arab-Israeli War (the Six-Day War), in July 1968, when the Ba'athists staged another coup, because of which, Ahmad Hasan al-Bakr became the President of Iraq (1968–1979) and the Chairman of the Revolutionary Command Council, with Saddam Husayn serving as his deputy.

In 1970, Bahrain, Algeria, Abu Dhabi, Dubai, and Qatar joined the OAPEC.

The Saudis were not pleased about Qadhafi's radicalizing effect on OAPEC. Indeed, Libya pressed hard for the use of oil as a political weapon and managed to renegotiate its oil agreements with the international oil companies. For most part, however, the Saudis were worried that the revolutionary regimes would harness the oil politics to threaten their interests. In fact, when Iraq applied for a membership in 1971, Saudi Arabia initially rejected its request. As it seemed, the Saudis were against Iraq's membership in OAPEC because it disliked its revolutionary regime and considered Iraq as a threat. Eventually, Iraq's membership request was approved in 1972. Syria joined the membership in 1972 and Egypt in 1973.

The radical regimes initiated a lobby to coordinate Arab oil producers' political interests in response to the unsuccessful 1967 oil embargo. Correspondingly, these regimes wanted to use oil embargo as an economic and political weapon against Israel, while looking for balance between the Arab states and Iran.[18] All in all, Qadhafi's rise to power, and his radicalizing impact on the oil politics, played a substantial role in the events that preceded the 1973 oil embargo.[19]

---

[18] Benjamin Shwadran, *Middle East Oil since 1973*, Boulder, CO: Westview Press, 1986, 46.

[19] The Arab oil producers had attempted to use the oil embargo already in 1956 and 1967. In response to the Arab-Israeli wars at the time, they had declared an oil embargo against the countries that they claimed had been supporting Israel. In 1967, the Arab oil producers (including Saudi Arabia, Kuwait, Iraq, Libya, and Algeria) declared an oil embargo to deter any country from providing support to Israel. Accordingly, the Arab oil producers banned oil shipments to the United States, the United Kingdom, and the Federal Republic of Germany (also known as West Germany). Nevertheless, the 1967 embargo was unsuccessful, mainly because it did not significantly reduce the amount of oil available to the key Western oil consumers, and because oil supplies were redistributed to the embargoed countries. For more on the oil policy and the Middle East oil, see: Daniel Yergin, *The Prize: The Epic Quest for Oil, Power & Money*, London: Simon & Schuster, 2008, 536–542, Benjamin Shwadran, *The Middle East, Oil, and the Great Powers*, Jerusalem: Israel Universities Press, 1973; Benjamin Shwadran, *The Growth and Power of the Middle Eastern Oil Producing Countries*, Tel-Aviv: The Shiloah Center for Middle Eastern and African Studies, Tel-Aviv University, 1974; Benjamin Shwadran, *Middle East Oil Crisis since 1973*, Boulder, CO: Westview Press, 1986; Fadhil, J. Chalabi, *Oil Policies and Myths: Analysis and Memoir of an OPEC Insider*, New York, NY: I.B. Tauris & Co, 2010.

4 EMERGING PAN-ARABISM AND THE POLITICIZATION OF ARAB OIL 41

THE RASHIDI UNREST AND THE REPERCUSSIONS OF THE 1970 'BLACK SEPTEMBER'

By the early 1970s, Egypt had ceased sponsoring revolutionary activity against Saudi Arabia and was now supporting the Saudi policy regarding the conflict in Yemen. While the Egyptian foreign policy had principally changed, however, the regimes in Baghdad and Tripoli were now the leading sponsors of anti-Saudi activity in the Arab world. In fact, by the eve of the 1973 Arab-Israeli War, these regimes had organized multiple sabotage and terror campaigns against the monarchy.

Indeed, the Saudis were troubled by the Iraqi-sponsored activities. In March 1970, Umar Saqqaf, the Saudi Minister of State for Foreign Affairs (1968–1974),[20] pointed out to the British officials that the Iraqis "were out to make trouble [for the Saudi monarchy]."[21] Moreover, Saqqaf had told that the Iraqis had attempted to stir unrest among the Rashidi tribe, which resided in the Shammar mountain range in the northwestern Saudi Arabia. Based on Saqqaf's comments, the British Embassy assessed that the Iraqis wanted to revive the Saudi-Rashid clash of tribal loyalties.[22] However, as it was later revealed, the tensions had died down and the Iraqis had lessened these tactics, "probably in realization that the Saudis, with more money in their disposal, can play the tribal game better [than the Iraqis]."[23]

---

[20] Umar Saqqaf was an experienced non-royal Saudi diplomat. "Omar Saqqaf Dies; Saudi Diplomat, 51," *The New York Times*, November 19, 1974, 34.

[21] "Saudi/Iraqi Relations" (confidential report), James Craig (Councilor, British Embassy, Jeddah) to W.H. Fullerton (Arabian Department, FCO, London), March 3, 1970, *FCO 8/1487.*

[22] As a point of historical interests, the British Defense Attaché wrote that the Iraqis made use of one of the surviving Rashidis—the tribe opposed to the Al Saud at the turn of the twentieth century—to stir up trouble. During the first decades of the twentieth century, there were series of armed conflicts between the Rashidis and the Saudi monarchy. In the early 1970s, "[the] Saudi military reaction to this was to send one National Guard company of 7 *firqa fedayeen* to Rafah in March 1971; later in September 1971 this was reinforced by 18 *firqa fedayeen*. It may be significant that Prince 'Abd-Allāh [...] departed hurriedly on a 'hunting trip' to this area, but the real reason was probably either to use his considerable influence with the tribes, or inspection and reconnaissance." The *firqa fedayeen* were small local military units with less than ten men who were loyal to Al Saud. See: "Annual Report for 1971 by Defense Attaché, Jeddah" (confidential report), R.M. Begbie (Colonel Defense Attaché, British Embassy, Jeddah) to Ministry of Defense (London), January 24, 1972, *FCO 8/1915.*

[23] "Annual Report for 1971 by Defense Attaché, Jeddah," January 24, 1972.

In addition to the above-mentioned activity, the Iraqis were disseminating hostile propaganda against the Saudis through the Baghdad press and radio. According to Ziyad Shawwaf, the Head of the Western Department of the Saudi Ministry of Foreign Affairs, "the Saudis could not understand the Iraqi attacks; presumably they were for domestic consumption [in Iraq],"[24] and therefore, possibly, intended to raise the internal popularity of the regime in Baghdad. Moreover, Saqqaf added that, despite Iraq's own problems with Israel, the Kurds, and Iran, Baghdad was trying to extend its influence in the Persian Gulf and the Arabian Peninsula.[25] Interestingly, the British Embassy had heard from anonymous sources that the Saudi security authorities had received instructions to "keep Iraqis in Jeddah under particular surveillance."[26] No specific threat was mentioned in the reports. Correspondingly, the Embassy noted that "there [had] been no public expression of Saudi suspicions but as you know it takes a lot to persuade the Saudis to say anything nasty about their brother Arabs in public."[27]

In October 1970, just few months after the above-mentioned security incidents, the British diplomatic sources reported that the Saudis were afraid that "Palestinian sabotage teams"[28] would be entering the kingdom to damage the oil fields. The Saudis seemed to have been particularly worried about the consequences of the events of the 'Black September,' which had occurred few weeks earlier.[29] Following these events, the Saudis took numerous precautions to secure the kingdom. For instance, on September 23, 1970, the Saudi oil company Aramco received orders from the Saudi security committee to remove all foreign personnel from the important oil installations in Ras Tanura. When Aramco asked clarifications from Prince

---

[24] "Saudi Arabia/Iraq" (confidential report), St. John Armitage to Stephen L. Egerton (Arabian Department, FCO, London), May 23, 1970, *FCO 8/1487*.

[25] "Saudi/Iraqi Relations," March 3, 1970.

[26] Ibid.

[27] Ibid.

[28] It is not specified which Palestinian groups the Saudis were referring to. See: "Palestinians in Saudi Arabia" (confidential report), John Armitage to Robert McGregor (Arabian Department, FCO, London), October 3, 1970, *FCO 8/1483*.

[29] In September 1970, several international civil airliners were hijacked by Palestinian terrorists and flown to Zarqa airfield in Jordan. To overthrow the monarchy in Jordan, the hijackings were soon followed by heavy fighting between guerrillas loyal to the PLO and the Jordanian military forces; an event, which came to be known as the 'Black September.' The monarchy won the battles, and the PLO forces were mostly crushed while some fled to Syria and Lebanon.

Nayif bin Abd al-Aziz, the Deputy Minister of Interior (1970–1975), he explained that "the order was aimed at the Palestinians but that the Saudis did not wish to appear to be discriminatory."[30] Few days after the order had been given, a bomb exploded near the entrance to the king's main residence, also known as the Sahari Palace. The Saudis blamed the Palestinians for the bomb incident.[31]

Saboteurs targeted Saudi oil infrastructure in numerous occasions. As was reported in January 1973, the Trans-Arabian Pipeline (TAP)[32] was damaged due to an explosion. According to the spokesman of that pipeline's company, sabotage was suspected to be the cause of the explosion and that the damage was on a section of the pipeline about 23 kilometers south of the Iraqi border inside Saudi territory. However, it was not the first time that the pipeline had been targeted. The previous sabotage had been claimed by Palestinian guerrillas, who, according to the information acquired by the *Financial Times*, were "dedicated to striking at US interests in the Arab world." Furthermore, some anonymous sources had informed the newspaper that the sabotage could have been timed to coincide with the inauguration of President Richard Nixon (1969–1974) for his second term in the White House.[33] The British foreign officials, on the other hand, suspected that the Iraqis were the ones behind the attack. Moreover, they assessed that the attack could indicate both the worsening of the Saudi-Iraqi relations and the weakening of the domestic security situation in the kingdom.[34] Interestingly, in July 1973, few months after these latest oil pipeline attacks, Prince Abd Allah told Robert Lindsay (aka. Lord Balniel), the British Minister of State for Foreign Affairs (1972–1974), that "the only real danger was from communism, [… and that Iraq and

---

[30] "Palestinians in Saudi Arabia," October 3, 1970.

[31] Ibid.

[32] The TAP is an American-owned oil pipeline, which conveyed oil from the Saudi Eastern Province oil fields to the Sidon seaport in Lebanon, and which traverses through Jordan. The pipeline began operation in 1950. In 1990, the Saudis completely ceased its operation in response to Jordan's support of Iraq during the 1990–1991 Gulf War.

[33] It reported that this incident was already the fifth time the TAP-line was damaged by sabotage since 1969; see: "Explosion Damages Saudi Pipeline," *Financial Times*, January 23, 1973.

[34] A comment by an unknown FCO officer indicated that "the attack could equally have been launched from Kuwait"; see: "untitled document" (unclassified), January 24, 1973, no. 3, *FCO 8/2119*.

PDRY] on their own were not important."[35] Although the Saudi communications often followed a pattern of emphasizing less important foreign policy issues, it is possible that the Saudis were, in fact, more concerned about the repercussions of the developing Arab-Israeli conflict.

The Saudis and the Threat Posed by the 'Palestine-Problem'

The Palestinian militant groups posed a major headache to the Saudis during the 1970s, especially because these groups were often sponsored by radical Arab states—including Libya and Iraq, to operate against the Saudi monarchy. As such, the true face of the 'Palestine-problem,' as will be further elaborated in the later chapters, was that the Palestinian terror groups used these attacks to blackmail funds from the Saudis so that they could finance their operations. While sponsoring these Palestinian groups, the radical Arab states attempted to force the Saudis to change their foreign and oil policy to anti-Western. In accordance with such terror activities that were perpetrated against the Saudis and other Arab monarchies, David Kimche, the former Director General of Israel's Ministry of Foreign Affairs (1980–1987) and the former Deputy Director of Mossad (unknown–1979), has revealed that the Saudis paid the Palestine Liberation Organization (PLO) [*Munazzamat at-Taḥrīr al-Filasṭīniyyah*] hundreds of millions of dollars in regular installments. He also expressed his frustration by pointing out that "the spinelessness of the Arab leaders in the face of the PLO-threat was difficult to comprehend."[36]

For the most part, the Saudi perspective to the whole Palestinian issue is well articulated by a senior Saudi government official during a meeting

[35] Prince Abd Allah had a meeting with Lord Balniel in London on July 4, 1973. See: "Record of conversation between the Minister of State and Prince Abd Allah bin Abd al-Aziz at the Dorchester Hotel on July 4, 1973" (memo), no. 43, *FCO 8/2125*; "Defense Attaché's Annual Report for 1972" (confidential report), R.G. Woodhouse (Lieutenant Colonel, Defense Attaché, British Embassy, Jeddah) to Ministry of Defense (London), June 16, 1973, *FCO 8/2118*. See also: Amatzia Baran, "Saddam Hussein: A Political Profile," *The Jerusalem Quarterly*, 17, 1980: 115–144.

[36] David Kimche, *The Last Option: After Nasser, Arafat, & Saddam Hussein: The Quest for Peace in the Middle East*. New York, NY: Charles Scribner's Sons, 1991, 39, 91. More on the PLO, see, for instance: Helene Cobban, *The Palestinian Liberation Organization: People, Power and Politics*, New York, NY: Cambridge University Press, 1984; Aryeh Yodfat, and Yuval Arnon-Ohanna, *PLO: Strategy and Tactics*, New York, NY: St. Martin's Press, 1981.

with the British officials in February 1972. Prior to this meeting the officials from the British Embassy had enquired about the Saudi decision to purchase American F-5 fighter jets instead of buying British planes. The British were arguing that selling planes to the Saudis while supplying weapons to Israel was quite a contradiction.[37] Sayid Abd al-Rahman Mansuri, a Legal Advisor at the Saudi Ministry of Foreign Affairs, responded to Willie Morris, the British Ambassador to Saudi Arabia (1968–1972), by saying that "what we say about the Palestine-problem is lip-service: it is not part of our bone, as the Gulf and the Buraimi problem are. Saudi Arabia is not directly involved with Israel." Here Mansuri referred to the 1968 British announcement of withdrawing its military forces by 1971, on the one hand, and the Buraimi oasis dispute between the kingdom and Oman and Abu Dhabi, which was mainly settled by an agreement in 1974, on the other hand. Mansuri also added that when Saudi Arabia was involved with Israel—while emphasizing that it had been only "in a minor way"—through the Israeli occupation of two Saudi islands of Tiran and Sanafir, "the Americans quietly arranged things and got the Israelis out."[38]

Mansuri's response indicates that the Saudis were mostly interested in issues, which had immediate security and political repercussions. Moreover, such a decision-making approach is in line with an ancient Bedouin proverb, which says that "glancing about breeds trouble" [*shaffit naẓar yuḥṣul minha ḍarār*].[39] In other words, the Saudis have always been cautious about the risks that they might face should they be drawn into other people's conflicts. This was a Saudi priority because they did not want to risk their own interests—most importantly, the survival of their monarchy. As it seems, beyond its national self-interests, the Saudi royal family—like most of the other Arab regimes—had little genuine sympathy for the Palestinians. Most of the public statements in support of the Palestinians seemed to have been lip-service while the financial support was more or less 'protection money' in order that the Palestinians would be less tempted to stage attacks against Saudi Arabia. Furthermore, the Saudis

---

[37] See for instance: Tad Szulc, "US is Planning Step-Up in Arms for Jordanians," *The New York Times*, April 8, 1971, 1; "Israel Asks U.S. for New Arms Aid," *The New York Times*, June 10, 1971, 9.

[38] "Saudi Arms Procurement: Conversation with Sayed Abdulrahman Mansuri on 5 February 1972" (confidential report), Willie Morris (Ambassador, British Embassy, Jeddah), February 8, 1972, *FCO 8/1912*.

[39] See: Bailey, *A Culture of Desert Survival*, 391.

46   S. E. WILLNER

were aware of PLO's and other radical factions' capacity to make troubles in the kingdom, especially among the Palestinians who worked in the oil fields.[40]

THE ATTACKS AGAINST THE SAUDI EMBASSIES IN KHARTOUM (MARCH 1973) AND PARIS (SEPTEMBER 1973)

While Saudi Arabia's oil income had gradually increased because of its growing petroleum exports,[41] the radical Arab regimes stepped up their subversive activities against the kingdom. As the details presented next seem to point out, Muammar Qadhafi—for his own self-interests—was one of the main sponsors of terrorist activities against the Saudi kingdom. Concerning the Libyan foreign policy, one can always speculate about what was going on in Qadhafi's mind when he decided to sponsor various Palestinian guerrilla groups to attack against Saudi Arabia. Due to his complex personality and mindset, Qadhafi was considered, as William Quandt puts it, "something of an enigma" among the Saudis.[42] Furthermore, as Millard Burr and Robert Collins describe, Qadhafi was "young, impetuous and unpredictable" who "never forgot or forgave."[43] Quandt writes that Qadhafi's political rhetoric included outspokenly pro-Palestinian statements and he used the language of Islamic revival. In addition, Qadhafi was an anti-Communist revolutionary with ambitions of

[40] See for instance: "Palestinians in Saudi Arabia," October 3, 1970. Furthermore, as Shulamit Binah has pointed out, the radical Arab regimes of Iraq, Syria, and Libya used Palestinian proxy factions throughout the 1970s and 1980s to carry out attacks against other Arab regimes, among which Saudi Arabia was a frequent target. Shulamit Binah, *United States-Iraq Bilateral Relations: Confusion and Misperception from 1967 to 1979*, London: Vallentine Mitchell, 2018, 138, 145.

[41] In 1970, Saudi Arabia's crude oil production stood at 3.8 million bpd. The production increased to 6 million bpd (1972), to 7.6 million bpd (1973) and to 8.5 million bpd (1974).

[42] Quandt, *Saudi Arabia in the 1980s*, 22.

[43] J. Millard Burr and Robert O. Collins, *Africa's Thirty Years War: Libya, Chad and the Sudan, 1963-1993*, Boulder, CO: Westview Press, 1999, 78–79, 213. As a point of interest, Qadhafi caused headaches also for other Arab leaders. For instance, in April 1975 President Sadat had stated that "Qadhafi was one hundred percent sick and possessed by a devil, which makes him imagine things" and that he "had a split personality." See: Haim Shaked and Yehudit Ronen, "Simmering Tension: Libyan-Egyptian Relations, 1954-86," in Gabriel Ben-Dor and David B. Dewitt, eds., *Conflict Management in the Middle East*, Lexington, MA: Lexington Books, 1987, 120.

4 EMERGING PAN-ARABISM AND THE POLITICIZATION OF ARAB OIL   47

obtaining leadership in the Islamic and Arab world.[44] That being said, Qadhafi was clearly an enemy of the Saudis.

Moreover, Qadhafi's desire to target the Saudis was partly based on his radical anti-Western mindset. For instance, Burr and Collins have argued that Qadhafi's foreign policy was "surprisingly consistent having been shaped by the pan-Arab views of [the former Egyptian President Abd al-Nasir]." Qadhafi wanted to unify the Arab world so that it would be able to stand up to the West. Primarily, he sponsored various anti-Western liberation movements and terror groups in his attempt to destabilize pro-Western regimes.[45] However, in terms of Saudi Arabia, Qadhafi wanted (perhaps most importantly) that the Saudi monarchy would support higher petroleum prices. This is because he needed more money to finance his anti-Western political and ideological aspirations in Africa and the Arab world. However, there are no records available that could indicate whether Qadhafi had made any demands to the Saudis concerning the oil price increase. Nevertheless, during 1973, the Libyan leader sponsored two high-profile attacks against the Saudi embassies in Khartoum (Sudan) and in Paris (France). Although there is no conclusive evidence available, it is quite possibly that Qadhafi wanted to destabilize the Saudi monarchy.[46]

The first Saudi Embassy attack, which took place in Khartoum on March 1, 1973, has primarily been attributed as an attempt by the Palestinian guerrillas to influence the American Middle East policy. However, the reasons behind the attack appear to be more complicated.

[44] See: Quandt, *Saudi Arabia in the 1980's*, 22; John Wright, *Libya: A Modern History*, Baltimore, MD: The Johns Hopkins University Press, 1981, 110, 146, 154–155.

[45] In 1986, the US Department of State published a report, which said that "Qadhafi's commitment of political, economic and military resources in support of anti-Western activities worldwide may be surpassed only by the Soviet Union, its East European allies and possible North Korea or Cuba." "Text of State Department Report in Libya under Qaddafi," *The New York Times*, January 9, 1986, A6.

[46] Qadhafi had been advocating more radical oil policy since the summer of 1970 when Libya decided to raise oil prices. Few months later in November 1970, also Iran raised posted prices. Although Qadhafi was outspokenly anti-Western and advocated for the oil embargo against the Unites States, Qadhafi's Libya secretly violated the 1973–1974 Arab oil embargo by selling oil to the United States to minimize the damages of the embargo to its economy. Yehudit Ronen, *Qaddafi's Libya in World Politics*, Boulder, CO: Lynne Rienner Publishers, 2008, 13. For more about Libyan foreign policy, see for instance: Mary Jane Deeb, *Libya's Foreign Policy in North Africa*, Boulder, CO: Westview Press, 1991; Dirk Vanderwalle, *A History of Modern Libya*, Cambridge: Cambridge University Press, 2006; and Ronald Bruce St John, *Qaddafi's World Design: Libyan Foreign Policy, 1969–1987*, London: Saqi Books, 1987.

48 S. E. WILLNER

As it seems, Qadhafi had additional agendas that encouraged him to sponsor this attack, in which a group of eight armed Palestinian terrorists from the Black September Organization [*Munaẓẓamat Aylūl al-Aswad*]—the secret arm of *Al-Fatah*[47]—stormed a diplomatic reception at the Saudi Embassy. This reception was attended by several ambassadors and other diplomats. During the attack the terrorists managed to seize five diplomats, including American Ambassador Cleo Noel (1972–1973), *Charge d'Affaires* George Moore (1972–1973), and Belgian *Charge d'Affaires* Guy Eid (unknown–1973). Although Saudi Ambassador Abd Allah al-Malhuq was among the seized diplomats, he was allowed to move freely in the embassy premises.[48]

The attackers demanded the release of several Palestinian militants that were held in prisons in Jordan, Israel, West Germany, and the United States. These incarcerated militants included high-profile prisoner Sirhan Bishara Sirhan, who was imprisoned in the United States for the 1968 murder of Democrat Senator Robert F. Kennedy (1965–1968). When the United States made it known that they would not pay blackmail and release Sirhan, the terrorists murdered Noel, Moore, and Eid. Although the attackers had made demands for the release of their fellows, intercepted messages,[49] which were sent from Tripoli (Libya)[50] and from the *Al-Fatah* headquarters in Beirut (Lebanon), indicate that orders had been given to kill the diplomats in any case.[51]

---

[47] *Al-Fatah* is the most significant organization behind the Palestinian Liberation Organization (PLO). *Al-Fatah* is a reverse acronym from the Arabic words *Ḥarakat al-Taḥrīr al-Filasṭīnī*. The word *fataḥa* ('to open') means also 'to conquer' and 'to capture.' For further reading on the Black September Organization and its connection to *Al-Fatah*, see, for instance: Eli Karmon, *Coalitions between Terrorist Organizations: Revolutionaries, Nationalists and Islamists*, Leiden: Martinus Nijhoff Publisher, 2005, 244.

[48] More on the attack against the Saudi Embassy in Khartoum; see: David Korn, *Assassination in Khartoum*, Bloomington, IN: Indiana University Press, 1993.

[49] Although there is no evidence to confirm, it is possible that the American or the Israeli intelligence services had intercepted the secret Libyan communications.

[50] It is not revealed whether the intercepted message sent from Tripoli came directly from Qadhafi's Chief of Staff, who had close relationship with the Black September Organization.

[51] Korn, *Assassination*, 168,

At this point it is very important to briefly analyze the Libyan connection to the Khartoum embassy attack.[52] In terms of the possible motive for the Khartoum attack, anonymous sources in Sudan indicated that the attack was indeed inspired and planned by Libya and had nothing to do with the issue of Palestine, despite the fact that the terrorists had been Palestinian.[53] As it appears, the primary reason why the Libyans had sponsored this attack was to cause fear among the Saudis, and thus push them to align with the revolutionary Arab regimes.[54] Therefore, the Black September Organization was a natural partner for Qadhafi due to their anti-Western and anti-Saudi agenda.

While Qadhafi was said to have been the largest single financial contributor to the Black September Organization—giving it some $30 million annually[55]—it was reported that a few months earlier Saudi Arabia had frozen its financial aid to *Al-Fatah* due to political differences. This was most likely a consequence to *Al-Fatah*'s failed attempt to overthrow King Husayn of Jordan in February 1973.[56] Two weeks after the Khartoum attack on March 14, 1973, King Faysal told Nicolas Thacher, the US Ambassador to Saudi Arabia (1970–1973), that "Saudi Arabia has stopped all aid to *Al-Fatah* and would continue to do so until assurances received that *Al-Fatah* would cleanse itself of bad ideas and practices." However, the Saudis were adamant about not making such a statement publicly. Faysal explained that if Saudi Arabia was to announce publicly its intention to stop all aid to *Al-Fatah*, "our Palestinian brothers would attack us with

---

[52] Interestingly, it was reported by the Khartoum newspaper *As-Sahafah* on March 3, 1973, that members of the Khartoum bureau of the *Al-Fatah* made up a part of the commando unit, and that all members of the local Palestinian organization's office disappeared. As was reported in the newspaper, Fuad Yassa—the *Al-Fatah* representative in Khartoum—together with his family, left for Libya shortly before the assault. Although several people involved—including two Sudanese that had been working for the Libyan Embassy—were arrested in the aftermath of the attack, most of them were released in 1974 due to the pressure from the revolutionary Arab regimes.

[53] Henry Tanner, "Sudan is Planning to Try Guerrillas for Capital Crime," *The New York Times*, March 6, 1973, 1.

[54] It has also been suggested that Qadhafi had sponsored the attack in Khartoum in response to the growing *rapprochement* between the Sudan and the United States. See: Burr and Collins, *Africa's Thirty Years War*, 4.

[55] Korn is quoting a document sent from the US Embassy in Khartoum; see Korn, *Assassination*, 49.

[56] Juan de Onis, "Jordan Declares Amnesty for Political Prisoners," *The New York Times*, September 19, 1973, 1.

50 S. E. WILLNER

much bitterness."[57] While the Arab governments—including Saudi Arabia—had mostly kept silent on the attacks, it remains unknown whether the Saudis took any action following the attack in Khartoum—and if they did, then it was done quietly behind the scenes.[58]

The second attack against the Saudi embassies took place in Paris on September 5, 1973—six months after the Khartoum attack. Again, the reason behind the attack was attributed to the Palestinian terrorists making demands to get prisoners released. However, the attack was widely condemned in many of the Arab capitals, including Cairo, of which radio had denounced it as "senseless, deplorable and harmful to the Palestinian cause."[59] Even in this case, the details, which have emerged, indicate that there might have been more sinister reasons behind the attack, of which main purpose was meant to cause distress among the Saudis.

The five Palestinian attackers who seized the Saudi Embassy in Paris and took hostages, claimed membership in a previously unknown group called *Al-Iqab*,[60] demanding the release of Muhammad Daud Udeh, also known as Abu Daud,[61] from a Jordanian prison. Two days later, on September 7, 1973, the terrorists released all but four Saudi diplomats with whom they departed from Paris onboard a Syrian passenger jet. The plane refueled at Cairo and continued its flight to Kuwait. The next day the attackers took off from Kuwait and threatened to throw their Saudi hostages out of the plane over Riyadh if Abu Daud was not freed. However, the hostages were not harmed, and the plane returned to Kuwait. Two days later, during which the airplane had stayed on the runway, the attackers finally freed the hostages and surrendered to the local police.[62] After a

---

[57] "Discussion With King Faisal re Support for BSO-Fatah" (secret telegram), Nicolas Thacher (US Ambassador, Jeddah) to US Department of State, March 14, 1973, no. 81, *FRUS*, vol. E-9 part 2, *Documents on the Middle East Region, 1973-1976*, 303–306. See also: The *Middle East Economic Digest (MEED)* quoted a report, which appeared in the Kuwaiti press. *MEED*, February 16, 1973, 192; Onis, "Jordan Declares Amnesty for Political Prisoners."

[58] Korn, *Assassination*, 88; "6 Sudanese Including 2 Who Worked for Libyan Embassy, Are Charged with Plotting Against Nation," *The New York Times*, March 10, 1973, 10.

[59] Henry Kamm, "Commandos Leave Embassy in Paris," *The New York Times*, September 7, 1973, 1.

[60] The Arabic word *'iqāb* is usually translated as 'punishment' or 'penalty.'

[61] Abu Daud was a leader of *Al-Fatah*, who was first condemned to death in Jordan, but later commuted to life imprisonment, for his alleged part to overthrow King Husayn.

[62] Juan de Onis, "Gunmen Threaten Lives of 4 Saudis," *The New York Times*, September 8, 1973, 1.

4 EMERGING PAN-ARABISM AND THE POLITICIZATION OF ARAB OIL   51

few weeks had passed, on September 19, 1973, Abu Daud was released from the Jordanian prison. Although the Saudis had denied paying the kidnappers, it is quite likely that the Saudis negotiated with the Jordanians and possibly paid them to get Abu Daud released.

Interestingly, it was not publicly known at the time that during the attack senior members of the Saudi royal family had been visiting the embassy compound. One of the people that that were at the embassy during the attack is Muhammad al-Fawzan, the Director of Foreign Broadcasting at the Saudi Ministry of Information. According to him, it had been fortunate for the embassy staff that the intruders had not known their way around the building. Because of this, the attackers had failed to catch Queen Iffat Al Thunayan Al Saud[63] and her three sons,[64] who had been in the Ambassador's residence adjoining. While adding that during the attack many outraged Saudis in Western Europe had been calling the embassy in Paris, Al-Fawzan told that "had something happened to the Saudi hostages, there could well have been reprisals against the Palestinians in Saudi [Arabia]." Al-Fawzan added that six months earlier, in March 1973, when the Saudi Embassy in Khartoum was attacked, the anti-Palestinian feeling in Saudi Arabia had been very high.[65] Al-Fawzan's remarks indicate that the Saudis had been very frustrated and angry because of the attack against their diplomatic mission and the subsequent kidnapping of their diplomats. Furthermore, it is possible that, by conveying such a message through Al-Fawzan, the Saudis wanted to send a warning saying that the Palestinian workers could lose their jobs and be sent away from Saudi Arabia if there were more attacks.

In terms of the survival of the Saudi monarchy, the attack against the Saudi Embassy in Paris was a significant reminder of how vulnerable the royal family was to the pressure from the revolutionary Arab regimes in their attempt to influence Saudi decisions. As a response to the attack, Aramco received orders to remove all the Palestinian employees from its

---

[63] Iffat Al Thunayan Al Saud was the last, and at the time the only wife of King Faysal. As reported in the press, she was an influential woman in Saudi Arabia. Joseph A. Kechichian, "Pioneer who gave wings to Saudi women's dreams," *Gulf News*, August 7, 2008, https://gulfnews.com/general/pioneer-who-gave-wings-to-saudi-womens-dreams-1.40588.   See also: Joseph A. Kechichian, *Iffat al Thunayan: An Arabian Queen*, Sussex: Sussex Academic Press, 2014.

[64] The report only mentions that Bandar al-Faysal was one of them.

[65] "Matters Saudi" (confidential report), David E. Tatham (MED, FCO, London) to Dando (MED, FCO), September 10, 1973, no. 14, *FCO 8/2105*.

52   S. E. WILLNER

most important oilfields in Abqaiq near Dhahran. According to the Lebanese newspaper *Al-Muharrir* reporting on September 8, 1973, the Palestinian employees were placed doing "clerical jobs [far] away from the oilfields and wells."[66]

The peculiar timing of the embassy attack raises several important and interesting questions. First, did the Palestinian terrorists know that King Faysal's wife Iffat and the king's three sons were at the embassy during the attack? Second, if they knew, who provided them the information, and for what purpose? These questions remain unanswered but there is a good reason to believe that the Libyan intelligence had been behind the attack. However, the failure to catch Iffat could indicate that the terrorists had no prior knowledge of her presence at the embassy compound. Whether that was the case, or if the terrorists' intention was not to kidnap Iffat, it is quite likely that just the mere fact that she had been at the embassy during the attack could have made Faysal think that she had been the attackers' primary target. In fact, King Faysal might have even thought that the attack in Paris had been a message to him saying that he should better side with the radical Arab regimes. Interestingly, but not surprisingly, there does not seem to be any Saudi response in the Arab press concerning the attack against its embassy in Paris.

In response to the series of above-discussed attacks, the Saudis wanted that the United States would provide them more comprehensive security guarantees. As I will discuss in the next chapter, the Americans declined (October 1972). In an apparent response, King Faysal started promoting a pro-radical Arab alignment, while some of the senior princes were against such an approach. As will be discussed next, Faysal's radicalized foreign policy approach contradicted with the principles of Saudi pragmatism.

[66] *FBIS*, September 11, 1973.

CHAPTER 5

Conflicting Interests and King Faysal's Decision to Support Egypt's War Efforts

The 1968 British decision to withdraw its military forces from the Persian Gulf by 1971 had inspired radical Arab attacks against Saudi Arabia, because the withdrawal was considered as a sign of weakness. As such, the kingdom was seen as an easier target of subversion. The British withdrawal had also created a strategic dilemma to the United States at the height of the Cold War US-Soviet rivalry. Thereupon, instead of committing its military to a direct intervention in the region (since the United States was deeply involved in the costly Vietnam War), the Nixon Administration formulated a 'Twin Pillars' policy of selling weapons and providing security assistance to its two principal Middle East allies, Iran and Saudi Arabia. In return, the United States expected Iran and Saudi Arabia to keep the region from the spread of Soviet influence. The doctrine argued that the United States should pursue its interests through a partnership of its local allies.[1]

---

[1] For further reading on the Soviet foreign policy in the Middle East, see, for instance: Robin Edmonds, *Soviet Foreign Policy: The Brezhnev Years*, Oxford: Oxford University Press, 1984; Mark N. Katz, *Russia and Arabia: Soviet Foreign Policy toward the Arabian Peninsula*, Baltimore, MA: The Johns Hopkins University Press, 1986; Jaan Pennar, *The U.S.S.R. and the Arabs: The Ideological Dimension*, New York, NY: Crane, Russak, 1973; Yevgeny Primakov, *Russia and the Arabs: Behind the Scenes in the Middle East from the Cold War to the Present*, Transl. Paul Gould. New York, NY: Basic Books, 2009; and Stephen Page, *The Soviet Union and the Yemens: Influence on Asymmetrical Relationships*, New York, NY: Praeger, 1985.

© The Author(s), under exclusive license to Springer Nature Switzerland AG 2023
S. E. Willner, *Preserving the Saudi Monarchy*,
https://Doi.org/10.1007/978-3-031-30006-6_5

53

In accordance with the 'Twin Pillars' policy, and due to the increased radical Arab threat against Saudi Arabia, the Saudis felt that the American security guarantees were required so that the royal family could maintain its rule. As was discussed in the previous chapter, the radical Arab regimes had already sponsored multiple attacks against Saudi Arabia, and that these attacks had further intensified following the British military withdrawal from the Persian Gulf. Consequently, in October 1972, the royal family dispatched Minister of Petroleum Ahmad Zaki Yamani (1962–1986) to visit the United States. The purpose of Yamani's trip was to seek American security guarantees for the survival of the Saudi monarchy.

The Saudis had attempted to establish a long-term strategic link between the two states, which according to Yamani's proposal, included using Saudi oil to make the Americans more dependent on the kingdom. During his visit to the United States, Yamani had proposed that Saudi Arabia and the United States should conclude a commercial oil agreement, which would grant the kingdom a "special place" in the US markets, allowing it to be free from duties and quota restrictions of all kinds. This then would have encouraged the Saudis to invest on American oil refineries and fuel distribution facilities. The British foreign officials in London described the Saudi decision to send Yamani to the United States as "calculative" and assessed that it was "possibly aimed at the preservation of the existing Saudi regime."[2] It would, therefore, seem that his visit to Washington was primarily motivated by Saudi Arabia's need to seek security guarantees from the United States considering the increasing radical Arab states-sponsored subversive activity. Indeed, the Saudis had proposed that in return for the kingdom's commitment to become a major long-term oil supplier to the United States, and in return for its investments in the United States, the Saudis expected to receive some American guarantees for the kingdom's future stability.[3]

According to anonymous US government sources, the Americans had indicated to the Saudis that they could not give them such a preferential treatment, which Yamani had asked for in his meetings with the American officials. Interestingly, the British officials had been quite skeptical about

---

[2] "The Saudi oil offer" (confidential report), Guy P. Lockton (Oil Department, FCO, London) to Tatham, December 1, 1972, *FCO 8/1918*.

[3] "Yamani's oil deal proposal to the USA" (confidential report), Rex M. Hunt (MED, FCO, London) to St. John Armitage, December 29, 1972, *FCO 8/1918*. See also: David Hirst, "Saudi search for a special relationship," *The Guardian*, October 12, 1972.

the American ability to ensure the stability of the Saudi kingdom beyond what they were already doing. In other words, selling Saudi Arabia advanced weapon systems, training its armed forces, and providing the Saudis intelligence of potential threats. The British regarded a hypothetical US military intervention in Saudi Arabia unthinkable and without such an option being available, then they assessed that it was difficult to see how the Americans could have saved the monarchy if a coup would have taken place in Saudi Arabia.[4] Although there is not enough documentation to fully support such conclusions, it is quite likely that the American unwillingness to provide more comprehensive security guarantees to the royal family made King Faysal think that he had no other choice but to side with the radical Arab regimes and to join the oil embargo one year later in October 1973.

THE SAUDI CONTEMPLATIONS OF WHETHER TO USE THE OIL WEAPON

Before the 1973 Arab-Israeli October War started, the Arab oil producers, including OAPEC's most important member Saudi Arabia, held discussions about how they could use the 'oil weapon' in the conflict against Israel. Although King Faysal might have been tempted to make more money by using the oil weapon, the main Saudi concern was how to appease the radical Arab states, and thus, how to confront the radical Arab threat. Prior to the launch of the Arab oil embargo, King Faysal had expressed, both publicly and privately, about his willingness to use the oil weapon in the framework of a future Arab-Israeli conflict—an event that seemed imminent at the time. However, the Saudis were quite hesitant to politicize the use of oil. As will be discussed and analyzed next, some of the statements made by the Saudis were quite perplexing, even conflicting. This could indicate that there were serious disagreements within the royal family concerning how big of a threat the possible Saudi participation in an Arab oil embargo against the United States could pose to the survival of the Saudi monarchy. The following are some examples of Saudi statements on the use of the 'oil weapon.'

In February 1973, Umar Saqqaf said in a press conference that "although the oil weapon could be used against one's enemies, it was a

[4] "Yamani's oil deal proposal to the USA," December 29, 1972.

56 S. E. WILLNER

double-edged weapon, which would also hurt the producing country using it as well as friendly states."[5] Saqqaf had also asserted that "if oil were to be used as a weapon in a conflict against Israel, it would cause a serious harm to the Arabs as it is one of the main sources, which has helped Arab steadfastness."[6] Few days later, Prince Saud al-Faysal, who at the time served as the Deputy Minister of Petroleum (1971–1975), assured Henry St. John Armitage, the First Secretary at the British Embassy in Jeddah, that the Saudis viewed oil commercially, not politically and that Saudi Arabia would not use oil as a political weapon.[7]

The heightened Israeli-Egyptian-Syrian tension was leading to a new war. Toward the end of April 1973, King Faysal was deliberating how to position his kingdom in terms of the possible oil embargo. Perhaps coinciding with the elevated pressure from the revolutionary Arab regimes, King Faysal was expressing increased willingness to use the oil weapon. Accordingly, Faysal sent messages to the Americans through diplomatic channels and through Aramco warning that oil production could be reduced, or at least it would not be expanded, if the United States did not change its Middle East policy, particularly, the part concerning Israel.[8] Also, in the same month, the CIA quoted classified sources saying that King Faysal had been impressed with Sadat's war plans and about his arguments concerning the initiation of hostilities with Israel. Furthermore, Faysal had expressed firm support for Egypt and had argued to his advisors

[5] "Saudi Arabia," *Middle East Economic Survey (MEES)*, February 16, 1973, 7.

[6] The British Embassy in Jeddah quoted the daily Saudi newspaper *Al-Madinah*. See: "Minister Saqqaf declares petroleum will never be used as a weapon" (unclassified report), British Embassy (Jeddah) to MED (FCO, London), February 7, 1973, *FCO 8/2119*.

[7] "Saudi Arabia—Yamani's oil deal" (confidential report), St. John Armitage to Hunt, February 24, 1973, *FCO 8/2119*.

[8] Morris Adelman, *Genie Out of the Bottle*, Cambridge, MA: The MIT Press, 1996, 106; "Anglo-Saudi Relations" (confidential report), Tatham to N. Pinch (Department of Trade and Industry, London), July 16, 1973, no. 20, *FCO 8/2107*; "Intelligence Précis" (secret memo), James Schlesinger (Director of Central Intelligence) to President Nixon, April 20, 1973, no. 178, in *Foreign Relations of the United States (FRUS)*, vol. XXXVI, *Energy Crisis*, Washington, D.C.: Government Printing Office, 2011, 454–455

5 CONFLICTING INTERESTS AND KING FAYSAL'S DECISION TO SUPPORT... 57

that he felt for the first time that war against Israel was necessary to "restore Arab self-respect."[9]

Based on Saudi logic of operation, and because the Saudi royal family has been very secretive of its decision-making and of its true intentions, it is quite possible that the royal family had purposefully 'leaked' King Faysal's remarks to the CIA. If the source of the leak was Faysal himself, then the possible motivation for such an action was to make sure that the Americans would take the Saudis more seriously. The Saudis were in a difficult place because of the inter-Arab dilemma. In the light of the earlier attacks against Saudi Arabia, it is possible that the royal family wanted to send a message to Washington saying that the United States were not doing enough to secure the Saudi monarchy and, therefore, that it was 'forced' to side with the Egyptians and the more radical Arab regimes. This could imply that it was a moment of choice between the radicals and the United States on the tactical level.

Yamani's and Saqqaf's statements demonstrate similar position. While Minister of Petroleum Yamani had said that Saudi Arabia would not expand its oil production to meet the United States' demand unless the US alters its pro-Israel stance, Umar Saqqaf had told Alan K. Rothnie, the British Ambassador to Saudi Arabia (1972–1976), that the Saudi were under "great and increasing pressure from her sister Arab States not to allow the prospects of a closer oil tie-up with the Americans to blind her to the power, which oil gave her to influence US policies *vis-à-vis* Israel."[10] Faysal's message, which no doubt was conveyed to the Americans through Yamani and Saqqaf, seems to have been such that if a war would come, he would be unable to resist the Arab demands for joining an embargo against the US oil interests.

In Quandt's view, King Faysal was publicly linking oil with the Arab-Israeli conflict. In fact, according to Quandt, Henry Kissinger, the US

---

[9] It is not mentioned when Faysal had expressed these views. The CIA document went even further by saying that in late-March 1973 Sadat had told an emissary of Faysal that fighting must begin "sometime within the next few months." See: "Intelligence Precis," April 20, 1973. Furthermore, in April 1973, Sadat created a Ministry of Petroleum in Egypt and appointed Ezz al-Din al-Hilal to head it. According to Pierre Terzian, Hilal's priority was to set up a study on how to use Arab oil as a political weapon. Pierre Terzian, *OPEC: The Inside Story*, London: Zed Books, 1985, 170.

[10] "Saudi Arabian Oil Policy" (confidential telegram), Alan K. Rothnie (Ambassador, British Embassy, Jeddah) to FCO (London), April 28, 1973, *FCO 8/2119*; "Chronology," *MEJ* 7, 3 (1973), 356.

58 S. E. WILLNER

Secretary of State (1973–1977), was concerned by signs of Faysal's growing involvement in the Arab-Israeli conflict, and "feared that [King Faysal's] Saudi activism would ultimately bring down the monarchy, which might then be replaced by a Qadhafi-like regime."[11] Although there is no publicly available record to prove it, it is possible that Kissinger had conveyed such a message to the Saudis, either directly to King Faysal or to the senior members of the royal family. Quandt also reveals that every time Faysal referred to the use of oil as a political weapon against the West, "one of his aides would hasten to inform United States officials that [...Faysal's statements were] meant only for domestic Arab consumption,"[12] primarily referring to the radical Arab leaders. It is possible that Faysal's advisers were tasked by his brothers to tone down his statements to turn them into empty threats because they thought they were detrimental to the Saudi-US relations. This, in turn, threatened the survival of the Saudi monarchy. For this reason, the Americans probably didn't take Faysal's threats that seriously. In turn, Harold B. Walker, the Political Councillor at the British Embassy in Jeddah (1973–1975) assessed that there was little doubt that the Saudi threats of using oil weapon should be taken seriously. He continued that if the Saudis would resort to using the oil weapon it would be because the royal family had concluded that such a decision was to prolong its survival. He added that "whether or not the Saudi regime may be said already to have decided to use oil as a weapon, the factors at work mean that they will do so."[13]

Yet, to add more contradiction to these statements, King Faysal had warned about the dangers of using Arab oil as a weapon in an interview which he gave to the Lebanese magazine *Al-Hawadith* in August 1973. In that interview he challenged that "no-one is asking: where would we get the money for providing assistance to our brothers on the frontlines?"[14] Around the same time, however, Faysal seemed to have assured President Sadat that he would use the oil weapon while contributing $500 million to his war efforts against Israel.[15] Whereas some of the conflicting state-

[11] William B. Quandt, *Decade of Decisions: American Policy Toward the Arab-Israeli Conflict, 1967-1976*, Berkeley, CA: University of California Press, 1977, 160.

[12] Ibid, 160.

[13] "Oil as a Weapon" (confidential report), Harold B Walker (Councilor, British Embassy, Jeddah) to Patrick Wright (MED, FCO, London), August 4, 1973, no. 40, *FCO 8/2119*.

[14] Beirut weekly *Al-Hawadith* published King Faysal's statement on 30 August 1973; see: *FBIS*, August 31, 1973, A1-A3.

[15] Safran, *Ceaseless Quest*, 155.

5 CONFLICTING INTERESTS AND KING FAYSAL'S DECISION TO SUPPORT... 59

ments might have been part of a coordinated disinformation campaign by the Egyptians and the Syrians, there is a strong possibility that due to internal disagreements within the Saudis about the viability, usefulness, and the possible danger posed by imposing of the oil weapon, no clear Saudi position existed.

THE 'OIL WEAPON' AND INCREASING SAUDI CONCERNS

The numerous attacks against the Saudis, together with the radical Arab states' rhetoric of imposing the oil weapon in a future Middle East conflict, probably made King Faysal to calculate that he needed to express more adamantly his intentions of joining the radical Arab front against Israel and its allies. To respond to the possibility of an Arab oil embargo, the United States, in return, increased its own psychological warfare against Saudi Arabia. Although the subject of American psychological warfare campaigns and the threats of using military force to influence Saudi decision-making will be discussed more in detail in Chap. 6, it is useful to raise the issue already here.

The possibility of using US military force in order to occupy foreign oil fields seems to have been publicly discussed in the US Senate for the first time on May 21, 1973, when Senator J. William Fulbright (Democrat, Arkansas), the Chairman of the US Senate Foreign Relations Committee, warned that he had apprehensions that the United States or its military allies "might secure oil supplies in the Middle East by military means."[16] Two days later, on May 23, 1973, Abd al-Rahman Helaissi, the Saudi Ambassador in London, phoned Patrick Wright, the Head of the FCO Middle East Department (1972–1974). During the conversation Helaissi informed Wright about his recent phone call with Lord Peter Carrington, the British Secretary of State for Defense (1970–1974), in which he had raised (possibly tasked to do so by Fahd or Sultan)[17] the question whether, in case of oil embargo, the United States would use force to ensure oil

---

[16] As will be explored in Chap. 6, the United States had such military plans already since the 1940s in the context of the Cold War. Senator Fulbright's remarks were reported in the *Washington Post* May 21, 1973; see: "Chronology," *MEJ* 27, 4 (1973), 484. See also: Fred Halliday, *Arabia without Sultans: A Political Survey of Instability in the Arab World*, New York, NY: Vantage Books, 1975, 17–18.

[17] At the time, Fahd served as the Deputy Crown Prince (1967–1975) while Sultan served as the Minister of Defense (1963–2001).

60 S. E. WILLNER

supplies from Saudi Arabia and other Arab oil-producing states.[18] As reported by Wright, the Saudi Ambassador had told him that Lord Carrington dismissed the idea as "inconceivable."[19]

Helaissi had also told Wright that he had thereupon been interested to see in the day's press the account of Senator Fulbright's suggestion that "the Americans or their friends in the Middle East might one day find it necessary to take over the Persian Gulf." Helaissi continued that the Saudis had come under strong pressure from the Americans to increase their oil production. According to Wright, Helaissi seemed to have been prepared to admit that "full-scale military occupation was unlikely but pointed out that the Americans might well achieve their aim by a show of force. As he [Helaissi] put it, all that would be needed would be for two or three American warships to appear off Dhahran."[20] There is a possibility that Al-Helaissi had raised the issue of the warships to send a message to Washington; perhaps to hint that they could try to convince King Faysal of not using the oil weapon by a show of military force.

Helaissi undoubtedly played a significant role *vis-à-vis* the Saudi foreign policy through his appointment as the Saudi Ambassador to London. Although there is always the possibility that Helaissi's remarks had been his own, I am not convinced that Helaissi would have independently suggested to the Americans of such an action unless he had been commissioned to do so by some of the senior princes. Instead, Helaissi was a loyal emissary, who would have only advanced policies that were in line with Saudi Arabia's pragmatic foreign policy approach. As this specific interaction with the British officials indicates, the Saudis used their relations with friendly governments to send messages to the United States. Therefore, it is possible that instead of communicating directly with the Americans, the Saudis wanted to use this indirect channel for at least two important reasons. First, those senior princes that had commissioned Helaissi wanted to avoid embarrassment and damage had such remarks been leaked. Second, it is possible that those senior princes (possibly Fahd and Sultan) had

---

[18] Such an option—even if merely psychological—indicates how energy needs of the United States and the West were, at the time, very much dependent on Saudi Arabia.

[19] "US/Saudi relations" (confidential report), Patrick Wright (FCO, London) to Parson (FCO), May 23, 1973, no. 11, *FCO 8/2107*.

[20] Ibid.

thought that their message could have better impact if their message went through the British diplomatic channels.[21]

In order to calm down the Saudis, on the same day a spokesman of the US Administration said that "the idea of using force [...] does not reflect in any way thought within this Administration."[22] One could always speculate with the possibility that what if the Nixon Administration had not made such a statement and had Helaissi's indirect message reached Washington before they decided to respond to Fulbright's remarks. In other words, would the Americans have sent warships to the Persian Gulf to pressure Faysal? Based on the 'Twin Pillars' doctrine, such a US military operation would have contradicted the US global interests.

Interestingly, Wright also noted that Fulbright had for years been at odds with the US Administration and "because of this suggestion by him of what might happen was not in any sense an indication of what the US Administration might do." Finally, it is useful to address that, although Wright seems to have played down Senator Fulbright's message, it was obvious that it was received in Riyadh.[23] Helaissi's phone calls to the British officials point out that the Saudis were worried about the consequences of the possible Arab oil embargo, for which King Faysal had been publicly and privately showing support. What seems to confirm such point of view is—as Wright had indicated in his report—that it was the first time, on which an Arab diplomatic representative had raised such an issue with the British officials.[24]

Disagreements Within the Royal Family and Apprehensions About King Faysal's Senility

The members of the Saudi monarchy did not seem to have been unified when it came to the decision of using oil as a political weapon. In general, their approach to making decisions was mostly pragmatic, reflecting their primary interest, which was to prolong the survival of the Saudi monarchy. Although it is not known who might have brought up the idea of using the oil weapon (and whether it was one of his advisors or perhaps the

---

[21] Al-Ḥelaissi's phone call with the British officials is a perfect example of how the Saudis used a friendly foreign government to convey a message to the Americans.

[22] "Chronology," *MEJ* 27 4, 1973, 484.

[23] See: "US/Saudi relations," May 23, 1973.

[24] "US/Saudi relations," May 23, 1973.

62 S. E. WILLNER

Egyptians or the Syrians), King Faysal was probably convinced that using the oil weapon might be the best available option, which he could use to manage his way out from the radical Arab threat, and which would help him to enrich the kingdom. Despite his commonly known conspiratorial anti-Communist and anti-Semitic opinions, King Faysal was in general considered a shrewd and pragmatic leader. Together with the senior princes he formulated Saudi Arabia's foreign and domestic policies.

Fahd and Sultan were part the seven full brothers, who were often referred to as the 'Sudayri Seven.' In addition to Fahd and Sultan, the 'Sudayri Seven' also included Abd al-Rahman, Nayif, Turki, Salman, and Ahmad. The Sudayris seemed to have represented a modern, cosmopolitan, carefully liberalizing, and pro-American tendency. Another group within the royal family was said to have been led by Prince Abd Allah, the Commander of the Saudi National Guard. Abd Allah's group consisted of several princes and powerful men and was said to have been more pro-European. It was also told that the princes he represented were more open to the idea of exploring diplomatic relations with the Soviet Union.[25] Nonetheless, whatever had been the political orientation of these princely coalitions, it was quite certain that their primary goal was to preserve the Saudi monarchy.

In accordance with an ancient Bedouin proverb, which says that "it is better to destroy with people's consent than to build on one's own initiative" [*takhrab bi-rei al-jamī'a walā ta'mar bi-rei wāḥad*],[26] the senior princes insist on consultations with the king before any important foreign policy initiative is decided even if the decision is ultimately not what they want. However, the described disagreements regarding the oil embargo could indicate that Faysal had decided to publicly support the idea of an oil embargo, which was against the interests of his senior brothers. This, in turn, had angered some senior members of the monarchy. Accordingly, Fahd and Sultan did not want Faysal to alienate the United States, which was a major supplier of weapons, and which was considered a sort of protector due to US strategic interests in the Saudi oil resources. On the one hand, Faysal wanted to balance between various political forces (the United States vs. the radical Arab regimes) but was inclining toward the

---

[25] "Planeettain taistelu" [The battle of the planets] (secret report), Carolus Lassila (Ambassador, Embassy of Finland, Jeddah) to Ahti Karjalainen (Minister of Foreign Affairs, Helsinki), May 24, 1975, no. R-382/66, *Saudi Arabia sisäpolitiikka 1975–1977, AMFAF*
[26] Bailey, *A Culture of Desert Survival*, 190.

radical Arab block. On the other hand, based on political pragmatism, his brothers, especially Fahd and Sultan, seem to have been against such an alignment and instead preferred a closer partnership with the United States.[27] In fact, all the public statements and interviews, which I have analyzed for this study, indicate that, within the senior members of the royal family, it was Faysal (and his advisors), and not the whole royal family, who promoted the idea of using the oil as a political weapon.

In July 1973 both Fahd and Sultan had come privately to the Americans and assured them that Saudi Arabia's petroleum resources would never be cut off or curtailed to the detriment of the United States, Western Europe, or Japan. Fahd had expressed in a private conversation his desire to strengthen the Saudi-US relations, while Sultan had indicated that the senior princes were quite worried about King Faysal's state of mind. They even expressed that his "senility and irascibility" could be detrimental to the monarchy.[28]

Such unusually harsh remarks imply that Fahd and Sultan were concerned about the implications of Faysal's earlier statements regarding the possible use of the oil weapon. They also thought that Faysal's statements would antagonize the United States and prejudice the special Saudi-US relationship, which they believed was critical to the long-term survival of their monarchy. Internally, they might have also been worried that Faysal was arrogant and disrespectful and was not listening to them. In addition to such concerns, the two senior princes also mentioned Ahmad Zaki Yamani and Umar Saqqaf by name, of whom they had misgivings because they claimed the two advisors were taking advantage of the king's 'emotional and psychological vulnerabilities.' Fahd and Sultan said that the two advisors were adopting public postures with respect to the Saudi American relationship that were against the interests of the Saudi monarchy.[29] Such remarks could indicate that some senior members of the royal family had noticed the weight that these high-raking civil servants (Yamani and Saqqaf) were gaining in matters of Saudi foreign policy. Given Yamani's position, and his global standing, he certainly had some influence on Faysal's decisions. Therefore, it would make more sense that Fahd and

---

[27] See, for instance: "Planeettain taistelu," May 24, 1975; Robert Lacey, *Inside the Kingdom: Kings, Clerics, Modernists, Terrorists, and the Struggle for Saudi Arabia*, New York, NY: Penguin Books, 2009, 186–187.

[28] "Memorandum of Conversation" (secret), US Embassy (Jeddah) to Henry Kissinger (Secretary of State), July 26, 1973, no. 234, *FRUS*, vol. XXXVI, *Energy Crisis*, 499–501.

[29] Ibid.

Sultan had been more upset about King Faysal's foreign policy approach, which Yamani's and Saqqaf's statements were reflecting, and which they thought was against the fundamental principles of Saudi pragmatism. Without knowing exactly how Saudi decision-making works and what its interests are, it would be challenging to analyze what Fahd and Sultan were in fact referring to when they presented their concerns. However, it is unlikely that Yamani and Saqqaf would have dared to conduct policies in the king's name, or make decisions, without first consulting Faysal, especially considering their reputation of being loyal to the Saudi monarchy. Besides, it is also very unlikely that they would have survived in their positions as long as they did, had their behavior not served the Saudi interests. They were well-aware of their position *vis-à-vis* the royal family, which they loyally served.[30] Instead, it seems more likely that Yamani and Saqqaf—just like the other commoner advisors—were on the one hand watching each other "like desert hawks"[31] and, on the other hand, "like palace doves keep weather eye on the king's mood."[32] Therefore, they knew well what Faysal's desires were and they also knew how to act in order to appease him. Thus, Fahd's and Sultan's criticism might have been aimed toward Faysal, but for the sake of respect toward King Faysal, they chose to blame his advisors for his problematic statements.

There were also other characteristics of King Faysal's behavior that were causing embarrassment within the Saudi monarchy. Within the Jeddah diplomatic community, King Faysal was also known for his

[30] In the spring of 1973, Wanda Jablonski of the *Petroleum Intelligence Weekly* wanted to call Yamani "Henry Kissinger of Saudi Arabia" into which Yamani responded that "Wanda, do you want to destroy me?" "Visit of Yamani" (confidential telegram), Alan Rothnie (British Ambassador, Jeddah) to FCO (London), November 23, 1973, no. 14, *FCO 8/2121*. Furthermore, in January 1974, US Ambassador James Akins (1973–1975) asked whether Yamani's presence would be necessary at an Arab oil ministers' conference in Cairo, into which Faysal had replied that "the presence or absence of Zakī Yamani was irrelevant, since decisions on petroleum were taken not by individual ministers but by His Majesty's own government." Such response suggests that Yamani was well aware of his position *vis-à-vis* the royal family. See: "Saudi Position on Lifting of Embargo" (secret telegram), James Akins (Ambassador, US Embassy, Jeddah) to Department of State (Washington, D.C.), January 23, 1974, no. 290, *FRUS*, vol. XXXVI, *Energy Crisis*, 811–816.

[31] Based on the several diplomatic reports, it was obvious that there was rivalry and jealousy between Yamani and Saqqaf. See, for instance: "Suomen maakohtainen kohtelu öljynostajana Saudi Arabiassa" [Finland's country classification as a buyer of Saudi oil] (secret report), Lassila to Karjalainen, June 1, 1974, no. J-69, *AMFAF*.

[32] "Saudi Arabian External Policies" (confidential report), Walker to Patrick R.H. Wright (MED, FCO, London), July 19, 1973, no. 1, *FCO 8/2106*.

anti-Semitic rhetoric. In fact, it was nearly public knowledge among the foreign diplomats that Faysal was obsessed with the discredited anti-Semitic forgery *The Protocols of the Elders of Zion*, which he distributed to his guests at the royal palace.[33] These anti-Semitic views were also reflected by King Faysal's envoys. For instance, in October 1972, Finnish Ambassador Lassila met with Muhammad Ibrahim Massud, who served as the Saudi Deputy Minister of Foreign Affairs. During the discussion, Massud had commented Finland's UN politics and said that Max Jakobson's (Finland's Ambassador to the UN during 1965–1971) candidacy for the post of UN Secretary General in 1971 had been very questionable because, as he pointed out, "a Jew is always a Jew." Interestingly, Massud repeated this sentence several times, which seemed to have shocked the Finnish Ambassador. As a point of historical interest, Ambassador Jakobson ended up not being elected because the Soviet Union had wanted Austrian Kurt Waldheim to be the UN Secretary General. Years later it was revealed that the Russians had insisted Waldheim to become the Secretary General because the Soviet intelligence KGB had obtained *kompromat* about Waldheim's Nazi past.[34]

Nevertheless, Hume A. Horan, who at the time had served as the Deputy Chief of Mission at the US Embassy in Jeddah (1972–1977), pointed out that "as the king grew older he really did have a worse than blind spot for Jews, not Israelis, but Jews."[35] The British Embassy in Jeddah, in turn, described Faysal's behavior as "mania."[36] Moreover, Horan indicated that Faysal's behavior regarding his decision to deliver copies of the anti-Semitic book was indeed an embarrassment to some of the king's staff. While Faysal's conduct seems to have reflected his personal hatred toward the Jewish people, Thomas Lippman recalls from his own observations that after Faysal's murder in 1975 "the bookshelf

[33] See, for instance: "King Faisal: Oil, Wealth and Power," *Time Magazine*, April 7, 1975, 24; "Saudi Internal—An Anti-Zionist-Imperialist Conspiracy or a Wahhabi Backlash" (confidential report), Anthony M. Layden (British Embassy, Jeddah) to Tatham, June 7, 1972, *FCO 8/1906.*

[34] "Untitled Letter" (secret), Lassila to Richard Tötterman (Secretary of State, Ministry of Foreign Affairs, Helsinki), October 10, 1972, no. J-68, *Saudi Arabia: Diplomaattisuhteet 1972, AMFAF.*

[35] Hume A. Horan was interviewed by Charles Stuart Kennedy, the Association for Diplomatic Studies and Training, Foreign Affairs Oral History Project, November 3, 2000.

[36] "King Faisal's annual tea party for Heads of Mission" (confidential report), Ian S. Winchester (Counselor, British Embassy, Jeddah) to Wright, June 10, 1972, *FCO 8/1906.*

66   S. E. WILLNER

containing the '*Protocols*' was gone from the royal reception room."[37] Faysal was likely a 'lone wolf' with such an obsession. Therefore, it seems that Faysal's actions in this respect represented his own narrow worldview and had very little to do with daily politics in Saudi Arabia. It would be reasonable to argue that King Faysal's decision to support Egypt's war efforts against Israel and his decision to join the oil embargo was reflecting his anti-Semitism.

To conclude, Faysal might have contemplated that in his opinion the Arab oil embargo was the best option based on his reasoning that he needed to side with the radical regimes in order to prolong his own rule and the survival of the Saudi monarchy. However, based on the messages that Fahd and Sultan had conveyed to the Nixon Administration, there were serious disagreements between Faysal and the two senior princes. Furthermore, Faysal might have dismissed his brothers' warnings and objections (at least some) concerning the dangers of Saudi involvement in the oil embargo.

START OF THE OCTOBER WAR

The Arab-Israeli October War was launched on the Jewish holy day of Yom Kippur on Saturday, October 6, 1973, at 14:00, when Egyptian forces crossed the Suez Canal to the east bank on the Sinai Peninsula, while Syrian troops began an assault on the Golan Heights. To assist Egypt, Saudi Arabia had made generous financial contributions for its war preparations. However, Saudi Arabia's main contribution to the war efforts was its decision to join the Arab oil embargo, which was declared 11 days later, on October 17, 1973, after it had become more evident that the Arab armies were going to lose the war against Israel. Although the oil embargo was initially imposed against all those states, which the Arab oil producers considered allies of Israel, namely, Canada, Japan, the Netherlands, the United Kingdom, the United States (and later extended to Portugal, Rhodesia, and South Africa), its main target was the United States. On this date, Prince Fahd told British Ambassador Rothnie that Saudi Arabia had drafted its oil policies based on the fact that it "could not afford to ignore either more radical Arab governments around her or

---

[37] Thomas Lippman, *Inside the Mirage: America's Fragile Partnership with Saudi Arabia*, Boulder, CO: Westview Press, 2004, 222.

5 CONFLICTING INTERESTS AND KING FAYSAL'S DECISION TO SUPPORT... 67

radical forces within her frontiers."[38] Following his discussion with Fahd, Rothnie reported to London that in formulating its oil policies the royal family showed great sensitivity to the risks that it might run if the radical Arab regimes could claim in their propaganda that the Saudi kingdom was not making proper contribution to the Arab cause.

The embargo, which was a political act taking advantage of prevailing economic circumstances, had two main elements. First were the initial production cutbacks followed by additional 5 percent cutbacks each month. Second was the ban on oil exports to the United States and the other above-mentioned embargoed states. By December 1973, the Arab oil producers had cut their oil production by 25 percent while the price of oil had nearly quadrupled (by early 1974), rising from below $3 per barrel (October 1973) to nearly $12 per barrel (December 1973).

For the most part, however, the Saudi policy in terms of the Arab-Israeli October War was founded on pragmatism. Based on such characteristics of their foreign policy, the Saudis responded in two major ways. First, despite the pressure from the radical regimes, the Saudis seemed to have chosen to play time, and second, the Saudis wanted to contribute as little as possible to the actual war efforts. In fact, it was much easier and safer for the Saudis to give out money than to send military forces to the battle. According to the information that Group Captain Ives, the British Defense Attaché in Jeddah, had obtained, the 1973 October War came as a complete surprise to the Saudi Ministry of Defense and the military headquarters. Ives assessed that "whatever their real intentions might have been, they were prevented by the unpreparedness [...] of making a major military contribution to the Arab cause."[39]

On the one hand, the Saudis had not been ready for the war because they had not known when the war was supposed to start, and therefore this could explain the lack of preparedness of the Saudi military. In this respect, a comprehensive study prepared by Uri Bar-Joseph on the surprise

[38] "Saudi Internal" (confidential report), Rothnie to Wright, December 22, 1973, no. 20, FCO 8/2105.

[39] "Defense Attaché's Annual Report for 1973" (confidential report), Group Captain Ives (Defense Attaché, British Embassy, Jeddah) to MOD, (London), March 16, 1974, FCO 8/2348. An interesting detail mentioned by Ambassador Rothnie is that the Saudi forces "managed to get lost" for some time while the Saudi brigade traversed Jordan to Syria. See: "Defense Attaché's Annual Report" (confidential report), Rothnie to James Callaghan (Secretary of State for Foreign and Commonwealth Affairs, FCO, London), March 9, 1974, FCO 8/2348.

68   S. E. WILLNER

of the Yom Kippur War, and the preceding Israeli intelligence failure, seems to support such a conclusion. According to his findings, the Egyptians and the Syrians did not share their plans concerning the timing of the planned war with any of the other Arab states (except with Jordan).[40] Perhaps the primary reason for that was their fear that the Saudis might share the information with the Americans.[41]

On the other hand, the Saudis had not prepared their army for the war because, based on their pragmatic foreign policy, they did not want to participate in it, and therefore, it was easier for them to play time. Rachel Bronson confirms similar view[42] who has interviewed Raymond Close, a former CIA Station Chief in Jeddah. Close said that Prince Fahd had summoned him and "made clear that Saudi troops were under strict instructions not to become involved in the fighting."[43] This, in turn, was probably meant as a carefully articulated message to Israel. In other words, although it was politically dangerous to stay out of the war, the Saudis knew that it was even riskier had they been directly involved in the battle. Furthermore, such a policy approach concerning the October War indicates that the Saudi monarchy was not interested in being involved in other people's wars unless they had direct security implications for them. And even if such situation would occur, the Saudis would prefer to pay others to do the fighting. For the royal family, its own security and survival always came first and the ideological preferences second.

In fact, the Saudi policy concerning the 1973 October War was reflecting similar pragmatism as expressed by Deputy Prime Minister Faysal in 1962 when he had opposed direct Saudi military intervention in Yemen. According to Sarah Yizraeli, Faysal had justified his decision by arguing that Saudi Arabia had to protect its own interests first before intervening beyond its borders. It would seem, as Yizraeli points out, that in 1962 Faysal was afraid that, had the Saudi military failed in Yemen against the Egyptian supported revolutionaries, it might have triggered a coup in

---

[40] Uri Bar-Joseph, *The Watchman Fell Asleep: The Surprise of Yom Kippur War and Its Sources*, Albany, NY: State University of New York Press, 2005.

[41] According to Moshe Maoz, the Syrian military commanders in the field were not shared the information about the war until one hour before the attack. See: Moshe Maoz, *Assad, the Sphinx of Damascus: A Political Biography*, London: Weidenfield & Nicolson, 1988, 92.

[42] Rachel Bronson is an American political scientist.

[43] Rachel Bronson, *Thicker than Oil: America's Uneasy Partnership with Saudi Arabia*, Oxford: Oxford University Press, 2006, 117.

5 CONFLICTING INTERESTS AND KING FAYSAL'S DECISION TO SUPPORT... 69

Saudi Arabia.[44] However, the threat of coup did not necessarily have to come from outside forces, but it could equally have emerged from within the royal family itself, which at the time was quite divided. Therefore, to conclude, one could say that as part of a sort of 'survival instinct,' it was critical for the ruler to know when to yield and when to fight.[45]

Finally, one should briefly discuss the economic implications of the oil price increases and the political ramifications of the Saudi participation in the oil embargo. First, the economic conditions in the international oil markets were ideal for a significant oil price increase. While the global economic growth had been close to surpassing oil demand, the oil producers had not increased their production enough to match up with the growing demand.[46] Therefore, the Arab oil embargo triggered an oil market supply shock relatively easily, which the other non-Arab oil producers, such as Iran and Venezuela, took full advantage, and consequently increased their oil prices.[47]

Second, and perhaps more importantly, without Saudi Arabia's participation the embargo would not have had as serious impact on the world economy as it ended up having. Therefore, King Faysal's decision to support OAPEC's resolution to declare the oil embargo was critical for the embargo's success because Saudi Arabia was world's largest oil exporter and a pivotal player in OPEC.

Although the main political aim of the 'oil weapon' was to achieve various objectives regarding Israel, Morris Adelman, an American energy economist, assessed in 1982 that the oil embargo was a political failure. Instead, he argued that the embargo was a "stunning economic success" for the Arab oil producers.[48] The main reason for the oil weapon's political failure was that, despite their anti-Israeli political rhetoric, most of the Arab oil producers were predominantly motivated to use the embargo to

[44] Yizraeli, *Remaking of Saudi Arabia*, 160.

[45] House, *On Saudi Arabia*, 18.

[46] Already in April 1973, James Akins, who at the time served as the Director of the Office of Fuels and Energy in the US Department of State (1968–1973), warned about the looming oil crisis. In his view, the economic conditions were ripe for such eventuality. See: Ian Skeet, *OPEC: Twenty-Five Years of Prices and Politics*, Cambridge: Cambridge University Press, 1988, 83–84.

[47] In fact, after the 1973 oil embargo, Muhammad Riza Pahlavi, the Shah of Iran, had been hawkish in his demands to increase the oil prices even further.

[48] Morris A. Adelman, "OPEC as Cartel" in *OPEC Behavior and World Oil Prices*, ed. James M. Griffin and David J. Teece, London: George Allen & Unwin, 1982, 44.

make more money as many of them had significant domestic development pressures. Perhaps the most important indication of such a domestic economy issue is that both Iraq and Libya—the two most radical Arab oil producers, and the two main enemies of Saudi Arabia, were secretly violating the embargo and sold oil to the embargoed countries, most notably, to the United States.

Conclusion of Part II The 1973 Arab–Israeli War and the Arab Oil Embargo

CONCLUSIONS

The decision to join the 1973 Arab oil embargo was a major turning point for the Saudi monarchy. Since the rise of radical Arabism in the late 1950s, Saudi Arabia has been a recurring target of subversive activity. The intensity of these attacks, which the revolutionary Arab regimes sponsored against Saudi Arabia prior to the 1973 embargo, indicates that the radical regimes attempted systematically to influence Saudi foreign policymaking. By analyzing these underlying circumstances, and the Saudi decision-making process in responding to these threats, one can discover several principal characteristics of the way the royal family makes its decisions based on its strategic interests.

The Saudi maneuvering around the events preceding the oil embargo strongly suggests that Saudi foreign policy is fundamentally pragmatic, and that its decision-making processes are based on tribal-familial principles where important decisions are usually made through the process of consultation and consensus. Despite facing serious objections from the senior princes, King Faysal was the ultimate decision-maker behind the ruling to join the oil embargo. Although there is reason to believe that Faysal's decision to join the embargo, and to support Egypt, was partially influenced by his anti-Semitic mindset, the rationale for his decision was his own political balancing, based on his calculation (and fear) of the possible repercussions from the revolutionary Arab regimes had he not done so.

As the available records point out, Faysal might have thought that the frequent attacks were meant to undermine the legitimacy of his leadership. In his conspiratorial mindset, the fact that his wife almost got kidnapped in Paris just one month before the start of the war might have reminded him of how fragile the Saudi monarchy truly was, and that he could not take its survival for granted. Furthermore, the royal family seems to have backed Faysal to limit the potential risk of revealing its weakness. In other words, the many conflicts within the Saudi monarchy could indicate that the royal family had backed Faysal's decision out of respect toward him, and not because his decision had been a right one. Had these internal disagreements been exposed to the public, this could have weakened the Saudi position even further. When the Saudis uncovered that the survival of their monarchy was at stake, they made the necessary decisions to safeguard it.

PART III

The End of the Oil Embargo and the Murder of King Faysal (1973–1976)

The Saudis decided to terminate the oil embargo in mid-March 1974—five months after it had been imposed. Before it was over, however, the price of oil had quadrupled from its pre-embargo levels and consequently, the world economies were seriously struggling due to the high fuel prices. The embargo even caused panic among some oil consumers, especially amid those nations that had no oil production of their own; who had no oil reserves; and who were almost completely dependent on the Middle East oil. Therefore, some buyers were willing to purchase crude oil from auctions for record-high prices.

At the time, the President Richard Nixon's administration (1969–1974) was somewhat paralyzed on the presidential level due to a political scandal, which came to be known as the Watergate scandal. The oil embargo almost fully coincided with the height of the affair. Nevertheless, due to the high economic stress and the fear of the embargo's increasingly negative impact on the political stability of several US allies, the Nixon Administration decided to apply pressure and adopt psychological warfare campaign against Saudi Arabia, which was the most important participant in the oil embargo. Without the Saudi participation, the embargo, and the oil crisis that followed, would most likely never have impacted the lives of hundreds of millions of people as seriously as it ended up doing. The US pressure made King Faysal nervous and worried, but it did not change his mind. Rather, it seems to have made him more stubborn and reluctant to terminate the embargo. When Faysal continued making more threats (despite his ruling to end the embargo in March 1974), the United States, in turn, intensified its political pressure on the royal family. The major event in Saudi foreign policy happened only after Faysal was murdered in March 1975 and a new rule was established in the kingdom.

CHAPTER 6

Towards the End of the Oil Embargo

THE ORIGINS OF THE US MILITARY PLANS
AND PSYCHOLOGICAL WARFARE AGAINST THE SAUDIS

The American psychological warfare campaign for changing the Saudi oil policy played a leading role in the US attempts to influence Saudi policy-making in the aftermath of the oil embargo. Although most of the threats discussed in this chapter were predominantly meant as psychological warfare tactics, it is useful to recall a quote from David Kimche, the former director general of Israel's Ministry of Foreign Affairs. In 1991, he wrote that "to be effective, even the most telling diplomatic moves had to be backed by commensurate power—real power; rhetoric was no substitute."[1] As will be deliberated next, since early 1950s there existed a top-secret American plan to take over Saudi Arabia's oil production areas, but for different reasons than what the Saudis were contemplating. In fact, the plans were a contingency against a hypothetical Soviet threat to occupy Saudi oil fields, not against the Arab states. However, it is unlikely that the Saudis knew the extent of the top-secret plans, and therefore it could not have taken the rumors and statements of the American military plans simply as empty threats.

The initial plans for an American military operation with the aim of taking over Saudi Arabia's oil fields were secretly deliberated in the years that

[1] Kimche, *The Last Option*, 35.

© The Author(s), under exclusive license to Springer Nature   75
Switzerland AG 2023
S. E. Willner, *Preserving the Saudi Monarchy*,
https://doi.org/10.1007/978-3-031-30006-6_6

76 S. E. WILLNER

followed the end of the Second World War. Such contingency plans emerged in the aftermath of the blockade of Berlin in 1948, during which the Soviet Union attempted to hinder the West's access to the Western part of the divided German city. The Berlin Blockade, which lasted from June 1948 to September 1949, was one of the first serious international confrontations of the Cold War. During the time when Berlin was divided between the Western allies (the United States, the United Kingdom, and France) and the Soviet Union, the Soviets blocked the Western allies' access through the Russian-occupied East Germany to the sectors of the city that were under Western control.[2] In addition to the repercussions of the Berlin Blockade, the Americans were troubled by the growing communist activity in the Iranian Azerbaijan and the Iranian Kurdistan. Consequently, the Americans were afraid that such communist activity could lead to the establishment of two pro-Soviet republics in these Iranian regions.[3]

Moreover, the above-mentioned developments made President Harry S. Truman's administration (1945–1953) increasingly worried about the possibility that the Soviet land forces could sweep through Iran and Iraq to the Persian Gulf to take over the region's petroleum resources. The Americans were concerned that the US troops and their allies would have been unable to stop such a Soviet invasion. As such, the United States developed a top-secret 'denial policy,' according to which Aramco—and in the later plans the US armed forces—would have either disabled or destroyed the oil fields with the aim of keeping the Soviet Union from using Saudi oil for up to one year in the event of a Soviet invasion. Since the top-secret 'denial policy' was very sensitive to Saudi-US relations, the policy was based on "concurrence obtained from the Saudi Arabian Government." However, if the Soviets would have attacked Saudi Arabia before the Americans had been able to obtain "the prior concurrence" from the Saudi government, the top-secret document suggested that the

[2] See, for instance: Avi Shlaim, *The United States and the Berlin Blockade, 1948–1949: A Study in Crisis Decision-Making*, Berkeley, CA: University of California Press, 1983; Michael D. Haydock, *City under Siege: The Berlin Blockade and Airlift, 1948–1949*, Washington, D.C.: Brassey's, 2000.

[3] See, for instance: Louise L'Estrange Fawcett, *Iran and the Cold War: the Azerbaijan Crisis of 1946*, Cambridge: Cambridge University Press, 1992; Archie Roosevelt, Jr., "The Kurdish Republic of Mahabad," *Middle East Journal*, 1, 3, 1947: 247–269; Mark Gasiorowski and Malcolm Byrne eds. *Mohammad Mosaddeq and the 1953 Coup in Iran*, Syracuse, NY: Syracuse University Press, 2004, 203–208.

United States should proceed to implement the "plans for selective surface demolitions and [oil] well-plugging."[4] These top-secret plans also suggested that instead of destroying the oil fields, the United States could use radiological weapons to poison the oil fields and therefore making the fields uninhabitable. In fact, the British military had concluded in 1955 that as a last resort the "most complete method of destroying [Saudi] oil installations would be by nuclear bombardment."[5] Had the plan been leaked to Saudi Arabia, it would have had grave economic and political repercussions affecting both American and British interests in the region.[6]

The Soviets ended up not invading Saudi Arabia, but the top-secret contingency plans remained in US drawers. In May 1973, when the possible military response to a looming oil embargo was first publicly discussed, the sensitive 'denial policy' was still a well-guarded secret. When the embargo commenced in October 1973, it appears that the Nixon Administration exploited part of these military plans in its psychological warfare operations against Saudi Arabia so that the Saudis would be more convinced to terminate any ideas about oil embargo. However, the archival sources indicate that the United States considered an actual military action a remote possibility. Therefore, it preferred to use all means of psychological warfare to influence Saudi decision-making with regards to the oil embargo.[7] As will be discussed later, these US efforts made the Saudis very anxious. Since the political discourse within the royal family has often been filled with conspiratorial interpretations of events, this contributed to these Saudi anxieties. Therefore, the main aim of the psychological warfare was to make some of the senior princes eager to convince King Faysal

[4] "Denial and Conservation of Middle East Oil Resources and Facilities in the Event of War" (top-secret report), NSC Planning Board (Washington D.C.), December 22, 1953, NSC0176, *Dwight D. Eisenhower Presidential Library.*

[5] "Oil Denial in the Middle East" (top-secret report), Joint Planning Staff (Ministry of Defense, London), December 12, 1955, *FCO.* A copy of the document is available at the National Security Archive of the George Washington University, Washington D.C.

[6] Due to the sensitivity of these contingency plans, most of the archival documents referring to military plans were not released until mid-2010s. Steve Everly has assessed the 'denial policy' in his following article: Steve Everly, "The Top-Secret Cold War Plan to Keep Soviet Hands Off Middle Eastern Oil," *Politico*, June 23, 2016; Steve Everly and Charles R.T. Crumpley, "Truman Ok'd Sabotage Plot," *The Kansas City Star*, February 25, 1996, A1.

[7] It is useful to note that the domestic opinion in the United States was firmly opposed to any new military ventures abroad due to the long Vietnam War. The conflict in Vietnam lasted from 1955 until 1975.

78   S. E. WILLNER

that the embargo was not in the long term, in the interest of the royal family. The Nixon Administration probably hoped that the pressure they put on the royal family would lead Faysal to terminate the embargo and sustain him from attempting it again.

FAYSAL'S CONFRONTATIONAL MESSAGES: THREATS AND COUNTERTHREATS

King Faysal had been a generous financial supporter of Egypt's war efforts against Israel.[8] Faysal told the Cairo newspaper *Al-Jumhuriyah* published on November 22, 1973 that during his meeting with Secretary of State Henry Kissinger (1973–1977) few weeks earlier (November 8, 1973), he had expressed to the secretary his unwillingness to terminate the oil embargo.[9] Faysal's message was threefold: first, there would be no return from the embargo until there were complete Israeli withdrawal from the territories conquered in 1967 war; second, there would be no compromise on "Arabism of Jerusalem"; and third, there would be no compromise over the "rights of the Palestinian people."[10] Although Faysal's main purpose must have been to assure the Egyptian government of his continuing financial support for Egypt, he must have also addressed the Americans that he was obliged to the Arab cause. Faysal told Kissinger that he wanted the United States to put more pressure on the Israelis. Kissinger responded to Faysal's demands by saying that they were "politically impossible."[11] Kissinger knew that Israel would refuse to give up territory without mutual concessions.

The Saudi monarchy was in a difficult position. On the one hand, as Faysal pointed out to Kissinger a few weeks later, on December 14, 1973, "[he] had no choice" but to join the embargo, because he was afraid of

---

[8] The Saudis assisted the Egyptian with hundreds of millions of dollars, although the exact amount is unknown. See, for instance: Safran, *Ceaseless Quest*, 155.

[9] Memorandum (top secret), Brent Scowcroft (President's Deputy Assistant for National Security Affairs) to President Nixon, November 9, 1973, no. 238, *FRUS*, vol. XXXVI, *Energy Crisis*, 675–676.

[10] "*Al-malik Faysal yu'alinu fi tasrīhāt tanfaridu biha 'al-Jumhūriyah'*" [King Faysal makes exclusive statement to "Al-Jumhuriyah"], *Al-Jumhuriyah*, November 22, 1973, 1, 7; *FBIS*, November 26, 1973.

[11] Memorandum, November 9, 1973.

the reactions in the radical camp in case he ruled otherwise.[12] On the other hand, the Saudi Ambassador in Beirut had recalled in another occasion— in a possible reference to the internal royal family objections and pressure—that Faysal had been very unwilling to join the embargo because joining it "risked his throne."[13] The Saudis seems to have been afraid of the consequences of its deteriorating relationship with the United States. As Ambassador Lassila assessed, the United States was the only foreign power at the time that could really threaten King Faysal's rule. Perhaps more importantly, Lassila indicated that the United States was the only foreign power that could severely pressure the royal family and, if needed, to confiscate the Saudi Arabia's financial assets deposited in the West. However, as will be discussed later, had the situation come to that point, it would have been in the interest of the Saudis to depose Faysal. Nonetheless, Kissinger increased his pressure on Riyadh and conveyed a message to the royal family (November 21, 1973) saying that the United States wanted it to end the embargo and if it would not, it would have to face serious consequences:

> It is clear that if pressures continue unreasonably and indefinitely, then the United States will have to consider what countermeasures it may have to take. We would do this with enormous reluctance, and we are still hopeful that matters will not reach that point.[14]

While the rumors of possible American military intervention began to circulate in the Arab capitals, Faysal conveyed another confrontational message through Minister of Petroleum Ahmad Zaki Yamani. In an interview with the Danish Television, on November 22, 1973, Yamani asserted that the Saudis had in their possession an oil weapon far greater than what they had been using. In fact, he was referring to the extreme option of destruction of the oil infrastructure. "What we did [embargo] was nothing at all," he said, and continued that if Washington was thinking about a military

---

[12] "Memorandum of Conversation" Riyadh, December 14, 1973, no. 267, *FRUS*, vol. XXXVI, *Energy Crisis*, 766–769.

[13] The Saudi Ambassador's name is not mentioned in the report. See: "Suomen öljykysymys ja Saudi-Arabia" [Finland's Oil Trade and Saudi Arabia] (report), Carolus Lassila (Ambassador, Embassy of Finland, Jeddah) Ahti Karjalainen (Minister of Foreign Affairs, Helsinki), April 16, 1976, no. J-46/19, *AMFAF*.

[14] Kissinger held the press conference on November 21, 1973. See: Henry Kissinger, *Years of Upheaval*, Boston, MA: Little, Brown & Company, 1982, 880.

80 S. E. WILLNER

action to take over the oil fields, then it would be a "suicide" by the United States. He added that if military force would be used, the Saudis would "immediately blow up" the installations.[15] The logic behind the threat was probably based on similar plans, which the Americans and the British had contemplated in the 1940s and 1950s, namely that the denial threat of Saudi petroleum resources would deter a foreign power from occupying the Saudi oil fields.

Although the threat of Saudis destroying their oil fields might sound absurd and unlikely, and although there is no record that could indicate how serious King Faysal had been with his threats (especially because they were totally against the Saudi guidelines of pragmatism and the survival of their monarchy), nevertheless the CIA took them seriously. In response, one week after Yamani's interview on November 30, 1973, the CIA recommended that the United States would need to assess the Saudi capacity to destroy its oil installations in the event of US military action.[16] However, there is no information available to suggest that by November 1973 the Saudis had implemented such a 'Samson Option'[17] and placed explosives in their oil installations. The Danish Television interviewer seemed to have been surprised by Yamani's answer and asked, "By yourself? By your people?," to which he answered, "of course, of course. [...] What will happen, [...Europe] must live without oil from Saudi Arabia for so many years, because it takes years to repair [the oil infrastructure...]."[18] Since Yamani was very loyal to the royal family, and since his communications were usually carefully articulated, he would not have conveyed such a confrontational message unless he had been commissioned to do so. Considering the otherwise pragmatic Saudi foreign policy approach and considering the conflicting interests within the royal family in relation to the oil

---

[15] "Interview on Danish Television with Saudi Arabian Minister of Petroleum, Shaikh Ahmad Zaki Yamani, November 22, 1973" (transcript) (confidential telegram), Danish Embassy (London) to FCO, November 29, 1973, *FCO 8/2121*.

[16] "CIA Study of US Options Toward Saudi Oil Embargo" (secret memorandum), Harold H. Saunders (National Security Council Staff) to Henry Kissinger (Secretary of State), November 30, 1973, no. 255, *FRUS*, vol. XXXVI: *Energy Crisis*, 717–718.

[17] In military doctrine, the 'Samson Option' refers to the alleged Israeli last resort deterrence strategy of using of nuclear weapons against an invading army that has already invaded and destroyed much of the country.

[18] "Interview on Danish Television with Saudi Arabian Minister of Petroleum, Shaikh Ahmad Zaki Yamani, November 22, 1973," November 29, 1973.

embargo, it is quite likely that King Faysal had instructed Yamani to make such remarks.

One can conclude that Yamani's threatening statement was completely against the pragmatic principles of Saudi foreign policy. Therefore, it was probably dictated by Faysal and not by most of the royal family. Furthermore, it is quite likely that Faysal was so frightened about the possibility of the US capture of the Saudi oil fields that he gave a counterthreat, which was based on emotions rather than cold calculation. As will be contemplated next, senior members of the royal family were very concerned about the escalating situation.

SENIOR MEMBERS OF THE ROYAL FAMILY CASTING THEIR DOUBTS ABOUT THE EMBARGO

While King Faysal seemed to have been more ready to side with the radical Arabs and was also seemingly more confrontational vis-à-vis the United States, his brothers, particularly Fahd and Sultan, were increasingly worried about the consequences of the embargo. According to Anwar Ali, the governor of the Saudi Arabian Monetary Authority (1958–1974), in November 1973, some of the senior princes were casting their doubts about the use of the oil weapon. Anwar Ali did not elaborate more but based on earlier statements by both Fahd and Sultan, they had been advocating against Faysal's decision to join the Arab oil embargo. David Tatham, a British diplomat in Jeddah, assessed Anwar Ali's comments by saying that "at first point this seems strange as from the Arab point of view, it [the embargo] has surely been a considerable success. However, there are many influential Saudis whose personal fortunes are closely tied to Western stock markets."[19] As it seems, the senior princes were afraid that a prolonged embargo was not only unsettling the established channels of business in the Middle East, but they were also afraid that it could lead into confiscation of their substantial personal foreign assets.[20] Based on such reasoning, it was in their interests to terminate the oil embargo as quickly as possible.

It seems probable that these increasing doubts about the continued oil embargo were a prime motivator, which led Khalid, Fahd, and Sultan to

---

[19] "Faint Hearts and the Oil Weapon" (confidential telegram), David E. Tatham (MED, FCO) to FCO, London, November 26, 1973, no. 151, *FCO 8/2109.*
[20] Ibid.

82 S. E. WILLNER

convey several back-channel messages to Washington. On November 27, 1973, the Americans received such a back-channel message from Deputy Prime Minister Khalid, who had told them that the Saudis were "very suspicious and nervous about rumors that the US [was] planning [...a military action concerning control of oil producing facilities in the kingdom].''[21] Khalid had asked whether "[President Richard] Nixon could make it clear to the Arab power bloc that the US plans [involved] no armed intervention in their countries; it would help melt tensions that now exist.''[22] Perhaps in response to a similar message from the royal family, James Akins, the US ambassador to Saudi Arabia (1973–1975), reported to Washington that the Arabs and the Americans were to be set on a "collision course" and that "Kissinger did not understand the Arabs at all and had got his heels dug in about forcing Faysal to agree to relax the oil embargo soon.''[23] As it appeared, Kissinger was preparing to add more pressure on the Saudis.

The US Deliberations and Kissinger's Response: "The Wilder Flights of Zumwaltery"

In November 1973, the American ambassador to Jeddah, Akins, told his British counterpart Alan K. Rothnie that "Kissinger might well resort to more direct means of pressure on Faysal over the oil." Rothnie commented that "Akins was not more specific than this, but I felt, from what he had said to me in the past weeks that *the wilder flights of Zumwaltery* were not entirely excluded from his [Kissinger's] mind.''[24] Akins did not elaborate what he meant by this expression "*the wilder flights of Zumwaltery*," but it is possible the reference was to Admiral Elmo Russell

---

[21] On November 27, 1973, Peter Rousel wrote to George H.B. Bush (chairman of the Republican National Council Committee) that King Faysal's aides had been getting "some bad information about US intentions" in Saudi Arabia and, more specifically, that it is considering military action concerning control of oil producing facilities in the kingdom; see: "Notes," Peter Rousel (Republican National Council Committee) to George H.W. Bush (chairman of the Republican National Committee, Washington, D.C.), November 27, 1973, no. 250, *FRUS*, vol. XXXVI: *Energy Crisis*, 704–705.

[22] Crown Prince Khalid to Bill Wittmer (the former president of Tennessee Gas Pipeline Company), (telephone call), "Notes," 704–705.

[23] "US Policy/Saudi Oil" (confidential report), Rothnie to FCO (London), November 30, 1973, no. 128, *FCO 8/2120*.

[24] Ibid.

Zumwalt. First, and perhaps most importantly, Akins could have been saying that, as a strategist Kissinger, like Zumwalt, believed that the Soviet Union was the number one threat to the United States, and therefore such a Cold War thinking had been dominating Kissinger's confrontational approach vis-à-vis King Faysal.[25] Second, Akins might have been saying that Kissinger sought to change the way the State Department Arabists had been doing things in Saudi Arabia for decades and because of this, in Akins' view, Kissinger was advocating a stricter policy towards the Saudis (in a similar fashion as Zumwalt had been advocating against the Soviet naval capabilities in the 1970s). This is what frustrated Akins.

It is also possible that Akins was protesting his dissatisfaction to the fact that the United States was not doing enough to satisfy the Arabs. This would fit to his earlier, highly questionable unofficial attempts to advocate Aramco executives to use their contacts in Washington to lobby for the Arabs and "to hammer home the point that oil restrictions [were] not going to be lifted unless political struggle [was] settled in a manner satisfactory to Arabs."[26] In retrospect, Rothnie seemed to have been puzzled by Ambassador Akins' remarks. At the end of his report, Rothnie concluded that "I am not sure quite what this all adds up to. Akins may have been suffering a bout of despondency, but he is not, as I have known him over the years, an alarmist."[27]

Nevertheless, on November 28, 1973, Secretary of State Henry Kissinger, and Secretary of Defense James R. Schlesinger (1973–1975) summoned a joint meeting with their senior staff. The discussion was about how to find ways to end the Arab oil embargo. As recorded in the

---

[25] Admiral Zumwalt was a highly decorated US naval officer, who played a major role in the US military history. He served in several roles, and before retiring, he served as Chief of Naval Operations in the US Department of Navy. Richard Goldstein, "Elmo R. Zumwalt Jr., Admiral Who Modernized the Navy, Is Dead at 79," *The New York Times*, January 3, 2000, A17; Joseph Y. Smith, "Navy Reformer Elmo Zumwalt Dies," *The Washington Post*, January 3, 2000, A1.

[26] Robert Kaplan has quoted an Aramco document printed in the US Senate Subcommittee on Multinational's hearings. See: "Multinational Corporations and United States Foreign Policy," Part 7, *U.S. Senate*, February 20–21, March 27–28, 1974, 517. See: Robert, D. Kaplan, *The Arabists: The Romance of an American Elite*, New York, NY: Free Press, 1993, 174.

[27] Rothnie also mentioned in his report that Akins was "an old friend from our Baghdad days [and] no doubt felt free to unburden himself a bit." Rothnie served as a Commercial Council at the British Embassy in Baghdad during 1963–1965. See: "US Policy/Saudi Oil," November 30, 1973.

meeting minutes, the administration had received another back-channel message, in which King Faysal and Second Deputy Prime Minister Fahd asked an intermediary to explore a mutually acceptable compromise to end the oil embargo. According to the same document, Fahd had also asked this anonymous intermediary to find out whether the United States was planning "to do to us what they did to King Idris in Libya."[28] The Saudis were referring to some crude conspiracy theories, which circulated among the Arab leaders, according to which the CIA had sponsored Colonel Muammar Qadhafi's military coup in 1969.[29] This eventuality was untrue, but it is possible that such rumors had been purposefully disseminated as a way to increase pressure on the Saudis.

Kissinger then said that "the Saudis are blinking," to which Schlesinger responded that "[the Saudis] think we knocked off Idris." Kissinger's reaction to Schlesinger's remarks was that "[the Saudis] have never played in this league before. They are scared." Kissinger also asked—perhaps jokingly, but his intention was quite clear—"can't we overthrow one of the sheikhs just to show that we can do it?" The part of the discussion that followed has not been declassified. However, it could fit into the picture that the senior members of the Nixon Administration were debating at the time about the implementation of psychological warfare campaign against the Saudis.

The CIA had also assessed how the United States could convey Faysal a message saying that it "was contemplating serious actions against Saudi Arabia." The report was most likely prepared in response to Yamani's earlier remarks about Saudi Arabia's readiness to go as far as destroying its own oil fields in case of a US invasion. Firstly, the CIA suggested two actions, which have not been declassified yet. It added that these options were "not analyzed carefully but [were] simply put forward as possibilities." However, as the circumstantial evidence suggests, the first option might have been to use the psychological warfare tactics to send a message saying the United States was serious about using military force. Furthermore, the second option could have been (in case the first did not work out) to push the Saudis to overthrow King Faysal. Secondly, and perhaps more importantly, the CIA recommended that the United States

---

[28] "Memorandum of Conversation" in the White House Map Room (Washington D.C.), November 29, 1973, no. 253, *FRUS*, vol. XXXVI: *Energy Crisis*, 711.

[29] Qadhafi's coup overthrew King Idris in September 1969 and replaced the Libyan monarchy with a socialist anti-Western Arab republic.

would need to assess the Saudi capability to destroy its oil installations in the event of American military action.[30]

On November 29, 1973, another meeting was held between senior US foreign and defense officials. There, Kissinger proclaimed that "we can't yield to blackmail. We can't tie ourselves to any scheme. We must show our muscle now or the Russians will take extreme positions and drive us right out of the Middle East."[31] Kissinger must have been referring to the revolutionary Arab regimes, which were aligned with the Soviet Union. The Soviets were pleased for the initiation of oil embargo against the United States and even encouraged its continuation as the embargo weakened the United States and its NATO allies' ability to supply fuel for their economies and militaries. However, perhaps most importantly for the benefit of the Soviets, the dramatic increase in the oil prices had a favorable effect on Soviet foreign currency reserves because it was supplying oil products to the United States and other Western economies.[32] For the US economy, like those of other world economies, the situation was grave. On November 30, 1973, James Akins estimated that if the embargo would continue until the spring of 1974, then there "could be widespread industrial shut-downs and heavy unemployment, affecting up to 10 million workers."[33] Kissinger, in turn, had warned that "our view has been that if we once begin to let ourselves be blackmailed, this weapon will be used time and time again at every stage of the negotiations."[34]

---

[30] "CIA Study of US Options toward Saudi Oil Embargo," November 30, 1973.

[31] "Arab Oil Embargo and Production Cutbacks" (memo), Charles A. Cooper (US National Security Council) to Kissinger, November 29, 1973, no. 234, *FRUS*, vol. XXXVI: *Energy Crisis*, 662.

[32] Aryeh Yodfat and Mordechai Abir, *In the Direction of the Persian Gulf: The Soviet Union and the Persian Gulf*, London: Frank Cass and Company, 1977, 16,19.

[33] "US Policy/Saudi Oil" (confidential report), Rothnie to FCO (London), November 30, 1973, no. 128, *FCO 8/2120*. Because of the high oil prices, deep recession began in the Western industrial countries. For instance, the US gross national product dropped 6 percent between 1973 and 1975, while unemployment in the United States doubled to around 9 percent. Yergin, *The Prize*, 616–617. For further reading on Akins' views about the oil crisis, see, for instance: James E. Akins, "The Oil Crisis: This time the wolf is here." *Foreign Affairs*. 51, 3 1973: 462–490.

[34] "Minutes of the Secretary of State's Staff Meeting" (memo), Department of State, Washington D.C. December 26, 1975, no. 270, *FRUS*, vol. XXXVI: *Energy Crisis*, 773. Kissinger also mentions the possibility of a "super cartel," which in his view would be a cooperative of several Third World raw material producers. See: Henry Kissinger, *Years of Renewal*, New York, NY: Touchstone, 2000, 692.

86   S. E. WILLNER

The psychological warfare campaign against the Saudis took an interesting turn on December 12, 1973, when Secretary of Defense Schlesinger briefed Rowland Baring, the British Ambassador in Washington (1971–1974), about the secret US plans of "taking the oil fields" in Saudi Arabia. The top-secret report prepared by the British ambassador after the meeting stated that "the US would rather risk military action than be held ransom by the Arabs and their oil weapon."[35] It is quite likely that the briefing was meant as a message to the Saudi monarchy. Accordingly, Gerald Posner, an American investigative journalist, interviewed an anonymous official at the US Department of State, who told that "if you really want to keep something secret you don't have the Secretary of Defense tell the British Ambassador that we are thinking of having a preemptive strike on the biggest oil producer in the world." The official continued elaborating that such was "a surefire way to make sure that the news gets broadcast, and gets back to the Saudis, which is probably what the game plan was all along."[36] The Americans probably chose such an indirect avenue to convey their message to Riyadh because the British had had an intimate role in creating the Kingdom of Saudi Arabia in the early 1930s.[37] Therefore, Washington might have thought that London would inform the Saudis of the 'US war plans' because the British wanted to portray an image that they were the protectors of the Saudi interests. This, in turn, was in the US interests because they wanted to increase their pressure on the Saudis. Two days later, on December 14, 1973, Secretary of State Kissinger met King Faysal in Riyadh. The message from Washington had not yet reached the Saudi capital. This could explain Faysal's comment that "nothing would please me more than to say that tomorrow morning we will lift the embargo. But, as the American expression goes, it does take 'two to tango'."[38] By saying so, and by adding that "I had no choice," it was obvious that Faysal was not yet ready to lift the embargo.

---

[35] As quoted by: Gerald Posner, *Secrets of the Kingdom*, New York, NY: Random House, 2005, 121.

[36] Posner, *Secrets*, 121.

[37] In the 1920s and early 1930s, the British had supported Abd al-Aziz ibn Saud (instead of Husayn ibn Ali al-Hashimi, also known as Sharif Husayn, the King of Hejaz (r.1916–1924) and the Emir of Mecca) to become the ruler of the region in the Arabian Peninsula that became known as Saudi Arabia.

[38] "Memorandum of Conversation," Riyadh, December 14, 1973, no. 267, *FRUS*, vol. XXXVI, *Energy Crisis*, 766–769.

Ambassador Akins reveal a perplexing detail of Kissinger's negotiation tactics. During Kissinger's visit to Saudi Arabia on December 14, 1973, he had made a puzzling revelation by telling the Saudis three times that he was "afraid of being assassinated by the Israelis."[39] The fact that he told this three times indicates that he wanted to make sure that the Saudis got his message. On the one hand, Kissinger might have wanted to impress the Saudis with the kind of intelligence they could get if they would end the embargo and if there ever were any assassination plans against a Saudi king. On the other hand, Kissinger perhaps wanted to distance himself from Israel and to exalt his own importance to the monarchy.

In any case, Kissinger's statements of his own assassination sound very absurd. In other words, such remarks would not have made any sense given the fact that the United States had provided Israel much needed arms, which proved so vital to winning of the 1973 October War. Therefore, could it have been possible that Kissinger intended to message the Saudis that he was under great pressure and that he did not have other alternative but to turn into a more serious measures against the kingdom (as Secretary Schlesinger had told the British Ambassador in Washington two days earlier)? Anyway, it is not reported how the members of the royal family reacted to Kissinger's mystifying message. They must have listened carefully, and were quite likely puzzled about his words, but certainly they were no fools.

What happened next indicates that few days after Kissinger's visit the British ambassador had warned the Saudis of the 'American war plans.' About a week after Kissinger's mid-December 1973 visit of Saudi Arabia, the king's mind seemed to have changed—perhaps after the American messages had reached Riyadh. On December 20, 1973, Minister Saqqaf told Akins that King Faysal "has now decided that the Arabs have made their point; that the world understands the ability of the Arabs to use their oil weapon effectively. [...] The king has therefore decided that the oil boycott must be lifted and limits on production removed." Nevertheless, Akins still had his doubts about Faysal's change of mind. At the end of his

---

[39] Ambassador James Akins revealed Kissinger's comments during his private visit to the United Kingdom in April 1974. He had unofficial meetings at the FCO on April 2, 1974. Over the meeting Akins told his British hosts, among other things, that "on his second visit to Saudi Arabia Kissinger had referred on three occasions to his fear [...that he could be] assassinated by the Israelis [...]." See: "Saudi Internal" (secret memo), FCO (London), April 2, 1973, no. 105, *FCO 8/2349*; "Visit of Mr. James Akins" (report, for eyes only), M.S. Weir (FCO, London) to Rothnie, April 5, 1974, no. 106, *FCO 8/2349*.

88 S. E. WILLNER

report, Akins commented that "there is no reason to believe that Saqqaf is not telling the truth, but this news should still be viewed with caution." He added that there remained a possibility that Faysal would back down from his decision to end the embargo if faced with strong opposition from the radical Arab states.[40] Akins' suspicion turned right: Faysal was not yet ready to end the embargo. On December 26, 1973, Minister Saqqaf told Akins that "the king was difficult." Saqqaf added that at times he thought Faysal "wanted to lift the boycott immediately; at other times he seemed morose, dispirited and hostile."[41]

NIXON'S MESSAGE TO KING FAYSAL: "RESTRICTIONS MUST BE ENDED IMMEDIATELY"

At the end of December 1973, Iranian oil had been auctioned on the free market for more than $17 per barrel. Such a price was an indication that in panic some of the oil consumers were willing to pay unforeseen amounts for their oil supply. Although the Saudis were selling their oil for much lower price, the level was still much higher than what it had been before the embargo (in April 1973, the price had been at $2.74). To restrain the drastic oil price increase, the Saudis had helped to negotiate a price of $11.65 per barrel for OPEC oil in December 1973.[42] In spite of King Faysal's earlier statements, there were no signs that the embargo would be lifted. On December 28, 1973, President Nixon sent a personal letter to King Faysal, in which he iterated that "it is absolutely essential that the oil embargo and oil production restrictions against the United States be ended immediately."[43] Similarly, Secretary of State Kissinger asked to convey another message to King Faysal, saying that he "cannot express too

[40] "Memorandum" (secret), Scowcroft to Nixon, December 20, 1973, no. 268, *FRUS*, vol. XXXVI, *Energy Crisis*, 770.

[41] "King Faysal's Letter to the President" (memo) (secret telegram), Akins to Department of State (Washington), December 26, 1973, no. 272, *FRUS*, vol. XXXVI, 776–777.

[42] Safran, *Saudi Arabia: Ceaseless Quest*, 160–164.

[43] "Letter from Nixon to Faisal" (secret), President Richard Nixon to King Faysal (Riyadh), December 28, 1973, no. 274, *FRUS*, vol. XXXVI, *Energy Crisis*, 779. Furthermore, Kissinger had written similar but less confrontational letter to the Shah of Iran. Although Iran did not participate in the oil embargo, the Shah's oil policy had contributed to the rise of oil prices. In his letter to the Shah, which Kissinger wrote in Nixon's name, Kissinger warned the Shah of the grave consequence of the rise in oil prices, which could cause a worldwide recession. See: Henry Kissinger, *Years of Upheaval*, Boston, MA: Little Brown, 1982, 888.

strongly his disappointment and dismay."[44] The next day, on December 29, 1973, Saqqaf told Akins that after he had reviewed Kissinger's letter to Faysal, the king had "expressed concern over tone of [the US] Secretary [of State]'s letter to Saqqaf; [and] wondered why US is resorting to threats."[45] Saqqaf continued saying that Faysal "made no comment about the President [Nixon]'s letter other than to ask what was meant by an 'immediate' lifting of the boycott; he said the President must know [that] such action could be taken by only an Arab consensus and it could not be achieved today."[46] Saqqaf added that Faysal had further "asked if the US were really trying to destroy Saudi Arabia or drive it into the camp of the radicals?" Akins wondered whether this was a rhetorical question and, as such, did not respond. Saqqaf reiterated that if the Saudis were to lift the embargo immediately, "it would appear as complete surrender to American pressure." He added that "the reaction in the Arab world against the king and against Saudi Arabia would be even stronger."[47] Although Second Deputy Prime Minister Fahd seems to have expressed his support for Faysal's policy, he wanted to assure the Americans that the Saudis desired to end the embargo as soon as possible. His defense for the Arab position was that if the embargo were lifted based on unconditional disengagement, then the "Arabs would be denying themselves their major political leverage."[48]

In mid-January 1974, few weeks after Fahd had made the above comments, Saqqaf and Kamal Adham, the director of the General Intelligence Directorate,[49] possibly following their observations of King Faysal's behavior and knowing how to read him, urged Akins to convey to Washington that "arguments for lifting of [the] boycott [should] be kept free of threat or menace." They said that otherwise Faysal would freeze into a negative and unhelpful posture. They also strongly advised Washington to "treat

[44] "Letter from Secretary Kissinger to Minister Saqqaf" (secret telegram), Kissinger to the US Embassy (Jeddah), December 28, 1973, no. 273, *FRUS*, vol. XXXVI, *Energy Crisis*, 777.

[45] "Saudi Reactions to President Nixon's and Secretary Kissinger's Letters" (secret telegram), Akins to the Department of State (Washington), December 30, 1973, *FRUS*, vol. XXXVI, *Energy Crisis*, 783.

[46] Ibid. 783.

[47] Ibid.

[48] Untitled, US Embassy (Jeddah) to Henry Kissinger (Washington), January 13, 1974, no. 282, *FRUS*, vol. XXXVI, *Energy Crisis*, 798–799.

[49] Kamal Adham was King Faysal's brother-in-law. See, for instance: Peter Hobday, *Saudi Arabia Today: An Introduction to the Richest Oil Power*, New York, NY: St. Martin's Press, 1978, 117–118.

90   S. E. WILLNER

the king with honey, not onions."[50] What one could learn from such statements is that Saqqaf and Adham were advising the United States to respect Faysal and not to threaten him. Akins, who was an experienced Arabist, had already written to the Department of State in a similar way weeks earlier noting that Faysal was "very sensitive to threats" and that he tended to get "stubborn when he [felt] he [was] being pushed." As such, Akins had recommended that the US administration should appeal the Saudis of their friendship and better nature instead of using threats of countermeasures.[51] Nevertheless, the line adopted by the United States was completely opposite.

There was little doubt that King Faysal was stubborn but also that he was a very traditional Saudi decision-maker. Such behavior would seem to explain Faysal's reaction when Minister of Petroleum Yamani met him in the morning of December 30, 1973, to brief him about the embargo's negative impact on the fuel supply of the US Navy. Yamani told Faysal that the embargo was benefiting the Soviets and that the US Navy needed special arrangement to secure its fuel supply. Yamani told Akins that the king did not respond to his request. When Yamani told Faysal that "he interpreted his silence as consent, [...] the king still did not respond."[52] Faysal's conduct could reflect his desire to play it safe and clear him from taking responsibility for bad decisions. Therefore, depending on the context of the matter, this means that if a person does not say anything, it usually implies his consent.

Ending the Embargo

One key characteristic of Saudi politics is that it tends to anchor political acts in personal relationships. Before King Faysal decided to end the oil embargo, he approached the Soviets through the Grand Mufti of Russia. Since the Mufti was a religious figure, it might have been easier and less problematic for Faysal to approach him, considering that Saudi Arabia and the Soviet Union had no diplomatic relations. Although there are no

---

[50] "Saudi Position on Lifting of Embargo" (report) (secret telegram), Akins to the Department of State (Washington), January 23, 1974, no. 290, *FRUS*, vol. XXXVI, *Energy Crisis*, 811.

[51] "Saudi Reactions to President Nixon's and Secretary Kissinger's Letters," 787.

[52] "Saudis to Supply Sixth and Seventh Fleets with Oil" (secret telegram), Akins to the Department of State (Washington), December 30, 1973, no. 275, *FRUS*, vol. XXXVI, *Energy Crisis*, 781.

6 TOWARDS THE END OF THE OIL EMBARGO   91

available records, it is possible that the Saudis had used the Mufti before as an unofficial conveyer of messages between the Saudis and the Russians. Nevertheless, it appears that the Grand Mufti of Russia first traveled to Sana (North Yemen), from where he flew to Saudi Arabia in a special aircraft that Faysal had sent for him.[53] The Mufti was reported to have had several secret sessions with Faysal. Although exact dates of these meetings are unknown, it would make sense that they took place around January–March 1974. Why would Faysal, who was obsessively anti-communist, meet with the Grand Mufti of Russia, whom he must have thought had close ties to the Soviet intelligence? As Faysal considered communist ideology a threat to his kingdom and especially because most of the revolutionary Arab regimes were aligned with the Soviet Union, it would seem unlikely that he was seeking closer relations with the Soviets. Instead, it is more likely that Faysal attempted to utilize his secret communication channels with the Soviets as bargaining points with the United States while possibly pursuing equilibrium in his relations with the two superpowers. In fact, Muhammad Riza Pahlavi, the Shah of Iran (r. 1941–1979), had attempted similar tactics in the end of 1950s and early 1960s.[54] Therefore, the purpose of Faysal's meetings with the Grand Mufti might have been to send a message to the Americans that the king could get closer with Moscow if Washington's Middle East policy would not change.[55]

The tension in the Persian Gulf had increased as the Iranians were more involved in the war in the Omani Province of Dhofar. As a response to the increased Soviet activity in the Indian Ocean region,[56] and in response to the latest Middle East war, the United States had decided to set up a

[53] The Grand Mufti's travel dates are unknown. "Saudi/Soviet Relations" (confidential report), Harold B. Walker (Counselor, British Embassy, Jeddah) to Stephen J.L. Wright (FCO, London), June 7, 1975, no. 57, *FCO 8/2574.*

[54] Aryeh Yodfat wrote that ties with the Soviets were also a part of the Shah's attempts to diversify Iran's foreign relations and avoid complete dependence on the United States; see: Aryeh Yodfat, *The Soviet Union and Revolutionary Iran,* London: Croom Helms, 1984, 32–33. For further reading, see also: Shahram Chubin, and Sepehr Zabih, *The Foreign Relations of Iran: A Developing State in a Zone of Great-Power Conflict,* Berkeley, CA: University of California Press, 1974.

[55] "Saudi/Soviet Relations," June 7, 1975.

[56] The Soviet Union increased its naval presence in the region in response to the 1971 Indo-Pakistan War, in which it supported India by selling it weapons.

permanent naval and air base on the island of Diego Garcia,[57] located some 1600 km south of the tip of India. The Saudis had not missed the news of this development. During a lunch meeting with Patrick Wright, the head of the FCO Middle East Department (1972–1974), Abd al-Rahman Helaissi, the Saudi ambassador to London, had raised the issue of Diego Garcia and "described it as 'proof' of American aggressive statements about the oil producers."[58] It is possible that the Saudis had been contemplating the US plans to invest some $30 million[59] on the island's infrastructure, and thought that one of the purposes of the military base was to put more pressure on their monarchy. The royal family was right that Washington was employing other methods to persuade Faysal to terminate the embargo. Rumors were spreading in Beirut that the CIA was planning to overthrow King Faysal. While residing in Beirut, Ambassador Lassila cabled to Helsinki an interesting story he had heard sometime earlier and most likely before the end of the oil embargo. Lassila's source was Mr. Shaibani, who was an advisor to Prince Abd Allah ibn Abd al- Aziz.[60] His exact position in Beirut is not revealed in the report, but it is possible he was a Saudi diplomat stationed in the city. According to Shaibani, there had been serious rumors circulating among the high-ranking Saudis in Beirut that the Saudi intelligence had spotted a team of CIA agents, whose aim was to overthrow King Faysal.[61] It is not known who had initiated such rumors, but it is possible that the CIA was behind them. It is also possible that the CIA wanted to convince the Saudis of its aims, and therefore, it wanted to make it look like its agents were ready to overthrow King Faysal if necessary.

In addition to the Americans, President Anwar al-Sadat of Egypt had also been advocating King Faysal to end the embargo. On February 14–15, 1974, Faysal met Al-Sadat, President Hafiz al-Asad of Syria, and

[57] According to *The New York Times*, Admiral Elmo R. Zumwalt Jr., the US Naval Chief of Operations, had said that "events such as the Arab-Israeli war, the oil embargo and ensuing price rises show that our interests in the Indian Ocean are directly linked with our interests in Europe and Asia, and, more broadly, with our fundamental interest in maintaining a stable, worldwide balance of power [...]." See: Bernard Weinraub, "The Value of Diego Garcia," *The New York Times*, June 2, 1974, 201.

[58] "Lunch with the Saudi Ambassador" (confidential report), Patrick Wright (Head, MED, FCO) to Mr. Young (FCO), February 8, 1974, no. 1, *FCO 8/2341*.

[59] Bernard Weinraub, "US Plan to Set Up Island Base Is Chilling Relations with India," *The New York Times*, February 8, 1974, 61.

[60] Shaibani's first name is not disclosed.

[61] "Suomen öljykysymys ja Saudi-Arabia," April 16, 1976.

6 TOWARDS THE END OF THE OIL EMBARGO   93

Chairman of Algerian Revolutionary Council Hawwari Bumedien in Algiers. During his meeting with King Faysal, Al-Sadat had articulated to him that the oil embargo had served its purpose, and therefore it might well turn against the Arab interests.[62] It is not revealed in what tone Al-Sadat had conveyed his message to Faysal. However, it is quite likely that Al-Sadat's discussion with King Faysal was a turning point in Faysal's decision-making with regards to the embargo's ending. If Al-Sadat's discussion with Faysal indeed was a turning point, it could indicate that the Egyptian president knew how to appeal the king. On the contrary, the Syrian president Al-Asad decided not to endorse an end to the embargo.[63]

Nevertheless, one can always speculate about the ultimate reasons that helped to terminate the oil embargo. Faysal met Kissinger for the third time on March 2, 1974. In his memoirs, Kissinger describes that Faysal "always spoke in a gentle voice even when making strong points. He loved elliptical comments capable of many interpretations, thus protecting himself against being quoted in contexts that he could not control and that might ultimately prove embarrassing."[64] In similar fashion, Quandt has described that in its decision-making, the royal family was "slow, reactive rather than assertive, and elliptical rather than direct."[65] Such conduct could imply just how fundamentally important it was for Faysal to avoid taking responsibility for bad decisions and to preserve his face and thus to protect his honor. King Faysal understood that Kissinger used press leaks to enforce his political message. Therefore, Faysal had told Kissinger that he would not lift the oil embargo, although, according to Saqqaf, he had meant the opposite. The embargo was terminated two weeks later, on March 17, 1974. Afterwards, on April 26 when Saqqaf met Kissinger, he told the secretary of state that he had considered the meeting on March 2 one of the best he had seen. Kissinger asked how he knew this. Saqqaf

---

[62] In fact, Al-Sadat had conveyed to Faysal on January 18, 1974, that he would travel to Arab capitals to obtain an approval of the other Arabs to terminate the embargo. See: Untitled message, Kamal Adham (Royal Advisor, Jeddah) and Saud al-Faysal (Deputy Minister of Petroleum, Jeddah) to Kissinger (Washington), January 22, 1974, *FRUS*, Vol. XXXVI, *Energy Crisis*, 808–809.

[63] Henry Tanner, "Four Arab States Seek Joint Policy," *The New York Times*, February 13, 1974, 6. See also: Yergin, *The Prize*, 612–613. For more on Hafiz al-Assad of Syria, see, for instance: Moshe Maoz and Avner Yaniv, *Syria under Assad: Domestic Constraints and Regional Risks*, London: Croom Helms, 1986; Moshe Maoz, *The Sphinx of Damascus: A Political Biography*, London: Weidenfeld and Nicolson, 1988.

[64] Kissinger, *Years of Upheaval*, 661.

[65] Quandt, *Saudi Arabia in the 1980s*, 108–109.

94 S. E. WILLNER

replied that "usually the king just stares at his lap [when he does not mean what he says]; this time he was looking straight ahead. [...] Usually, the king sits there picking lint off his robe [to avoid eye contact, when he was not saying what he meant]; this time he didn't."[66] Then Saqqaf told Kissinger that it was clear that the embargo would be lifted. Kissinger then asked, "How?" "Because the king said it would not. [...] The king was afraid you would leak it, so he told you the opposite," Saqqaf explained.[67] Faysal's behavior indicates that he wished to play it safe, and thus he wanted to end the embargo in an opportune time. In addition, the Saudis might have calculated that the oil embargo could get out of hand.

[66] Kissinger had also recalled that "In talking to me he [King Faysal] would look straight ahead, occasionally peeking from around his headdress to make sure I had understood the drift of some particular conundrum." Quoted in: Yergin, *The Prize*, 612.

[67] "Minutes of Meeting" (secret memo), Riyadh, March 2, 1974, *FRUS*, vol. XXXVI, *Energy Crisis*, 925, footnotes.

CHAPTER 7

Threats of a New Oil Embargo

FAYSAL'S THREATS OF A NEW OIL EMBARGO AND HIS CONFLICT WITH FAHD

As the months passed, the specter of an oil embargo remained while high oil prices persisted around the level of $11 per barrel. Whereas the cease-fire negotiations had made some progress between Israel and Egypt and between Israel and Syria, Israel had not been willing to give up the conquered territory without mutual concessions from the Arabs. It was not long after the oil embargo was terminated (March 1974) that King Faysal returned to his public rhetoric of threatening to impose another embargo. According to Raymond Close, a former CIA Station Chief in Jeddah during 1970s, when Faysal finally decided to terminate the embargo, it was not "because of our [American] baby blue eyes," but rather because he "expected to get something in return for a Saudi Arabian contribution."[1] Although the Unites States had been clear about its resolution against the oil embargo, it would seem that Faysal was still convinced that he could use the oil weapon-threats to gain more concessions from the Americans. Therefore, On July 21, 1974, after the two interim agreements with Israel were signed (between Israel and Egypt in January 1974 and between Israel and Syria in May 1974), Minister of Petroleum Yamani delivered a press statement, probably by the request of King Faysal, saying that the oil

[1] Bronson, *Thicker Than Oil*, 138.

© The Author(s), under exclusive license to Springer Nature Switzerland AG 2023
S. E. Willner, *Preserving the Saudi Monarchy*,
https://doi.org/10.1007/978-3-031-30006-6_7

95

embargo could be re-imposed unless the Arabs receive assurances that Israel will give up territory conquered during the 1967 and the 1973 wars. Yamani's statement coincided with US Secretary of Treasury William Simon's (1974–1977) official visit to Saudi Arabia, which took place during July 18–20, 1974. However, Simon told reporters that the subject of possible resumption of the embargo never came up in his discussions with King Faysal or other top Saudi officials.[2] Still, the statements regarding possible resumption of the oil embargo were causing worry in Washington. On August 13, 1974, Kissinger told in a meeting with Secretary Simon that he did not think the United States could take another embargo. He continued that "it would lead to economic collapse in Europe. It would lead to the collapse of NATO. If it comes to that…"[3] Several paragraphs of the report that follow have not been declassified yet, but it seems that Kissinger and his administration were discussing the possible contingency plans and further steps in case the Saudis would re-impose the oil embargo. Although there are no declassified sources available, it is possible that Kissinger had pressured the Saudis to balance Faysal's acts and alter his confrontational foreign policy.

The Americans were becoming increasingly concerned because of King Faysal's threats of re-imposing the oil embargo. At the end of August 1974, a few weeks after Kissinger had met with Secretary Simon, Senator J. William Fulbright paid a visit to Saudi Arabia.[4] According to a commentary that appeared in the Saudi newspaper *Al-Madinah*, Fulbright had warned "his Arab friends of the possibility that a country like America might resort to military force in order to control the oil fields and ensure

---

[2] "Saudi warning to US on renewal of oil embargo," *Financial Times*, July 22, 1974.

[3] "Oil Price Strategy" (secret memo), Washington D.C., August 13, 1974, *FRUS*, vol. XXXVII, *Energy Crisis*, 3. Furthermore, Kissinger was especially afraid that communists could gain power in Italy, Greece, and Portugal—a development, which would have benefitted the Soviets immensely. A US official had commented on Kissinger's earlier remarks on the long-range implications of the oil price crisis by saying that "you [observers] must look upon him [Kissinger] in this case as a historian. He grew up in Nazi Germany and knows how economic depressions can lead to acceptance of authoritarian regimes, and he fears that this could happen in the West if something is not done to solve the problem." Bernard Gwerzman, "Kissinger Sees Oil Crisis Periling Western Society," *The New York Times*, September 27, 1974, 1.

[4] The exact dates of Senator Fulbright's visit are unknown.

the continued flow of oil should there be an embargo."[5] This was not the first time that Fulbright had hinted of such eventuality. Interestingly, the fact that the royal family had conveyed such a message in a Saudi newspaper could indicate that some of the powerful princes intended to balance Faysal's policies *vis-à-vis* the United States.[6] It is also possible that the purpose of such an article was to reveal to the radical Arab regimes that the United States and the West were putting great pressure on the Saudis.

If aforementioned had been the purpose of such an approach, it no doubt had failed to change Faysal's policies and statements. Consequently, to the US threats, the oil producers had decided to enforce their own countermeasures, or at least they were implying such intent. In October 1974 unconfirmed reports emerged that Kuwait had mined its oil fields and tightened security around its oil infrastructure.[7] In November 1974 Ambassador Lassila reported that the Saudis acted in a similar manner. Shaibani had told him that the Saudi security forces had placed mines and other explosives in the proximity to their oil installations and that he had seen these 'explosive devices.' Shaibani emphasized that "if the America means business, so do the Arabs mean business" and added that, if necessary, the Saudis could "explode the oil fields in five minutes."[8]

An interesting question here is to whom Shaibani's message was meant? It would be reasonable to assume that it was intended for the United States. However, since the Saudis had earlier been suspicious[9] about Finland's close relations with the Soviets, it is possible that his message was meant for the Russians. However, there is no evidence to suggest that the Finnish government had passed such a message to Moscow or to Washington.

King Faysal's public statements continued to be confrontational. For instance, on September 13, 1974, Faysal told the Lebanese newspaper

---

[5] "Saudi Oil Policy" (unclassified, translation of commentaries), Ahmad Muhammad Mahmud (Foreign Affairs Editor, *Al-Madinah*, Jeddah), September 3, 1974, no. 184, *FCO 8/2350*.

[6] Another possibility is that the commentary in *Al-Madinah* was a warning to the Soviets to refrain from intervening in what the United States saw as its immediate sphere of influence.

[7] "Trying to cope with the looming crisis," *Time*, October 14, 1974, 47–53.

[8] "Mitä puhe USA:n sotilaallisesta interventiosta saattaisi tarkoittaa?" [What the US military intervention could mean?], Lassila to Karjalainen, November 24, 1974, no. R-129/37, *AMFAF*.

[9] See: "Muistiinpano" [notes] (confidential telegram), Pentti Uusivirta (Counselor, Embassy of Finland in Washington) to Veli Helenius (Minister, Ministry of Foreign Affairs, Helsinki), March 10, 1967, no. 804, *Saudi-Arabia: Diplomaattisuhteet 1966–1971, AMFAF*.

98   S. E. WILLNER

Al-Anwar that Arab unity and consensus were essential when taking political or military steps against one's enemies. He added that "when the Arabs were united, they reached Europe and China. They lost only when they were divided." The king was probably referring to Abbasid Arab Muslim caliphate, which ruled from the eighth century until the thirteenth century (750–1258 CE). In any case, such statements could indicate that Faysal wanted to cover his back against possible critics in the radical Arab camp. Furthermore, such statements could also imply that he aspired for Arab leadership, although such a policy was clearly against the pragmatic Saudi foreign policy approach. On another occasion King Faysal had told *Newsweek* that "we do not want to impose or re-impose the oil embargo on our friends, but our friends must realize where their strategic interests lie. They must decide this."[10]

Although King Faysal continued delivering his threats through the international and Arab press, the entire Saudi monarchy did not seem to agree with his confrontational messages. According to an interview with Beirut weekly newspaper *Al-Hawadith* in October 1974, Second Deputy Prime Minister Fahd had said that "the oil card is [a] dangerous one and should not be used without sufficient justification. It is not at all in the Arab interest to deal with this subject emotionally or rigidly, or to bring up the subject on every occasion."[11] It appears that Fahd had been criticizing Faysal and possibly also the other radical Arab leaders. Based on Finnish diplomatic reports, Fahd had developed a serious conflict with the king. The latest storm seemed to have emerged after Prince Fahd had reportedly lost six million dollars during one of his gambling trips to Monte Carlo, Monaco. Faysal had also been very upset at Fahd, apparently because Fahd had made a personnel appointment within the Saudi administration when the king had been away without first consulting him. Ambassador Lassila did not specify when the incident had taken place or what kind of a

---

[10] King Faysal was interviewed by *Newsweek* and the full interview was broadcasted on radio on September 22, 1974. King Faysal's interview was published in the Beirut daily newspaper *Al-Anwar*: "*Khilāl istiqbālihi lil-duktur 'Amīn Al-Ḥāfiz al-malik Faysal: 'ala al-'Arab 'an ya'malū lis-silm bayad wa-lil-ḥarb bayad 'ukhra*" [King Faysal during his meeting with Dr. Amin al-Hafiz: The Arabs must be prepared for the peace, on the one hand, and for the war, on the other hand], *Al-Anwar*, September 13, 1974, 1,16; *FBIS*, September 16, 1974, C1; *FBIS*, September 24, 1974, C2.

[11] Prince Fahd's interview was published in the Beirut weekly newspaper *Al-Hawadith* on October 18, 1974; see: "Prince Fahd Hints Saudi Arabia Could Use Oil Weapon Again," *MEES*, October 25, 1974.

decision it had been. Although that appointment was probably not an important one, it is quite likely that, in principle, Faysal had protested because Fahd had not asked his opinion on the matter. Lassila's report also suggests that there had been several other similar disagreements. Possibly because of these frequent conflicts between the two Saudi royals, rumors had emerged according to which Faysal wanted to remove Fahd from his post as the Second Deputy Prime Minister. Had he been removed from the post at the time, it is unlikely that he would have become the king few years later in 1982.[12] If such deliberations were in fact taking place at the king's court, it would only indicate that there were serious tensions between King Faysal and various members of the royal family.

Faysal Is Worried About the US Psychological Pressure

Saudi Arabia is not a single ruler dictatorship, nor has it ever been one. The Saudi monarchy is kind of a 'desert democracy' where consultation and consensus plays a key role in its decision-making process. While King Faysal continued to rule Saudi Arabia and was repeating his threats of a possible new oil embargo, the economic situation was worsening around the world. Although the 1973–1974 oil crisis had a painful effect on the Western economies, the Soviet Union, on the contrary, had immensely benefitted from the high oil prices because of its petroleum export revenues from the West.[13] As a result of the high oil prices, the price of manufactured goods increased, which, in turn, led to high worldwide inflation.

While the possibility of new oil embargo persisted, Washington was increasingly worried about these developments in the world economy. In

---

[12] "Huipulla tuulee" [The wind is blowing at the top] (secret report), Lassila to Karjalainen, October 29, 1974, no. R-78/23, *Saudi Arabia sisäpolitiikka 1969–1974, AMFAF.*

[13] Soviet Union's oil production was around 8.1 million bpd (1972), 8.7 million bpd (1973), 9.3 million bpd (1974) and 9.9 million bpd (1975). Moreover, the oil exports from the Soviet Union are estimated to have been around 2.6 million bpd (1972), 2.6 million bpd (1973), 2.7 million bpd (1974), and 3 million bpd (1975). The exact oil export revenues are unknown. The oil statistics are available at: "Statistical Review of World Energy," British Petroleum, accessed December 15, 2019, https://www.bp.com/en/global/corporate/energy-economics/statistical-review-of-world-energy.html. See also: Alexei Vassiliev, *Russian Policy in the Middle East: From Messianism to Pragmatism*, Reading: Ithaca Press, 1993, 102.

100   S. E. WILLNER

January 1975 Walter Levy,[14] an oil analyst and consultant, warned that "the world economy cannot survive in a healthy, or remotely healthy condition, if cartel pricing and actual or threatened supply restraints of oil continue,"[15] while the *Newsweek* forecasted that the Western democracies were facing "a wartime-like crisis."[16] Since King Faysal's decision to join the oil embargo had been fundamentally important for the successful launch of the 1973 Arab oil embargo, the *Time* magazine recognized him as one of the principal personalities in quadrupling oil prices.[17] This earned him the *Time* magazine's title 'Man of the Year.' The title was not flattering considering the circumstances under which it was 'awarded' to Faysal. He was the person who had "most significantly affected—for good or ill—the course of events,"[18] which had led into the oil embargo in October 1973. Despite OAPEC's petroleum production cuts, which reduced Saudi Arabia's oil production, the kingdom's oil revenues grew more than what was the effect of the reduced production. Accordingly, Saudi Arabia's oil revenues grew from $2.7 billion (1972) to $4.3 billion (1973) and to $22.6 billion (1974). The oil embargo, and the consequent increase in oil price, made Saudi Arabia immensely rich.[19] Yet, Faysal continued his confrontational foreign policy. As discussed earlier, there were senior members of the royal family that had been against the oil embargo. They might have contemplated that it was not worthwhile for the Saudi monarchy to risk its survival for additional financial gain.

The survival of the monarchy is a paramount objective for the Saudi royal family. In the beginning of January 1975 *Business Week* published an interview with Secretary of State Kissinger. The fundamental message that Kissinger wanted to convey to the Saudis was that "there is no circumstances where we would not use force," but the circumstances that would warrant such an action were extremely remote.[20] Although Kissinger had stressed that such a move would be undertaken only as a last resort to save the Western world in the gravest emergency, his aides had told *The New York Times* that Kissinger probably wanted to let the possibility of military

---

[14] Walter Levy was a former oil analyst at the Office of Strategic Services (OSS). He was recruited in 1943 and served until around 1945. OSS is the predecessor of the CIA. He was also a New York-based oil consultant and energy economist.

[15] "Faysal and Oil: Driving Toward a New World Order," *Time*, January 6, 1975, 10.

[16] Ibid.

[17] "*Time* Names Faysal 'Man of the Year'," *The New York Times*, December 30, 1974. See also discussion on pages 64–67.

[18] "A Letter for the Publisher," *Time*, January 6, 1975, 10.

[19] See Appendix.

[20] "Kissinger on Oil, Food and Trade," *Business Week*, January 13, 1975, 66–76.

action "hang there in front of the oil producers as a kind of inducement for not pushing prices any higher, and maybe bringing them down." The article also quoted anonymous officials (in fact, possibly Kissinger himself) at the Department of State theorizing that Kissinger's words might have been "a form of psychological pressure on the oil producers to take a more conciliatory attitude on [oil] prices."[21]

King Faysal was very worried about Kissinger's statements. On January 5, 1975, Ambassador Akins reported to Washington that Minister of Petroleum Yamani had told him that King Faysal was "depressed and worried by 'American threats' against Saudi Arabia." He also told Akins that he had never seen Faysal "so worried and so questioning of his relationship with the United States." Later on that same day King Faysal expressed Akins that he was "extremely disturbed" by the "series of 'American threats' against Saudi Arabia that culminated in the *Business Week* interview."[22] Yamani had also iterated to Akins that the prospect of occupying the oil fields was not good because: first, succeeding in occupying them was difficult; second, that the oil fields could be sabotaged easily; third, that a quick surgical military operation would be impossible; and fourth, that the outcome of such operation would be the "loss of Saudi production for years."[23]

The episode of new threats and counter-threats (of another oil embargo) seems to point out that King Faysal was developing deep rift not only between himself and the US Administration but also between himself and at least some of his senior family members. What was Faysal thinking when he decided to conduct such a policy: was he making decisions based on his emotions rather than using cold calculation; was his support for the Arab unity and the Palestinians just lip service; was he pressured by the radical Arabs; was he in conflict with his brothers in essence, and particularly in matters related to the embargo; did he possibly desire leadership in the Arab world; and did his brothers think he was about to bring a catastrophe to the kingdom? The answer to all these questions was probably affirmative, which would indicate that King Faysal was navigating in deeply dangerous waters.

---

[21] Bernard Gwerzman, "Kissinger Speaks of Force as Last Step 'In the Gravest Emergency' Over Oil," *The New York Times*, January 3, 1975, 2.

[22] "Editorial Note," *FRUS*, vol. XXXVII, *Energy Crisis*, 108–109.

[23] Ibid.

CHAPTER 8

The Murder of King Faysal

Washington continued its psychological warfare campaign against the Saudis. In early March 1975, just few weeks before King Faysal's murder, a provocative article 'Seizing Arab Oil' was published in the *Harper's Magazine*. The bottom-line message was that Faysal was still stuck in his old thinking and was about to bring disaster to Saudi Arabia. Another embargo would justify the United States to launch a military action to control the Saudi oil fields. The message was clear: The Saudis needed to change their political discourse and continue to be a partner to the United States if they desired to survive. Unfortunately, Faysal was unwilling to change his mind concerning his confrontational policy. This chapter investigates how King Faysal's murder was a major turning point in Saudi decision-making.

Advocating for 'a New Economic Order'

In November 1974, the industrialized nations established the International Energy Agency (IEA) in response to the possibility of new oil supply disruptions. One of the IEA's aims was to establish an emergency oil sharing mechanism designed to prevent panic of competitive crude oil buying, which had happened in late 1973, following the embargo and the oil production cuts. Naturally, the oil producers did not like the idea, because

© The Author(s), under exclusive license to Springer Nature Switzerland AG 2023
S. E. Willner, *Preserving the Saudi Monarchy*,
https://doi.org/10.1007/978-3-031-30006-6_8

103

they were afraid it would establish a united oil consumer front against the producers, and thus reduce their influence in the world oil markets.[1]

The petroleum producers' response to Washington's threats of military action, and to the establishment of the IEA, was to convene the OPEC Summit, officially known as the 'Conference of Sovereigns and Heads of State of OPEC Member Countries.' This summit convened in Algiers in early March 1975. The agenda of this OPEC meeting was mostly political in nature, and it reflected the political tensions that the 1973 oil crisis had created. Some of the OPEC members feared a potential economic or military confrontation with the petroleum importers. At the end of the conference, its participants published a declaration, which noted that "the cartel would take immediate and effective measures to counteract such threats with a united response."[2] Furthermore, the declaration condemned any economic or military plan that was designed for aggression against the OPEC oil producers.[3] However, despite the attempts to strengthen the petroleum producers' position against the Western industrialized nations— especially against the United States—the summit did not bring OPEC more influence or prestige. The Saudis were most likely against such a development as it could have posed a strategic threat to Riyadh's interests. There are two main reasons why the Saudis demurred from making OPEC more powerful as well as from imposing another oil embargo. First, such a development would have given the radical Arab states more power to threaten the Saudi interests, and second, it would have put Saudi Arabia on a major collision course with the United States.[4]

[1] See for instance: Skeet, *OPEC*, 166–167; Kissinger, *Years of Renewal*, 664–700; Shwadran, *Middle East Oil since 1973*, 93–98.

[2] "Searching for Stability," *Time*, March 17, 1975, 33.

[3] OPEC, *OPEC Solemn Declarations: 1974 Algiers, 2000 Caracas and 2007 Riyadh*, Vienna: OPEC, March 2009.

[4] See, for instance: Pierre Terzian, *OPEC: The Inside Story*, London: Zed Books Ltd, 1985, 214.

THE MESSAGE FROM HENRY KISSINGER AKA "MILES IGNOTUS" TO THE SAUDIS

Secretary of State Kissinger liked using Machiavellian[5] philosophy in his dealings with the Saudis. In his memoirs, Kissinger writes—quoting the ancient Chinese general and military strategist Sun Tzu—that "all warfare is based on deception."[6] During his term as the secretary of state, Kissinger knew how to manipulate the press to convey messages to foreign governments. On the eve of the March 1975 OPEC Summit, *Harper's Magazine* published an article under a nom de plume 'Miles Ignotus,'[7] which Ambassador James Akins had claimed was authored by Henry Kissinger. On March 12, 1975, few days after the article in *Harper's Magazine* was published, Akins said, in an interview with the official *Saudi Press Agency*, that "the threats of an invasion of the oil fields [which the article was pointing] and the accompanying press campaign have been planned by the sick minds of people who do not know what they are saying."[8] In Akins' view, such statements were worsening the Saudi-US relations. Because of the article's far-reaching implications on Saudi decision-making, the content and the message of the *Harper's* article will be discussed in this section.

It appears that the article published in the *Harper's Magazine* was a carefully articulated message addressed to the "military dictators and megalomaniac kings of OPEC." However, more importantly its message was meant for the Saudi monarchy. The message that 'Miles Ignotus' attempted to convey to the Saudis was that another oil embargo was no longer a threat but an opportunity for the United States to justifiably intervene

---

[5] A Machiavellian person is defined as "politically cunning and unscrupulous, seeking power or advantage at any price; amoral and opportunist." See: Robert Allen ed., *Chambers Encyclopedic English Dictionary*, Edinburgh: Chambers, 1994, 768. Machiavellianism has also been defined with the words: "to deceive and manipulate"; ibid.

[6] Henry Kissinger, *Years of Upheaval*, Boston, MA: Little Brown, 1982, 459.

[7] In Latin, 'Miles Ignotus' means 'unknown soldier.' Following its publication, there were rumors circulating about who was behind the penname 'Miles Ignotus,' who claimed to be "the pseudonym of a Washington-based professor and defense consultant with intimate links to high-level US policy makers." See: Miles Ignotus, "Seizing Arab Oil: The Case for U.S. Intervention: Why, How, Where" *Harper's Magazine*, March 1975, 42–62.

[8] "Saudi Arabia," *MEES*, March 14, 1975, 3. In August 1975, Akins was dismissed from his position. Three decades later in 2003, in an interview with Robert Dreyfus, Akins said that he thought the reason why he was dismissed was because he was critical of Kissinger's Middle East policy. See: Robert Dreyfus, "The Thirty-Year Itch," *Mother Jones*, March 2003.

106   S. E. WILLNER

militarily. Possibly referring to King Faysal, it stated that "some captive to the old politics, fail to make the connection." It was time for the Saudis to act before it was too late.[9]

The article started by explaining the background of the oil crisis and declared that the world economic situation was serious. It manifested that "while all members of OPEC are extortionists, some [of] the Arabs are also blackmailers." The article stated that "with the oil-price crisis compounding every human misery, the time for action has surely come. [...] Why should we countenance the transfer of hundreds of billions of dollars' worth of real estate and industry to the ownership of reverse colonialists?"[10]

The author argued that the "dictatorial elites" considered OPEC a force "that can humiliate the West." His message was clear: the power of OPEC should be broken because it was destroying West's prosperity. The author listed numerous ways this could happen, including the nonviolent methods of financial denial, ownership denial and market manipulation: "Some of these nonviolent strategies are more plausible than others, but all would in fact be utterly ineffectual." Accordingly, the author claimed that "the only feasible countervailing power to OPEC's control of oil is power itself—military power." He also argued that the lack of any other alternative does not mean that the use of force is feasible by the fact itself.[11]

If a decision for a military action had to be taken, the only feasible target—when the goal is to break OPEC and to end the artificial scarcity of oil—would be Saudi Arabia. The author explained that "if the use of military force is to be limited and therefore efficient, the real leverage must come from market pressures, and only the Saudi oil fields can provide the means."[12]

In many ways, the article in *Harper's Magazine* painted a very gloomy—nearly nightmarish, picture for Saudi Arabia, had it to decide to confront the United States. The author of the article speculated that the situation on the ground was already heading towards another Middle East war. He assessed that sooner or later the demands on Israel—something that King Faysal was stubbornly clinging to—would become excessive; the Israelis would refuse to give up further territory without mutual concessions. He added that since the 1973 October War ended with the Arab armies in

[9] "Seizing Arab Oil."
[10] Ibid.
[11] Ibid.
[12] Ibid.

chaos, with both Damascus and Cairo under great threat, "the next [war] was likely to end with the same result, but sooner." The author predicted that under such circumstances there would probably be another oil embargo, which would trigger the US forces to enter Saudi Arabia and take over the oil fields.

Through his emissaries, King Faysal had numerous times threatened to destroy Saudi oil fields in case there was a military action to take over the oil production areas.[13] The author labeled such plans unfeasible. He iterated that the Saudis could try to booby-trap the oil fields but that they would not have enough time to do it thoroughly. If they would decide to commence with their plans and plant explosives at their oil fields, they would face several disquieting issues. In reference to the threat of militant Palestinian guerrillas, who on many occasions had been tormenting the Saudis, the article debated that if the Saudis decided to place plastic charges "pre-set to demolish oil facilities, they would be apt to go off whether there was an invasion or not."[14]

In attempt to gain bargaining points with the Americans, King Faysal had secretly approached the Soviets on several occasions before he decided to end the oil embargo in March 1974. In response to the possibility of inviting Soviet troops into the kingdom to prevent a possible US military action, the author judged such a move fatal to the survival of the Saudi monarchy. In the past, the monarchies in the Middle East had been afraid of the revolutionary forces because of their desire to overthrow them. Furthermore, the new (revolutionary) regimes were often anti-Western, and more favorable to the Soviets, which served the interests of the Russians. The author even predicted that a Soviet presence in the kingdom would ensure the overthrow of the Saudi monarchy by the Soviets, and that "it would mean defenestration and mutilation by the mob, as when the Hashemites of Iraq were overthrown [in 1958]." This was probably

---

[13] See, for instance: "Interview on Danish Television with Saudi Arabian Minister of Petroleum, Shaikh Ahmad Zaki Yamani, November 22, 1973" (transcript) (confidential telegram), Danish Embassy (London) to FCO, November 29, 1973, *FCO 8/2121*.

[14] Ibid. The evidence points out that the CIA had seriously evaluated these Saudi threats. However, it is unknown whether the Americans had raised with the Saudis the possibility, where their kingdom would have to live without the oil income in case the Saudis decided to implement their threat.

108   S. E. WILLNER

one of the worst fears of the monarchy. As such, the author considered it an unimaginable scenario.[15]

The author of the *Harper*'s article also addressed what would happen in the aftermath of a possible US military intervention. The damaged or destroyed oil fields would be swiftly repaired and funded by future petroleum sales. It even proposed the establishment of a fictional 'International Oil and Aid Organization' that would be established to pump and market the oil and allocate funds for investments. The purpose of such organization, according to the author, would also be to allocate some of the money to the Saudis to pay "essential imports," while rest of the oil income would be distributed to the poorest Third World countries. The oil production would be radically increased, which would lower the price of oil and consume the oil reserves much faster than what was the current rate. This, in turn, would stop the massive transfer of funds to OPEC, which consecutively would cripple its ability to influence the oil markets.[16]

As Kissinger had articulated in his earlier press statements, domestic opinion was a principal factor when the United States was deliberating its foreign policy actions. He had said, for instance, that it had been difficult for the United States to get out of the long Vietnam War.[17] In reference to such deliberations, the author argued that if the American public had questioned the US national interest of the Vietnam War, then it might not be the case with a possible military action against Saudi Arabia. The author argued that "all those affected by inflation and unemployment [...] would understand [the reason behind such an operation]."[18]

The author concluded that "mindful of all political costs and all the strategic risks, [the military action] can be done." He wrote that if the Americans would not act, almost the entire world could turn into an "authoritarian slum." It added that United States could in fact comply with political extortion and that it could afford to pay economic extortion.

---

[15] "Seizing Arab Oil." Although the Saudis had approached the Soviets during 1973–1974, one of the key reasons why King Faysal didn't sign commercial agreements with the Soviets was probably due to his conspiratorial mindset concerning communism and the Soviet intentions. Unlike Faysal, the Shah of Iran had made several commercial agreements with the USSR in the 1950s and early 1960s. His aim was to pressure Washington to provide him more favorable economic agreements and defense assistance.

[16] Ibid.

[17] "Kissinger on Oil, Food and Trade," 66–76.

[18] "Seizing Arab Oil."

8 THE MURDER OF KING FAYSAL   109

However, "the price—moral, political, and social —would be far too high."[19]

The author's message seemed to have been such that another embargo was not an option and that if the Saudis desired to survive and avoid humiliation, then there was no other meaningful option, but to be with the United States: "With Americans some compromise might well be possible," but not with anyone else.[20]

If Kissinger was in fact the author of the *Harper's Magazine* piece, it would only prove how grave the situation indeed was. According to Akins, the article "had to have been the result of a deep background briefing. [...] You don't have eight people coming up with the same screwy idea at the same time, independently."[21] According to a diplomatic report quoted by Andrew Scott Cooper, the Saudi cabinet had convened for a special session (March 1975) to discuss the *Harper's* article and its implications on Saudi Arabia. Based on these reports, Prince Fahd had been "deeply concerned" about the possible US military intervention concerning the Saudi oil fields.[22] It is quite likely that the Saudis had concluded that the article had been authored by a high-level official in President Gerald Ford's administration (1974–1977).

However, as it seems, even the *Harper's Magazine* article did not change King Faysal's mind. Two days before his murder, on March 23, 1975, King Faysal declared, in a television interview with the American CBS, that he was not willing to compromise on the status of Jerusalem; and second, that, at least publicly, he did not want to take seriously the threats of potential American military intervention. Regarding Jerusalem, Faysal said that "our viewpoint is that the return of Jerusalem to Arab administration is vital, and we shall not accept anything short of that." Regarding the possible US military threat to occupy the oil fields, he commented that "we do not believe that any government with a little sense would accept to drag the world to total destruction."[23] That being said, it

---

[19] Ibid.

[20] Ibid.

[21] However, Dreyfus has emphasized that "Kissinger has never acknowledged having planted the seeds for the article" See: Dreyfus, "The Thirty-Year Itch."

[22] Andrew Scott Cooper, *The Oil Kings: How the U.S., Iran & Saudi Arabia Changed the Balance of Power in the Middle East*, London: OneWorld Publications, 2011, 235.

[23] King Faysal's interview was conducted by the US television network *CBS*, and it was distributed by the *Saudi Press Agency*, See: "Faisal's last interview," *MEES*, April 4, 1975, ii–iii.

110   S. E. WILLNER

was becoming more and more obvious that Faysal's comments resounded the radical Arab rhetoric, which was not in line with Saudi strategic interests. The deadlock was obvious.

The Murder and the Succession

On Tuesday March 25, 1975, King Faysal was murdered at a reception in Riyadh, which he had organized to honor the visit of Kuwaiti Minister of Petroleum Abd al-Mutalib al-Qazimi. It has been argued that Faysal's murder had nothing to do with succession rivalry and that the transition from Faysal to Khalid was smooth.[24] In light of the reports that I have reviewed, both observations were probably correct. However, such conclusion was not necessary an indication that the murder was a random incident, which was claimed to have been planned and executed solely by his mentally deranged nephew Prince Faysal al-Musaid. As it seems, there could have been other sinister reasons that led to this tragic incident.

As contemplated earlier, Saudi Arabia had been heading towards serious confrontation with the United States ever since it had joined the Arab oil embargo in October 1973. Although most of the US messages to the Saudis about the possible military action were part of psychological warfare to influence the royal family's decision-making, the royal family must have taken them very seriously. The Saudis were known for deliberating very carefully before making any decisions. If the Saudis had carefully deliberated on the message of 'Miles Ignotus,' they must have come into a conclusion that another oil embargo was completely out of the question and that to survive, they needed to change the monarchy's political discourse immediately. Unfortunately, as the archived documents reveal, King Faysal was unwilling to change his mind.

Although the king is the final arbiter of the royal family politics, however, according to the traditional patterns of Saudi tribal-familial decision-making, major decisions should go through the process of consultation and consensus. When the king makes decisions against the will of the powerful princes, and if he continuously tends to make fatal miscalculations, he may eventually have to pay for the consequences. The same applies also to other members of the royal family if their actions threaten the collective interests of its senior members. For instance, in 1951 Defense Minister

---

[24] Bligh, *From Prince to King,* 90. See also: Mordechai Abir, *Saudi Arabia: Government, Society and the Gulf Crisis,* London: Routledge, 1993, 67.

Prince Mansur ibn Abd al-Aziz (1943–1951) died under mysterious circumstances after allegedly being poisoned by unknown members of the royal family.[25] Another story went to say that he had suffered from alcohol poisoning at a party, which was hosted by his brother Nasir ibn Abd al-Aziz.[26] It was suggested that Prince Mansur was planning to seize the power in the army, and, in order to do so, he had already formed military units loyal to him. There were also claims that he had challenged the royal succession based on which his older brother Saud was slated to become the next king after his father King Abd al-Aziz (r. 1932–1953).[27]

In fact, succession rivalry has always existed within the senior ranks of the royal family. However, Prince Mansur, whose mother was an Armenian concubine, did not have the backing of *akhwāl*, maternal uncles. In other words, those royal princes whose mothers were from prominent families displayed stronger political credentials. If it is true that Mansur had been preparing to seize the power in Saudi Arabia, then it could indicate that his actions were threatening the interests of some of the more powerful branches of the royal family.

The reign of King Saud (1953–1964) is another example. It has been widely recorded how King Saud severely mismanaged Saudi Arabia's finances, and as a result he had nearly bankrupted the monarchy. In addition to his bad fiscal management, Saud had also concentrated power to his sons and to his branch of the family (Banu Khalid).[28] Again, such conduct conflicted with the interests of the other influential members of the royal family. Eventually the family had had enough, and it reached a consensus to abdicate King Saud. Following Saud's abdication, which took place in November 1964, an anonymous senior prince commented that "we preferred to sacrifice Saud rather than the country."[29] In saying so he indicated that the royal family's interests always lay first with the survival of the Saudi monarchy. As the records seem to point out, the common

---

[25] Peter W. Wilson and Douglas F. Graham, *Saudi Arabia: The Coming Storm*, Armonk, NY: M.E. Sharpe, 1994, 145.

[26] "The New Succession Law Preserves the Monarchy while Reducing the King's Prerogatives" (confidential telegram), James C. Oberwetter (Ambassador, US Embassy, Riyadh) to CIA (Langley), November 22, 2006, *WikiLeaks*, https://wikileaks.org/plusd/cables/06RIYADH8921_a.html, accessed: January 21, 2019.

[27] Wilson and Graham, *Saudi Arabia: The Coming Storm*, 145.

[28] See a chart of the most important branches of the sons of Al Saud in the Appendix.

[29] Paul L. Montgomery, "Faisal, Rich and Powerful, Led Saudis into 20th Century and to Arab Forefront," *The New York Times*, March 26, 1975, 10.

112   S. E. WILLNER

denominator, which led into King Saud's abdication, on the one hand, and King Faysal's assassination, on the other hand, is that both Saud and Faysal had failed to protect the principal interests of the monarchy, and thus they had lost their support within the senior ranks of the royal family.

The circumstances that surrounded King Faysal's death throw several unanswered questions of his murder, yet no 'smoking gun' has ever been presented to the public. There is no record that could indicate how the assassin Prince Faysal came to know about the reception, in which he murdered the king, and how it was possible that the security at the royal palace was lax on that day. Although the Kuwaiti minister had no part in the murder, it was known that the king's assassin and Abd al-Mutalib al-Qazimi had studied at the same university in Colorado few years earlier, and that they might to have known each other from the times of their studies.[30]

If Prince Faysal al-Musaid was indeed used as an executor of the state assassination, then there would have been at least two substantial factors that could have made him an ideal recruit for such conspirators. First, the assassin had a possible motive, and second, he had a history of misbehavior. Regarding the first point, one of the theories was that the young prince was holding grudge against the king because his brother Khalid al-Musaid had been killed by a Saudi policeman in 1965, after leading an abortive attempt to destroy the capital Riyadh's new television transmitter.[31] Regarding the second point, he had been arrested and pleaded guilty to a charge of selling drugs while residing in the United States. Because of his unlawful conduct, he had received a criminal record, and was sent back to Saudi Arabia. Additionally, it was rumored that the young prince had associated himself with radical Arab students during his studies and had possibly absorbed some of their revolutionary ideology.[32]

---

[30] Robert Lacey, *The Kingdom*, New York, NY: Harcourt Brace Jovanovich, 1982, 426.

[31] Prince Musaid, the father of Faysal, claimed subsequently that the king had instigated the killing of his son, Prince Khalid, and that Musaid remained resentful. See: Holden and Johns, *House of Saud*, 380.

[32] "The Death of a Desert Monarch," *Time*, April 7, 1975, 20; Holden and Johns, *House of Saud*, 379–280.

According to several official Saudi statements, the royal family announced that Prince Faysal had acted alone.[33] However, the possible number of perpetrators and the alleged insanity of Prince Faysal have been questioned. For instance, Ihsan Abd al-Quddus, the chairman of the Board of the Cairo newspaper *Al-Ahram*, wrote in a front-page editorial day after the murder, on March 26, 1975, about his suspicions regarding the hidden rationale of the assassin. He wrote, "I hope the mentally deranged nephew of the king was not incited by the sane. I am worried. This is just a warning."[34] Contrary to Abd al-Quddus' comments on the assassin's insanity, Minister of Petroleum Yamani, who was with the king when he was murdered, told the press after the assassination, "I really have no answer whether he did it on his behalf or someone else encouraged him to do it […] But what I can say positively is that the boy is not insane."[35] If Yamani's observation of Prince Faysal's mental state was correct, it could indicate that the murder indeed was carefully premeditated.

It was becoming obvious that the details of Faysal's murder were raising suspicions among several observers, and as a result, numerous suggestions of possible conspiracies emerged. None of them, however, pointed towards the royal family. Some were suggesting the involvement of foreign intelligence services, while others were contemplating the possibility of the radical Arab involvement. The Russians had claimed, possibly citing reports in the Arab press, that the CIA had been involved.[36] However, the *Time* magazine utterly dismissed such rumors by saying that "in light of Washington's well-documented concern for keeping King Faysal's

---

[33] See, for instance: "*Walī 'ahd al-Sa'ūdiyyah yudlī "lil-Anwār" bi-awwal ḥadīth lil-ṣaḥāfa al-'Arabiyah "siyāsat al-malik Faysal mustamirratun*" [The Saudi Crown Prince gives *Al-Anwar* a statement to the Arab press: "King Faysal's policies continue"], *Al-Anwar*, April 1, 1975, 1,7. See English translation: "Beirut Paper Interviews Prince Fahd," *FBIS*, April 2, 1975, C1-C5.

[34] "*Mādhā ba'da Faysal*" [What after Faysal], *Al-Ahram*, March 26, 1975, 1.

[35] "Text of Yamani Interview with CBS," *MEES*, May 2, 1975, 1–8. See also: "*Riwāyāt mukhtalifa 'an maṣīr al-qātil*" [Differing Reports about the fate of the murderer], *Al-Ahram*, March 27, 1975, 1.

[36] The *Time* magazine, in an article titled "The View from Moscow," wrote on April 7, 1975: "at week's end, however, the Soviet press agency *Tass* cited charges published in some Arab newspapers that the CIA was involved in the assassination of Saudi Arabian King Faysal. Since quoting from the foreign press is a common Soviet way of expressing official views, the repetition of this patently absurd accusation was a measure of how far the Kremlin is prepared to go to exploit Middle Eastern paranoia for its own advantage."

114   S. E. WILLNER

friendship, the accusation seemed absurd."[37] Such assessment, however, was only partially true. As has been discussed earlier, even some senior princes had indicated to the Americans of Faysal's problematic mindset. It was also evident that Faysal's relationship with Washington was not warm. In fact, as Holden and Johns wrote, "such conjecture could only be reinforced by language such as *The Washington Post* used in its editorial commenting Faysal's death. It said: 'Faysal probably did more damage to the West than any other single man since Adolf Hitler'."[38] Such a commentary indicates that King Faysal was not a liked leader in Washington.[39]

Even though the Americans seemed to have wanted Faysal deposed, it was probable that there were powerful Saudi royals who wanted him gone even more. For the royal family, a major problem with Faysal's mindset and behavior was that although he had never been an easy person to deal with, his "obsession with Zionism and Communism" was "getting far worse" than what it had previously been. In other words, as Akins had reported almost a year before Faysal's murder (April 1974), King Faysal's obsession had become so much deeper and worrisome that it had started to paralyze his decision-making. Akins added that "Faysal makes a miserable impression on those he sees" and that the king's advisors "are embarrassed by the meetings and they realize that nothing positive comes out of them; indeed, that definite harm is done the country." When Faysal had meetings with foreign delegations, most of the discussions were around the topic of his obsession. There were several examples of such behavior. For instance, when Ahmad Muhammad Numan, the special advisor to the president of YAR, met Faysal in the early 1974, almost all the meeting time was devoted to the king's account of his "mother-daughter, daughter-mother" theme, namely that "Communism is the daughter (or mother) of Zionism." Furthermore, the same had happened when Faysal had met with Parker Hart, the vice president of Bechtel Corporation (1974–1990) and the former US ambassador to Saudi Arabia (1961–1965). Hart said that some of the senior members of the royal family had tried to change the subject to other topics, such as economic development, but they failed. Consequently, after his 45-minute meeting with the king, "Hart left the

[37] "The Death of a Desert Monarch," *Time*, April 7, 1975, 20.

[38] *Arab Record and Report*, March 16–31, 1975, 199–200; Holden and Johns, *House of Saud*, 382.

[39] Holden and Johns wrote that "it could be and was tortuously argued that it was in the interests of the US to remove a king who was so intransigent on the question of Jerusalem and replace him with more amenable leadership." See: Holden and Johns, *House of Saud*, 382.

8 THE MURDER OF KING FAYSAL   115

audience with no other subject having been touched." Furthermore, due to King Faysal's behavior, several senior princes were expressing their frustration. As Akins reported, in private, these anonymous senior princes were talking about the future succession and about Faysal's "rigidity and his imperfect understanding of the changing world."[40]

Similarly, in May 1974, an anonymous Saudi advisor had characterized King Faysal's communications and decision-making as *nubbūwah*. The Arabic word *nubbūwah* refers to 'prophecy' and 'prophethood.' Furthermore, the verb of the same root *nabā* can refer 'to disagree' or 'to be in conflict,' or 'to be offensive.' In other words, as the anonymous royal advisor put it, one would almost have to be like a "prophet" in order to "guess what [Faysal's] Saudi policies were going to turn out to be."[41] These comments signify that Faysal's policies were in serious conflict with some members of the royal family.

Since the senior members of the Saudi monarchy were trying to avoid criticizing King Faysal openly, and therefore trying not to dishonor him, they were saying that the princes were worried that the king's nonroyal advisors would take advantage of the king's vulnerability and conduct policies that were against the interests of the Saudi monarchy. The princes had also expressed their concerns that some of Faysal's emissaries were not only filtering information that reached the king, but they were also limiting some of the senior princes' access to the king. However, it is possible that due to the internal disagreements, the king requested such procedure. This could indicate that Faysal did not want to meet up with some of his brothers.

Perhaps another reason why many senior princes saw Faysal's advisors in negative light was because they had been very loyal to the king, and as such they had also delivered messages from the king, which had been against the interests of the powerful princes. Prince Saud al-Faysal, who at the time served as the assistant minister of petroleum (1971–1975), had once said to Ambassador Lassila—although the exact time of the discussion is unknown, it certainly took place before the murder—that "one day they [the foreign advisors] will take the kingdom away from us."[42] This

---

[40] "Possible Change in Power Structure in Saudi Arabia" (secret telegram), Akins to Joseph Sisco (assistant secretary of state for Near Eastern and South Asian Affairs), April 10, 1974, no. 107, *FRUS*, vol. E-9 part 2, *Documents on the Middle East Region, 1973–1976*, 379–383.

[41] "Nature of Saudi Policies," May 25, 1974.

[42] "Planeettain taistelu," May 24, 1975.

116   S. E. WILLNER

might have been exaggeration, because the advisors were the king's emissaries and reflected his mindset. Moreover, it is doubtful that there had been any reason to question their loyalty to the royal family, but rather it is possible that they just reminded too much of the late King Faysal. In accordance with Lassila's notes about his discussion with Saud al-Faysal, Akins wrote already in April 1974 that "even those tied most closely to Faysal, even his sons, must know that there's no hope for his [the king's] improvement."[43] As Shaibani had cryptically put it, "when every sun falls, so does its planets."[44] In fact, as discussed earlier, such indirect remarks of dissatisfaction towards the king could indicate that out of respect towards Faysal, the members of the royal family did not directly accuse the king. Based on my analysis of Saudi communications, such statements imply that the main problem emerged from King Faysal himself.

When King Faysal decided something that was or was not to be done, he usually refused to discuss the subject any further.[45] In this respect, the dispute between King Faysal and Prince Fahd should be addressed. As the available records suggest, King Faysal had argued with some of his senior brothers about the oil embargo's usefulness both before and after the embargo had been declared. In addition, it appears that the king's decision to continue supporting Egypt had also been questioned. According to American press reports, Fahd had expressed his dissatisfaction over Saudi Arabia's financial support to Egypt by saying that it was a bottomless pit.[46] The disagreements between Fahd and Faysal seemed to have boiled over to a point where the king was contemplating removing him from the position of second deputy prime minister and thus denying him the succession to the crown. It is also possible that Faysal's main concern with Fahd was his moral conduct (drinking, gambling), and therefore he wanted to replace him with another member of the Sudayri-branch of the royal family to preserve his alliance with the group.

Finally, a few words need to be said about the succession itself. Some foreign observers wondered how it was possible that the succession had been surprisingly smooth after King Faysal's assassination. *Newsweek* pointed out that the most striking aspect of the assassination was how the Saudis managed with the tragedy. "In almost any other state in the volatile

[43] "Possible Change in Power Structure in Saudi Arabia," April 10, 1974.
[44] "Planeettain taistelu," May 24, 1975.
[45] "Possible Change in Power Structure in Saudi Arabia," April 10, 1974.
[46] "The Murder of King Faysal," *Newsweek*, April 7, 1975, 21.

8 THE MURDER OF KING FAYSAL   117

Arab world and even in many supposedly more advanced, the ruler's murder would probably have brought troops and tanks out into the streets. [...] Instead, Saudi Arabia arranged a swift transfer of power."[47] In contrast, Ambassador Akins wrote in April 1974 that the royal family has "an acute sense of self-preservation and the change [... in power] will probably not be dramatic."[48]

The royal succession was probably settled much before Faysal's murder had been conspired. It is useful to note that this above-discussed 'surprise' by Westerners of the 'smooth succession' is mainly because of their misunderstanding of the dynastic monarchy and, furthermore, of the importance of the shared interests of the royal family. Interestingly, it was reported that Prince Muhammad ibn Abd al-Aziz—often referred to as *kabīr al-ʿāʾila* (the tribe's elder) or "the strong Muhammad,"[49] and who was the full-brother of King Khalid—was the main architect in arranging the family consensus behind the succession process. According to Kamal Adham, Muhammad "had been an important figure during the trouble with Saud, and after the assassination of Faysal."[50] As it seems, Khalid preferred to consult his full-brother Muhammad in all important issues and tended to follow his advice. Until Khalid's death in 1982, Muhammad remained a powerful figure behind the scenes.[51]

After King Faysal's assassination, the Saudis revised their policy vis-à-vis the United States, and stopped altogether making threats of renewing the oil embargo. This policy change was not because the Saudis had suddenly gone through a major revival, but rather because stubborn and

[47] Milton R. Benjamin, Barry Came and Nicholas C. Profitt, "The Murder of King Faisal," *Newsweek*, April 7, 1975, 21.

[48] "Possible Change in Power Structure in Saudi Arabia," April 10, 1974.

[49] "Perheriidan perspektiiveja" [Perspectives of family dispute] (secret report), Lassila to Karjalainen, June 26, 1976, no. R-344-76, *Saudi Arabia sisäpolitiikka 1975–1977, AMFAF.*

[50] "Succession" (confidential report), James Craig (Ambassador, British Embassy, Jeddah) to Adams (Staff Member, MED, FCO, London), August 9, 1982, no. 27, *FCO 8/4770.*

[51] Prince Muhammad was known as "The Father of Two Evils" [*Abu Sharain*], which was a reference to his violent temper and drinking, which made him less eligible to head the Al Saud, although he was senior to his full-brother Khalid. See for instance: Said Aburish, *The Rise, Corruption and Coming Fall of the House of Saud*, New York, NY: St. Martin's Press, 1996, 78; Yizraeli, *Remaking of Saudi Arabia*, 81; "Perheriidan perspektiiveja," June 26, 1976; "The New Succession Law Preserves the Monarchy while Reducing the King's Prerogatives," November 22, 2006. See also: "Faisalismista post-faisalismiin," [From Faysalism to post-Faysalism] (secret report), Lassila to Karjalainen, April 8, 1975, no. R-283/50, *Saudi Arabia sisäpolitiikka 1975–1977, AMFAF.*

118 S. E. WILLNER

confrontational Faysal was no longer ruling the Saudi monarchy. Thus, final question needs to be addressed: Is it possible that King Faysal's murder could have been a state assassination, and if yes, who could have benefitted from his murder?

Based on the declassified records, I find it highly perplexing what Akins has reported about his discussions with the Saudis following Faysal's assassination. Akins told that in 1975 he "had to spend an awful lot of effort arguing with the Saudis that Kissinger was not behind the killing of Faysal."[52] At this point, such an accusation sounds so absurd that it convinces me to believe that some of the senior princes wanted to shift the blame (and the possible suspicion) from themselves to the United States. In addition, some of these princes were probably also ashamed by the way Faysal was murdered, and, therefore, they wanted to distance the blame. Although the analysis lacks direct proof, there is still plentiful circumstantial evidence, which points out that some of the senior princes had conspired behind the scenes and had pushed Prince Faysal al-Musaid to murder the king. Interestingly, a Saudi scholar Madawi al-Rasheed has quoted an unnamed senior Saudi official, who has revealed some thought-provoking details about the assassination. This anonymous official, whom Al-Rasheed has interviewed had served King Faysal during the 1970s, claims that prior to the assassination he had been delivered a message from "a Western intelligence source" saying that the king would be assassinated, and that Prince Fahd had been one of the key conspirators behind the assassination. Although Al-Rasheed does not reveal the identity of the Saudi official, nevertheless his account seems credible, and supports the evidence that I have acquired during my investigation.[53]

AFTER KING FAYSAL

The succession process following King Faysal's murder was completed in just few hours. After the enthronement of the new king, the Saudi monarchy, under the leadership of King Khalid and Crown Prince Fahd, wanted to convey two key foreign policy messages: one, to assure that nothing would change; and another clearly showing that Saudi Arabia was going to be more cooperative and that the relations with the United States would

---

[52] Kaplan, *The Arabists*, 174.
[53] Madawi al-Rasheed, *The Son King: Reform and Repression in Saudi Arabia*, Oxford, Oxford University Press, 2021, 61–62.

"be even much better."[54] Such statements might sound perplexing, especially after King Faysal's earlier confrontational approach to using the oil embargo against the United States. However, if one interprets the Saudi communications correctly, its fundamental approach to decision-making—and especially how the members of the royal family see what is best for their survival—had not changed over the years.

In one of his first statements as the new King of Saudi Arabia, Khalid announced that nothing would change in the Saudi policies and that it would follow the old policies.[55] Furthermore, according to British ambassador Rothnie, the royal family had emphasized the continuity of the late king's policies so much that it had led him to doubt if that was what they really meant when the Saudis said so.[56] Nevertheless, King Khalid's statements could be interpreted as follows: First, it is possible that Khalid's statements were meant to assure the Saudi public that the kingdom was stable and that the succession had been completed in unity. Second, and perhaps more importantly, King Khalid's statement could have also meant that King Faysal was an exception to the old policies. Therefore, by returning to the old policies, the Saudi monarchy was going back to what has been its policy before Faysal.

Perhaps mistakenly, Rothnie predicted that, because of the change in the leadership, the Saudi monarchy would be more preoccupied with its survival. He assessed that the Saudis would rather have to focus on internal affairs than foreign policy. He added that "they will be less likely to wish to confront the Shah, or even the Iraqis, over minor matters such as the price of oil." However, such an assessment is inaccurate. It was true that almost constantly the Saudi monarchy has needed to secure its survival, but as my assessment in the coming chapters indicate, the Saudis did not have to worry as much about the threats arising internally than about external threats.

Furthermore, Ian Skeet, a British energy expert, has argued that the leadership change in Saudi Arabia had significant repercussions for the Saudi policy and the Saudi-US dialogue, which he contributed to Fahd being the new deputy prime minister.[57] His observation seems correct.

---

[54] "Text of Yamani Interview with CBS," *MEES*, May 2, 1975, 1–8.
[55] "Death of a Desert Monarch."
[56] "Saudi Oil Policy" (confidential report), Rothnie to MED (FCO, London), April 26, 1975, no. 28, *FCO 8/2592*.
[57] Skeet, *OPEC*, 128.

120   S. E. WILLNER

However, it was not only Fahd who had been pursuing closer relations with the United States. Good relations between Riyadh and Washington were important for the political and economic interests of the Saudi monarchy, which, in turn, had significant implications for its survival.

If something indeed had changed within the Saudi monarchy, however, it might have been the atmosphere between the various members of the royal family. It was reported by some of the foreign observers that the senior princes had become more relaxed following Faysal's death. Mark Herdman, a British diplomat in Jeddah, reported about his discussion with James Fox, a correspondent of the British daily newspaper *Sunday Times*, and two unnamed American reporters. According to their observations, both Deputy Prime Minister Fahd and Prince Saud al-Faysal had been surprisingly easy and free when they had discussed Saudi government policy.[58] Such behavior could indicate—and possibly also confirm—that during Faysal's reign there had been significant tensions between Faysal and Fahd. Finally, few words should be said about the dynamics between Fahd and Khalid. Although Muhammad was a strong figure behind the scenes, his full-brother Khalid was still a weak ruler, probably controlled by Fahd. Therefore, from the beginning of Khalid's rule, the Sudayris seemed to have taken control, which could also explain the relaxed atmosphere within the royal family.

THE END TO OIL WEAPON THREAT

As it was explored earlier, the murder of King Faysal, and the consequent change in the kingdom's leadership, was a significant turning point for Saudi decision-making. The climax of tensions, that had shadowed the Saudi-US relations, seemed to have been a consequence of Faysal's continuous stubbornness not to receive the US messages to stop threatening with another oil embargo, and his determination not to consult the royal family. Especially the senior princes Fahd and Sultan seem to have insisted that Faysal had to change the course of the Saudi foreign policy, which in their eyes was heading towards a serious collision with the United States. In other words, another oil embargo would have been a major threat to its monarchy's survival. Instead, Faysal continued his rhetoric saying that he

[58] "Saudi Government Policy Following the Death of King Faysal" (confidential report), Mark Herdman (British Embassy, Jeddah) to James C. Radcliffe (MED, FCO, London), April 5, 1975, no. 35, *FCO 8/2570.*

could restore the oil embargo if his demands were not met. Following Faysal's death, the Saudis made statements to the press about the use of "oil weapon," but as will be discussed next, the royal family almost entirely subsided its threats of initiating another embargo.

In November 1975, Minister of Petroleum Yamani said in an interview that "the question of using oil as a weapon in the Arab battle is settled in principle, but the use of this weapon should be effective and at the right time."[59] A few months earlier, Israel and Egypt had advanced in the post-1973 war talks to conclude an interim accord over Sinai and in September 1975 the two nations signed an agreement, which provided for Israeli withdrawal from parts of the Sinai Peninsula. The agreement had been a continuation of diplomatic developments, which had led to the opening of the Suez Canal in June 1975 after eight years of closure following the June 1967 War. However, despite the advance in the Egyptian front, the negotiations between Israel and Syria over the possible withdrawal of Israeli forces from the Golan Heights, which it had conquered in 1967, had not shown any considerable progress. Although Yamani was referring to the Israeli presence in the Golan and the possible use of oil weapon, his remarks point out that the Saudis were not willing to enter another confrontation with the United States and thus sacrifice its primary interests, which were intimately related to the survival of the Saudi monarchy.

In fact, in August 1975, during his visit to the Foreign and Commonwealth Office in London, Helaissi, the Saudi ambassador to the United Kingdom, had expressed that "[the Saudi] government did not seek trouble with Israel." He continued by saying that Saudi Arabia's main interest was to settle the Israel issue "in order to put an end to Russian [Soviet] trouble making in the Middle East." Such remarks could indicate that the Saudis were looking for a way to get out of dangerous promises and to detach Saudi Arabia from the Arab-Israeli conflict. The Saudis knew that the Soviets used the Palestinian issue to counter the American influence and to promote Marxist ideology in the Middle East. Additionally, the Saudis wanted to approach the issue carefully and to manage the

---

[59] *"Al-Yamani fī ar-Ra'y Al-'ām: Nad'amu al-Kuwait qawlān wa-'amalān fī mufāwaḍātihā ma'a ash-sharikāt"* [Yamani to *Ar-Ray Al-am*: We support Kuwait by saying nothing about the negotiations with the [oil] companies], *Ar-Ray Al-am*, November 22, 1975, 14; *FBIS Middle East & North Africa*, November 28, 1975, A1-A3.

122   S. E. WILLNER

possible domestic public opinion regarding the Saudi position vis-à-vis the Arab-Israeli conflict.

Alan Phillips, an official at the FCO, assessed Helaissi's remarks and reported that the royal family was less concerned over Israel than the dispute between Iran and Iraq over the waters of the Shatt al-Arab bordering the two countries.[60] In fact, following a series of negotiations an agreement was signed in March 1975 to settle the border conflict between the two states. Therefore, it is likely that the Saudis were more worried that after settling the border dispute, Iraq would contribute more of its resources to threaten Saudi Arabia.[61]

NEW ATTACKS, THREATS EMERGE

The signing of the border agreement between Iraq and Iran in March 1975,[62] the start of the civil war in Lebanon in mid-1975, and the Syrian intervention in that conflict, had a considerable impact on Saudi royal family's sense of security. While the Saudis had acquired significant financial assets following the 1973–1974 oil embargo, the kingdom continued to be a tempting target for the radical Arab regimes, who wanted Saudi Arabia to endorse even higher oil prices and support pan-Arab causes.

Until 1975, Iraqis were committed to undermine the Saudi monarchy. However, due to Saddam Husayn's political pragmatism, Iraq's relations with Saudi Arabia improved after mid-1970s, especially following the signing of the 1975 border treaty. From Saddam Husayn's point of view, the agreement with Iran helped to reduce the internal and external pressure that had challenged his leadership. Therefore, to satisfy Iraqi internal and international expectations, he was able to justify his political pragmatism, and thus limit Iraq's revolutionary Ba'thi activity against the

---

[60] "Visit of the Saudi Arabian Ambassador" (confidential note for record), Alan Phillips (Private Secretary to the Secretary of State, FCO, London), August 11, 1975, no. 51, *FCO 8/2592.*

[61] Baram, *Saddam Husayn and Islam*, 122–124; "Iraq and Iran Sign Accord to Settle Border Dispute," *The New York Times*, March 7, 1975, 1.

[62] It was also known as the 1975 Algiers Agreement. Iran and Iraq had had several border disputes and conflicts since the late-1960s, mainly over the control of the strategic waterway of Shatt al-Arab. To put pressure on the Iraqis, the Iranians had supported the Kurdish revolt against the Iraqi government. Although the agreement was to settle the border dispute between Iraq and Iran, the main reason for Iraq to sign the accord was to end the Iranian support for the Kurdish rebellion in northern Iraq.

pro-Western Arab monarchies. According to Amatzia Baram, Saddam had concluded that Iraq could not jeopardize the Ba'th regime to promote revolution, and therefore Saddam thought Iraq needed to normalize relations with its neighbors. Interestingly, Baram adds that there were hints, which suggested that "Iraq could influence the monarchies to change their internal nature and international orientation through long-term pressures and persuasion, thus avoiding the need for revolution." Therefore, based on Baghdad's changed policy, the socialist Ba'th revolution in the Arab monarchies "[had] to wait for a more opportune moment."[63]

To finance their domestic development programs and military buildup, both Iraq and Libya needed to increase the income from their oil exports. Especially Libya's Qadhafi needed cash to finance his foreign policy and military adventures in Africa.[64] However, contrary to the revolutionary Arab regimes, Saudi Arabia's long-term strategic interest was to support a pro-Western oil policy, which translated into lower oil prices. Naturally, from the Saudi point of view, the more money the Iraqis and the Libyans had, the more they could: invest in their defensive and offensive military capabilities; sponsor the revolutionary activities around the kingdom; and therefore, threaten the Saudi interests. Such a policy had angered the regimes in Baghdad and Tripoli, who, in turn, intensified their attacks against the Saudis.

Naturally, Saddam's political pragmatism did not exclude the possibility of using other means of pressure (other than the export of revolution) on the Saudis. Tayeh Abd al-Karim, the Iraqi Minister of Petroleum, (1974–1982) had accused Saudi Arabia of supporting a plan developed by the International Energy Agency (IEA) to reduce global dependence on oil and to hold down prices. He had also accused that the Saudis were trying to take away "political power as well as revenue" from the oil

---

[63] Amatzia Baran, "Saddam Hussein: A Political Profile," *The Jerusalem Quarterly*, 17, 1980: 115–144; Amatzia Baran, "Qawmiyya and Wataniyya in Ba'thi Iraq: The Search for a New Balance," *Middle Eastern Studies*, 19, 2, 1983: 188–200.

[64] During 1978–1987, Libya was fighting against its poor southern neighbor Chad. Saudi Arabia was allegedly financing the Chadian military to defend against Qadhafi's invading forces. In 1978–1979, Qadhafi sent his army to assist the Ugandan president Idi Amin to fight against Tanzania. Burr, *Africa's Thirty-Year War*, 176–177.

producing countries.[65] Moreover, on July 17, 1976, during the festivities of the anniversary of the 1968 Ba'athist coup, Baghdad warned the monarchies of the region that it was committed to supporting the radical and revolutionary movements throughout the Arab world. This, the Iraqis said, included both economic and military aid. The Iraqi announcement was most likely intended for the Arab monarchies, saying that if the latter would not alter their pro-Western oil policy and increase the petroleum price, the revolutionary forces could try to overthrow them. Moreover, the statements by Iraqi Minister of Information Tariq Aziz (1974–1977)[66] conveyed similar message. He said that the Saudi government was following an oil policy, which Iraq could not accept, and that Iraq was supporting the rebel movement in the Omani province of Dhofar, which is bordering with South Yemen (PDRY).[67] Although there is no record of public Saudi response to the Iraqi threats, behind the scenes the Saudis were putting pressure on the United States that it would provide the kingdom more weapons.

[65] Thomas W. Lippman, "Iraqi-Saudi Relations under Strain Again," *The Washington Post*, July 28, 1976. Newspaper cut. *FCO 8/2809*; Peter Hobday, *Saudi Arabia Today: An Introduction to the Richest Oil Power*, New York, NY: St. Martin's Press, 1978, 114. See also: Kissinger, *Years of Renewal*, 898–899.

[66] Tariq Aziz was one of the most loyal men to Saddam Husayn. He served as the deputy prime minister of Iraq (1979–2003) and as the minister of foreign affairs (1983–1991).

[67] Lippman, "Iraqi-Saudi Relations under Strain Again."

CHAPTER 9

The Top-Secret Saudi Plan to Use the USSR to Pressure the United States

As discussed in the previous chapters, Iraq had a history of sponsoring revolutionary forces against Saudi Arabia. One of the Iraqi aims was to alter Saudi Arabia's oil policy in such a way that the monarchy would support higher oil prices. To defend itself against the revolutionary forces, the Saudis wanted the United States to supply advanced weapon systems. Thereupon, instead of committing its military to a direct intervention in the region, the Nixon Administration had formulated the so-called Twin Pillars policy of selling weapons and providing security assistance to its two principal Middle East allies, Iran, and Saudi Arabia. In return, the United States expected Iran and Saudi Arabia to keep the region from the spread of Soviet influence. Despite Riyadh's close relationship with Washington, the Saudis were not satisfied about the level of military assistance that the United States was willing to supply. To improve the situation, the Saudis decided to put pressure on the United States and launched a secretive disinformation operation to make it look as if the monarchy was in a process of establishing relations with Moscow. The challenge, of course, was how to convince the United States that the Saudis were planning to make a radical change into their earlier anti-communist policy. In this chapter, I will discuss some of these details.

During the 1970s, the Saudi royal family repeatedly voiced that communism and the Soviet Union represented a danger to the survival of its monarchy. Such statements were probably (at least partly) due to a genuine fear because the Soviets were backing the radical Arab regimes. These

© The Author(s), under exclusive license to Springer Nature   125
Switzerland AG 2023
S. E. Willner, *Preserving the Saudi Monarchy*,
https://doi.org/10.1007/978-3-031-30006-6_9

126   S. E. WILLNER

included regimes such as Baʻathist socialist Iraq and communist South Yemen (PDRY). Despite such Saudi fears, it is also quite likely that the Saudis purposefully disseminated these 'Soviet-threat' statements to get better weapon supplies from the United States. However, in the 1920s and 1930s the Saudis were having diplomatic relations with the Soviets, and initially Saudi Arabia had benefitted from its relationship with the Soviet Union. Accordingly, in February 1926, the USSR became the first country to recognize Abd al-Aziz Ibn Saud's conquest of Hejaz. In fact, in 1925 Abd al-Aziz had taken over Hejaz from its Hashemite ruler King Husayn, and in January 1926 he had assumed the title of king.

In 1926, in response to USSR's diplomatic recognition, Abd al-Aziz allowed the Soviets to establish a diplomatic mission in Jeddah,[1] which remained open until the eve of the Second World War in 1938. At the time, the Soviets mostly sought trade relations with the Saudis, which remained relatively inactive. Although the Saudis probably were suspicious about the Soviet activities in the Arabian Peninsula (concerning the spreading of Marxist ideology), it is more likely that the Soviets reduced their diplomatic activity and closed their consulate because of insignificant commercial relations. Another reason for closing the Soviet consulate was because the USSR was placing more resources on the European front because of the growing power of the Nazi Germany. In 1938, the USSR withdrew its diplomatic mission from Saudi Arabia.[2]

---

[1] Until 1980s, all the foreign embassies were in Jeddah. At the time of the creation of the modern Saudi Arabia in the 1930s, Jeddah was chosen as a location for foreign diplomatic missions and the Saudi Ministry of Foreign Affairs because of the city's accessibility to foreigners (Riyadh was located inlands far from the coast). Another reason could also be because the Saudis wanted to limit the presence of foreign agents in Riyadh.

[2] The Soviet decision to close their consulate might have been due to their attempts to improve relations with the British as the power of Germany grew stronger in Europe. To allow greater flexibility in foreign policy, the Soviets preferred to keep their options open and not commit themselves to positions. See: Mark N. Katz, *Russia and Arabia: Soviet Foreign Policy toward the Arabian Peninsula*, Baltimore, MA: The Johns Hopkins University Press, 1986, 132–133; Yodfat and Abir, *The Soviet Union*, 86, 154; Yodfat, *Soviet Union and Revolutionary Iran*, 147. See also: ʻAli Muhammad ʻAḥmad Shahrī, *Al-ʻAlāqāt al- Saʻūdiyyah al-Sūfiatiyyah wa-al- Saʻūdiyyah al-Rūsīyah*, 1926–1997 [The Saudi-Soviet and the Saudi-Russian Relations, 1926–1997]. Riyadh: Dar Ashbīlīyah, 2001.

JORDAN IN TALKS TO BUY SOVIET ARMS

By 1976, Saudi Arabia had acquired significant financial assets. According to the Saudi Arabian Monetary Authority (SAMA), Saudi Arabia's oil revenues grew from $2.7 billion (1972) to $4.3 billion (1973). When the oil prices quadrupled in 1973–1974 as a result of the oil embargo, the Saudi oil revenues spiked to $22.6 billion (1974), to $25.7 billion (1975), and to $30.8 billion (1976).[3] At the time, it was estimated that SAMA had increased its overseas investments and convertible foreign currencies from $20 billion (end of 1974) to an estimated value of $45 billion (end of 1975).

Following Saudi Arabia's strong financial position, both Egypt and Jordan had approached the Saudis to get finance for their military purchases from the United States.[4] In the 1970s, both Saudi Arabia and Jordan were purchasing primarily US-made weapons. Accordingly, King Husayn of Jordan (r. 1952–1999) was negotiating with the Ford Administration (1974–1977) about his desire to purchase American weapon systems, which then would be financed by the Saudis. Although such systems were considered technologically advanced and of high quality, it seems that the Saudis considered the deal too expensive. Therefore, to change the financial conditions of the weapons deal, King Husayn decided to turn to Moscow for alternative systems. The Soviet weapon systems were cheaper, but their quality did not match the American ones.

In May 1976, Jordan hosted a high-level Soviet delegation, and in response King Husayn made an 11-day official visit to Moscow a month later (June 1976). This development alarmed Washington. The Americans believed that if Jordan would buy Soviet-made weapons, the move would increase the Soviet influence in the traditionally pro-Western and pro-American kingdom.[5] In response, the United States warned King Husayn before he embarked for his trip to Moscow that he could lose American military and economic assistance worth millions of dollars in case he

---

[3] Kingdom of Saudi Arabia, *Saudi Arabian Monetary Agency: Annual Report 1979*, Riyadh: Saudi Arabian Printing Company, 1979, 22–23; "Saudis Widening World Holdings," *The New York Times*, April 7, 1976, 61.

[4] "Sadat Starts Tour to Seek Aid from Arab Oil States," *The New York Times*, February 22, 1976, 20.

[5] Bernard Gwertzman, "Jordan-Soviet Arms Talk Arouses Concern in US," *The New York Times*, May 16, 1976, 1.

128 S. E. WILLNER

decided to buy Russian systems.[6] It is not reported how Husayn had deliberated his decision. However, one can always speculate whether it was the American threats that changed King Husayn's mind regarding the weapons purchase. Instead of being serious about buying Soviet-made weapons, it is quite likely that the whole episode was his plan to pressure the Ford Administration so that it would provide him a better arms deal. After King Husayn's trip to Moscow, the Jordanians decided to purchase US-made air defense system worth some $540 million that was Saudi-financed. This system was like the one King Husayn had intended to buy from Moscow.[7] Considering Washington's response, it is quite possible that the United States decided to provide Jordan better weapons with reduced price after it was announced that King Husayn would travel to Moscow. Interestingly, the Iranians had used similar tactics in the late 1950s and early 1960s. Given the close relations between the Shah and King Husayn, the Shah might have advised Husayn to use similar tactics.

That being said, it is unlikely that the Jordanians had ultimate intentions of buying sophisticated weapon systems from the Soviet Union, especially because the Soviet arms had not helped to bring victory to neither Egypt nor Syria in the previous wars against Israel, and because such purchase would have led to significant Soviet military advisor presence in the kingdom.[8] Also, since the basic armament the Saudis had purchased was American, mixing it with utterly different Soviet-made weapon systems would have been complicated and expensive (mainly due to technical incompatibility of such advanced systems). Although there is no documentation that could confirm such a conclusion, it is reasonable to assume that King Husayn suspected that Soviet presence could encourage revolutionary pro-Syrian and pro-Iraqi activity in the kingdom. Based on King Husayn's experience, could the Saudis attempt similar tactics?

[6] "US is Said to Caution Jordan against Buying Soviet Missiles," *The New York Times*, June 17, 1976, 10.
[7] See: Bernard Gwertzman, "U.S. Says Jordan Bars Soviet Arms for Air Defenses," *The New York Times*, August 1, 1976, 1.
[8] Similarly, in 1972, Sadat expelled all Soviet advisors from Egypt.

THE TOP-SECRET SAUDI PLAN

Secrecy has been an essential element of Saudi decision-making processes. In such a context, a secret message often is the surest message to reach the target party. Therefore, the value of such a message could become multi-fold in comparison to public statements. As Uri Bar-Joseph puts it, "a high-level deception operation seeks to use the most secure channels available in order to transmit the deceptive information to the opponent so that it is less suspicious."[9]

According to British sources in Saudi Arabia, the Russians had attempted to establish new contacts with the Saudis following the murder of King Faysal. The British reported that an anonymous Arab diplomat had told the French Ambassador in Moscow that the Soviet government had taken steps to establish diplomatic relations with Saudi Arabia through King Husayn of Jordan.[10] There is no record available that could indicate how the Saudis responded to such Soviet approaches if they existed at all. However, it is quite possible that Crown Prince Fahd's interview with the North Yemeni newspaper *Al-Thawrah* in July 1975 was meant as a message to both Washington and Moscow. In this interview Fahd had iterated that Saudi Arabia was open to establish economic relations with all countries in the world, possibly in reference that it could consider buying advanced weapons from the Soviets. In the above-mentioned interview Fahd did not indicate that the Saudis would be ready to establish diplomatic relations with the Soviet Union.[11] On the contrary, the Saudis had expressed multiple times in the past that the Marxist ideology, which the Soviets were actively spreading in the Middle East, was a threat to its monarchy's survival. Considering the Saudi suspicions regarding the Soviet activity in the Middle East, hence, what could explain a sudden Saudi approach towards the USSR?

As I have previously mentioned, it seems that during the reign of King Faysal the Grand Mufti of Russia played a role in mediating between Moscow and Riyadh; and it could be that he played once again as a secret

---

[9] Bar-Joseph, *Watchman Fell Asleep*, 25.

[10] "Saudi/Soviet Relations" (confidential report), Harold B. Walker (Counselor, British Embassy, Jeddah) to S.J.L. Wright (Staff Member, FCO, London), June 7, 1975, no. 57, *FCO 8/2574.*

[11] Crown Prince Fahd's interview with the official YAR newspaper *Al-Thawrah* was published on July 3, 1975; see: "Crown Prince Fahd Interviewed by Yemeni Paper," *FBIS Daily Reports*, July 9, 1975, C4.

130 S. E. WILLNER

channel to avoid open-media contact between the Saudis and the Soviets. Also, the diplomatic reports from Helsinki, Finland, seem to suggest that the Saudis had intended to approach the Government of Finland to explore possible Saudi-Soviet relations. It appears that one reason why the Saudis had chosen Finland for such an intermediary role was because Finland had relatively close relations with the Russians due to the 'Agreement of Friendship, Cooperation, and Mutual Assistance,' which was signed between the two states in 1948.[12] Another reason was that by the mid-1970s it was clear that the royal family's earlier suspicions that Finland was a communist country were a mistake.[13] Another factor in support of the Finnish channel could be the fact that some Saudi businessmen had used Finland to travel to the Soviet Union so that they could do business discreetly without upsetting the United States. To understand the fundamental reasons why the Saudis approached the Finnish government, it is imperative to address how this Saudi initiative took place.

In June 1976, the diplomatic community in Jeddah had heard rumors about serious disagreements within the royal family. The Finnish ambassador Lassila reported that Crown Prince Fahd had been very upset

[12] The Agreement of Friendship, Cooperation, and Mutual Assistance was the foundation of Finland-Soviet relations during 1948–1992. Under the treaty, on the one hand, the Soviets intended to deter Western nations from attacking the Soviet Union through Finland. On the other hand, through the treaty, Finland secured its independency and survival as a democracy. The full text of the agreement is available at: "Asetus Asetus Suomen ja Sosialististen Neuvostotasavaltain Liiton välillä ystävyydestä, yhteistoiminnasta ja keskinäisestä avunannosta Moskovassa 6 päivänä huhtikuuta 1948 allekirjoitetun sopimuksen voimaansaattamisesta." [Decree on the Agreement between Finland and the USSR on Friendship, Cooperation and Mutual Assistance signed in Moscow on 6 April 1948.], *Finlex*, accessed November 26, 2019, https://www.finlex.fi/fi/sopimukset/sopsteksti/1948/19480017

[13] Finland was a very small player in the Middle East political affairs. In fact, in the late 1960s King Faysal seemed to have been convinced that Finland was a communist country, which made it difficult at first for Finland to establish diplomatic relations with Saudi Arabia. It is not completely clear how this misinformation (or disinformation) started spreading, but the Finnish diplomatic documents reveal that there had been a certain Saudi individual that had purposefully spread disinformation saying that Finland was a communist country. These documents also reveal that the reason why he was spreading such disinformation was because of his anger towards the Finns after they had decided not to use his services as a middleman for making oil trades. Eventually, the facts were made clear by the Finnish Foreign Ministry officials, who managed to convince their Saudi counterparts of the political orientation of the Finnish government. See, for instance: Letter, Henrik Blomsted (Embassy of Finland, Addis Ababa) to Martti Ingman (Minister, Ministry for Foreign Affairs, Helsinki), March 8, 1968, no. 182, *Diplomaattisuhteet 1966–1971, AMFAF.*

9 THE TOP-SECRET SAUDI PLAN TO USE THE USSR TO PRESSURE... 131

because the royal family had decided to purchase an aircraft fitted with special medical equipment to treat King Khalid's heart condition. Lassila also revealed that Crown Prince Fahd had disappeared from the public for several days, which raised the suspicions that a power struggle was taking place within the royal family, and this, he thought, could explain Fahd's sudden disappearance. Interestingly, Lassila also revealed that Fahd's disappearance from public eye took place a few days before Prince Muhammad embarked on a private trip to Sweden. Lassila asked Bengt Rösiö, the Swedish ambassador in Jeddah (1974–1977), if he knew anything about the purpose of Prince Muhammad's trip, but his Swedish counterpart did not seem to have any clues about this.[14]

As it seems, Prince Muhammad traveled to Stockholm to meet up with Shaikh Ziyad Shawwaf, the ambassador of Saudi Arabia to Sweden and Finland. Moreover, the diplomatic correspondence suggests that in Stockholm Prince Muhammad ordered the Saudi ambassador to set up a top-secret meeting in Helsinki with Urho Kekkonen, the president of Finland (1956–1982). Three months later, on September 13, 1976, a top-secret[15] meeting took place in Helsinki between the Saudi ambassador and President Kekkonen. During the meeting, Ambassador Shawwaf told Kekkonen that Saudi Arabia had gone through several changes since King Faysal's death. Shawwaf then started to talk about Saudi relations with the Soviet Union and said that the kingdom would like to explore developing these relations. The Saudi ambassador then told President Kekkonen that there were already several Saudis that have been traveling through Finland to the Soviet Union. He did not reveal what was the purpose of their travel, but it is quite possible that the Saudi businessmen intended to establish barter oil deals with the Soviets.[16]

---

[14] "Perheriidan perspektiivejä" [Perspectives of family dispute] (secret report), Carolus Lassila (ambassador, Embassy of Finland, Jeddah) to Ahti Karjalainen (minister of foreign affairs, Helsinki), June 26, 1976, no. R-344-76, *Saudi Arabia sisäpolitiikka 1975–1977, AMFAF.*

[15] Usually, the most sensitive diplomatic documents were classified as 'top secret.' In the case of the Ministry for Foreign Affairs of Finland, this classification was most often given to documents related to its relations with the Soviet Union.

[16] "Saudi Arabian Tukholmassa olevan suurlähettilään, sheikki Ziad Shawwaf'in käynti Tasavallan presidentin luona Tamminiemessä" [Shaikh Ziyad Shawwaf, the Saudi Ambassador in Stockholm, meeting with President of Finland in Tamminiemi] (top secret memo), Ministry of Foreign Affairs (Helsinki), September 12, 1976, *AMFAF.*

132 S. E. WILLNER

The Saudi ambassador also said that establishing government relations with the Soviet Union was a very sensitive and difficult subject for the Saudis, because "Saudi Arabia lacked experience in this issue," and as such he asked to keep their request highly confidential. President Kekkonen responded favorably to Shawwaf's request by saying that "[he] would be glad to help Saudi Arabia to establish government relations with the Soviet Union."[17] The first step, according to the report, was to prepare a letter to King Khalid. The Finns were probably very careful regarding their response due to the sensitivity of the Saudi request and since Finland was very eager to develop commercial relations with the Saudis. Unfortunately, the trail of currently available declassified archive material in Finland, the United Kingdom, and the United States ended there, with no documentation available that would indicate how the Saudi request progressed, if at all.

As discussed earlier, the Saudis had portrayed communism as one of the greatest threats to its survival because the communists had supported revolutionary forces around the world. Revolutionary forces, in turn, had overthrown several monarchies in the region surrounding Saudi Arabia.[18] According to Vladimir N. Sakharov, a former Middle East specialist who defected to the United States from the Soviet intelligence agency KGB[19] in 1971, Moscow had coordinated insurgencies against Washington's interests (and its allies) with "top operatives of insurgent groups operating on the Arabian Peninsula and in the Persian Gulf emirates."[20] In all its absurdity and perplexity, an outside observer should have concluded that, in a conspiratorial Saudi mindset, a possible Soviet military advisor presence in the kingdom would have equaled a major threat to the Saudi monarchy's survival. Thence, to explore a sensible reason for the Saudi move, it is useful to examine how the Ford Administration responded after the Saudi-Finnish contact had been established in this matter. When the royal family decided to put up such a secretive political plan, it must have drawn CIA's curiosity, which probably closely tailed Prince Muhammad while he was in Stockholm setting up the meeting with the Finnish

---

[17] Ibid.

[18] For example, the Marxist tribal revolt in Dhofar region of Oman and Yemen.

[19] The KGB [*Komitet Gosudarstvennoy Bezopasnosti*] has been translated into English as the Committee for State Security, and it was the main security agency in the Soviet Union.

[20] Supporting the PLO against the Saudis was ideal for the Russians since the Soviets had failed to form an effective Saudi Communist Party that could challenge the monarchy. Robert Moss, "Terror: A Soviet Export," *The New York Times*, November 2, 1980, 42.

government through the Saudi ambassador.[21] If this is what had happened, and if the CIA had concluded that, in utmost secrecy, the Saudis were attempting to establish relations with Moscow, then it might have pushed Washington to consider offering the Saudis a better arms deal.

At the end of July 1976, it was reported in the US press that the Ford Administration had decided to sell Saudis a massive amount of new generation missiles. The deal also included a proposal to modernize the Saudi National Guard so that it would be better equipped to respond to various internal threats. Based on reports published in the American press, the officials in Washington had justified the enormous weapons sale to Saudi Arabia by stating that the kingdom needed to defend itself against a simultaneous attacks from both Iraq and South Yemen (PDRY).[22] Nonetheless, if such was the Saudi intention all along—namely, to pressure the United States to make a better deal with the Saudis by making it look as if they were setting up secret relations with the Soviets—then it could indicate that the Saudis had truly mastered the use of deception and secrecy in pursuing their political aims. In the end, the question whether Washington called the Saudi 'bluff,' is less meaningful. Perhaps what is more important is that the move succeeded. The outcome of the operation was that Riyadh signed a major weapons deal with Washington and no Saudi-Soviet relations were established.

[21] It is also possible that there were CIA informants in the Swedish establishment as well. Nevertheless, one could always speculate whether the Finnish government had informed the Americans about the meeting that the Finnish president had with the Saudi ambassador. However, based on the logic of operation of the Finnish foreign policy officials, it is very unlikely that they had informed the Americans. Although there is no source for reference, one can claim that, in general, the Finns have been quite good at keeping secrets.

[22] Leslie H. Gelb, "U.S. Ready to Sell Missiles to Saudis," *The New York Times,* August 1, 1976, 14; "U.S. Arms Deal with Saudis Said to Include Base Facilities," *The New York Times,* September 4, 1976, 5.

Conclusion of Part III The End of the Oil Embargo and the Murder of King Faysal (1973–1976)

CONCLUSIONS

In March 1974, King Faysal ruled that Saudi Arabia would terminate its participation in the Arab oil embargo, which had seriously crippled the world economy. However, the embargo had already created cracks in the Saudi–US relations. At the height of the tensions, King Faysal had even sent his emissaries to convey that Saudi Arabia could destroy its oil installations in case the United States would intervene militarily and take over the petroleum facilities. In response, Washington examined these Saudi threats and commissioned the CIA to use various methods of psychological warfare, including the use of disinformation, so that Riyadh would conclude the embargo. The more Faysal was pushed and threatened, the more stubborn he became. Although the US threats worried Faysal, he was not willing to end the embargo, and once he did end it, was later thinking of renewing it. Hence, when Faysal finally decided to terminate the embargo, he wanted the United States to put more pressure on Israel in return for his decision. Therefore, he continued to deliver his threats of the possibility that there could be another embargo if his demands were not met.

From the point of Saudi decision-making, Faysal's threats were against pragmatism, which had been the Saudi policy in its desire for survival. Publicly, the senior princes wanted to portray the royal family as a united front, as unity in decision-making reflected internal cohesion and strength. However, privately several senior princes strongly disagreed with Faysal's policies, which had deteriorated the Saudi–US relations. For the royal

136   CONCLUSION OF PART III THE END OF THE OIL EMBARGO...

family, a major problem with Faysal's mindset and behavior was that although he had never been an easy person to work with, his obsession with Zionism and Communism had become so much deeper and worrisome that it had started to paralyze Saudi decision-making. Due to Faysal's behavior, several anonymous members of the royal family were expressing their frustration about his stubbornness and his flawed understanding of the changing world. It is very possible that Faysal's rigidity and arrogance [1] had blinded him from seeing, firstly, what the royal family's strategic interests were and, secondly, how most of the family might have disagreed with him on how such interests should be achieved. Faysal's inability to understand the importance of the Saudi–US relationship in the aftermath of the oil embargo turned him into a major liability to the rest of the royal family. In private, these senior princes were talking about the future succession.

Washington continued its psychological warfare operation against Riyadh. In early March 1975, just few weeks before King Faysal's murder, a provocative article "Seizing Arab Oil" was published in *Harper's Magazine*. If Secretary of State Kissinger indeed had authored the article, as claimed by US Ambassador Akins, it would only show how serious the situation was at the time. The fundamental message was that Faysal was still stuck in his old thinking and was about to bring disaster to Saudi Arabia. Another oil embargo would justify the United States to launch a military action to control the Saudi oil fields. Accordingly, the article presented a possible scenario for the war plans, which was so candid that it would have been hard to dismiss in Riyadh. The message was clear: The Saudis needed to change their political discourse and continue to be a partner to the United States if they desired to survive.

The murder of King Faysal was a major turning point in Saudi decision-making. The embargo affair, and the murder of Faysal that followed, seem to have clarified for the Saudis that their closest partner United States could become their biggest threat if its core interests were severely endangered. It is also possible that the senior members of the royal family were convinced that their survival and fate were intertwined with their maintenance of a close relationship with the United States. When King Khalid

---

[1] As hinted by Crown Prince Fahd, "Any ruler who believes he can make decisions without consultation is suffering from arrogance." Fahd made his statements in an interview with the Kuwaiti newspaper *As-Siyasah*. The interview was published jointly by the Saudi newspapers *Ukaz* and *Al-Jazirah*, March 29, 1982. See: *FBIS*, March 30, 1982, C6–C9.

was sworn in, it had become obvious that the new leadership had become much less confrontational *vis-à-vis* the United States. Since the Saudis had many times earlier proven to be pragmatic in their decision-making— while following the patterns of tribalism in such processes, it would not be meaningful to attribute this change because of a major revival within the royal family, but rather because King Faysal was gone.

PART IV

The Survival of the Saudi Monarchy During the Carter Administration (1977–1981)

The political events of Iran's Islamic Revolution (1978–1979), which led to major disruptions in the Iranian oil exports, and which created chaos in the oil markets, were a major trigger for global financial instability. Despite Saudi Arabia's attempts to stabilize the oil markets by increasing its oil exports, the oil prices kept going up under the circumstances that the *Petroleum Intelligence Weekly* described as "totally irrational market climate." [1] Eventually, this triggered an economic recession in the Western world. As such, this event has often been referred to as an oil crisis. The revolution in Iran brought to power a Shi'i theocratic regime that was heavily anti-American and anti-Saudi. Due to the revolutionary character of the new regime in Tehran, on the one hand, and because of the Saudi distrust in the Carter Administration's willingness to provide adequate security assistance to Saudi Arabia in the worsened geopolitical situation, on the other hand, the royal family needed to build a coalition against Iran. To do so, the Saudis successfully manipulated political events by spreading disinformation. They also increased communications with Iraq and began grooming Saddam Husayn, who shared similar concerns with the Saudis, to act militarily against the Iranians. As I will elaborate throughout the coming chapters, most of the Saudi decisions during these years can be described as pragmatic with the aim of securing the survival of the Saudi monarchy. Ultimately, every key foreign policy decision in Saudi Arabia has served this purpose.

---

[1] John Evans and Gavin Brown have quoted *Petroleum Intelligence Weekly*: John Evans and Gavin Brown, *OPEC and the World Energy Market*, Essex: Longman Industry and Public Service Management, 1993, 524.

CHAPTER 10

Saudi Concerns of the Marxist and Arab Revolutionary Threats (1977–1978)

President Jimmy Carter's Foreign Policy

President Jimmy Carter's term (1977–1981) in the White House was not an easy period for the Saudi monarchy. As I will elaborate in the coming chapters, the Saudis accused the Carter Administration of being unwilling to provide satisfactory guarantees to preserve their monarchy.

Before assuming the presidency of the United States in January 1977, Jimmy Carter had been a one-term governor of Georgia (1971–1975) with no international experience. Although Carter lacked experience in international relations, he did have his own (ideological) foreign policy goals. Most importantly, during his term in the White House, Carter realigned American foreign policy toward a new emphasis on universal human rights, liberalism, democratic values, nuclear nonproliferation, and global poverty. Moreover, Carter was a true believer in a world where perfect democracy would prevail. However, such foreign policy goals were in sharp contrast with the policies of the undemocratic Middle East regimes.

In many ways, the Saudis considered that President Carter's personal ideology was the main reason that portrayed his Middle East policy as weak and indecisive. Moreover, the Saudis were quite skeptical about Carter's ideological and arguably *naïve* foreign policy orientation because he pushed for democratization in traditional Middle Eastern societies without really understanding how such systems operate or the hostile

© The Author(s), under exclusive license to Springer Nature Switzerland AG 2023
S. E. Willner, *Preserving the Saudi Monarchy*,
https://doi.org/10.1007/978-3-031-30006-6_10

141

political forces taking advantage of that *naïveté*. In addition, the Saudis were convinced that the United States was more interested in Saudi oil reserves than preserving the Saudi monarchy. Furthermore, the Saudis blamed that Carter's unwillingness to help the Shah of Iran led to the Pahlavi-dynasty's downfall (January 1979). Especially toward the end of the Carter Administration, the Saudis indicated quite openly that they were very disappointed with the American foreign policy. For the Saudis, one of the most alarming policy issues was that, by pursuing his ideological foreign policy, Carter was willing to risk straining relations with US allies and friends (while widening existing rifts with its foes).

Another major issue, which alarmed the Saudis, was that Carter believed the United States should avoid military interventions as much as possible and that the United States' foreign policy should not strengthen dictatorial, undemocratic regimes (which also included the two core states of the 'Twin Pillar' strategy, namely, Saudi Arabia and Iran). In fact, already in May 1975 during his bid for the Democratic presidential nomination, Carter had declared that "never again should [...the United States] become militarily involved in the internal affairs of another nation unless there is a direct and obvious threat to the security of the United States or its people." He also added that "[the US] must not use the CIA or other covert means to effect violent change in any government or government policy."[1] Although Carter had made his statements early on his presidential campaign, they were consistent with his foreign policy as the President of the United States. It is quite likely that Carter's policy statements had raised serious alarms in Riyadh, especially because his statements contradicted with the Cold War-concerns of the earlier Republican Nixon and Ford Administrations.[2]

---

[1] Jimmy Carter, "New Approach to Foreign Policy" (Address to the American Chamber of Commerce in Tokyo), May 28, 1975, no. 2, *FRUS*, vol. I *Foundations of Foreign Policy, 1977-1980*, Washington D.C.: US Government Printing Office, 2014, 4. See also: David Collier, *Democracy and the Nature of American Influence in Iran, 1941–1979*, Syracuse, NY: Syracuse University Press, 2017, 276.

[2] For further reading, see, for instance: Jimmy Carter, *Keeping Faith: Memoirs of a President*, New York, NY: Bantam Books, 1995.

SABOTAGE OF OIL INSTALLATIONS AND FAILED COUP ATTEMPTS

In May 1977, two major fires broke out in the Abqaiq oil fields. These fires caused severe damage and massive financial losses to Saudi Arabia. It was estimated in 1977 that as a result Saudi Arabia had lost over 60 million barrels of oil production, while the repairs could have cost more than $100 million.[3] Eventually it took six months to repair the damage. Following the incident, Minister of Petroleum Yamani claimed that the fire at the oil installations had been an accident while Fahd had stated that what had happened "was normal and natural and could occur at any place."[4] Interestingly, a report prepared by the British Embassy commented on the fire incident by saying that it had been "more serious than Aramco or the Saudis were letting on." Mike Ameen, who served as the President of Mobil Middle East Development Corporation in London (1975–1988), had wondered "how it would have been possible to rule out sabotage as early as the official Saudi statements had done." He added that Abd al-Aziz al-Turki[5] had told him a few months earlier (February 1977) that the Saudis were worried about the vulnerability of their oil installations to Iraqi sabotage.[6] Days after the massive fires broke out, *The New York Times* reported from Beirut that the fire was suspected to have been a work of sabotage, and that Arab and African communists had been recruited by the Iraqis for sabotage operations against Saudi Arabia. According to the news report, the Saudis had received a warning of the attacks, but based on the anonymous source, the Saudis had dismissed it. The same source also claimed that the perpetrators had arrived at Saudi Arabia already a month prior to the attacks.[7]

An interesting question inevitably arises: If the Saudis had indeed been warned about these attacks, could it be true that they had not taken the warnings seriously despite the fact the Saudis had expressed their concerns that Iraqis were planning attacks against them? Amid such perplexity, there is a possibility that the warning had originated from a source that did not

---

[3] See: Untitled (confidential report), Jolyon C. Kay (British Embassy, Jeddah) to Robin A. Kealy (MED, FCO, London), May 19, 1977, no. 15, *FCO 8/3032*.

[4] Hobday, *Saudi Arabia Today*, 60, 99; "Prince Fahd Makes a Statement to Newsmen in Riyadh," *FBIS*, May 20, 1977, C1-C2.

[5] Abd al-Aziz al-Turki's affiliation is unknown.

[6] Untitled, May 19, 1977.

[7] "Fire Halts Oil Flow in Major Saudi Line," *The New York Times*, May 13, 1977, 1.

144 S. E. WILLNER

have diplomatic relations with Saudi Arabia. Accordingly, Israel had been closely monitoring the same radical Palestinian groups that were also threatening Saudi Arabia. Moreover, the cautious Saudi response and the desire to downplay the significance of the incident could indicate that the Saudis did not want to worsen their relations with Iraq.

The radical elements did not only target the oil installations. As it was reported, a failed coup attempt took place in mid-1977, just a few months after the disastrous fire in the Abqaiq oil installations. Adeed Dawisha revealed that 17 Saudi military officers and many civilians were tried around October and November 1977 for plotting against the Saudi royal family. As it seems, the objective of the failed coup was to overthrow the royal family and establish a revolutionary and republican Arab regime instead.[8] Mordechai Abir, in turn, claimed that the conspirators had been Ba'athists connected to Iraq, but the plot was masterminded and financed by Libya. Abir added that the CIA had monitored the secret communications of the Libyan intelligence, and therefore it had been able to warn the Saudis about this Libyan-sponsored plot.[9]

THE SAUDI RESPONSES TO THE SOVIET-SPONSORED MARXIST THREAT

The Soviet-sponsored revolutionary movements and the subsequent spread of what looked like communism or Marxism in the region surrounding Saudi Arabia posed a significant threat to Saudis during the second half of the 1970s. Based on the available archival records, the Saudi monarchy was seriously afraid that the Soviets were capable of not only overthrowing it but also of turning the kingdom into a socialist state. There were legitimate reasons for such Saudi concerns. In the southeast of the kingdom, Marxist revolutionaries had dominated the government of South Yemen (PDRY) since 1969, while Ethiopia in the southwest, across the Red Sea, had fallen into the hands of a Marxist military government in February 1977.[10] Although the Soviets—together with their communist allies from Cuba, East Germany, and North Korea—had been building up

---

[8] Adeed Dawisha, "Saudi Arabia's Search for Security," *Adelphi Papers*, 158, 7.

[9] Abir, *Saudi Arabia: Government, Society*, 75.

[10] Three years earlier in 1974, Emperor Haile Selassie (r. 1916–1974) was overthrown because of a mutiny in the military. A socialist military government came to power in Ethiopia.

10 SAUDI CONCERNS OF THE MARXIST AND ARAB REVOLUTIONARY... 145

their military capacity in the Horn of Africa and in Yemen for several years since the end of 1960s, it was not until the communist coup in Afghanistan in April 1978[11] that the Saudi sense of security seemed to have been dramatically shaken up. These events made the Saudis suspicious about the possible Soviet intentions concerning the Middle East petroleum.[12]

David B. Ottaway of *The Washington Post* assessed that the encirclement of communist forces around Saudi Arabia helped to "explain why the Saudis [were] pressing the Carter Administration to adopt a more aggressive posture in Africa [and] even hinting at the need for a direct American intervention to counter the expanding Soviet-Cuban military presence."[13] In addition to the Marxist activity in Africa, the Saudis were concerned about the warfare and terror sponsored by Libya's Muammar Qadhafi, who was following his own foreign policy designs in the poverty-stricken continent. The Saudis wanted that its partner United States would act more firmly against these threats. However, they ended up being disappointed in the American unwillingness to prevent the Soviet advance and in its subsequent undesirability to commit protecting the kingdom against the revolutionary forces.

At the end of May 1978, just one month after the coup in Afghanistan, King Khalid made an official visit to Paris, during which his entourage had several meetings with French officials. King Khalid's meeting with Valery Giscard d'Estaing, the President of France (1974–1981), coincided with the president's return from Washington, where his delegation had met with President Carter a few days earlier. As indicated by the British

---

[11] On April 27, 1978, a violent communist coup took place in Afghanistan overthrowing President Muhammad Daud (r. 1973–1978). The revolutionary People's Democratic Party of Afghanistan (PDPA) took power. William Borders, "Coup is Reported in Afghanistan," *The New York Times*, April 28, 1978, 1.

[12] Although Leonid Brezhnev, who served as the General Secretary of the Communist Party of the Soviet Union (1964–1982), had declared in 1976 that capitalism was "without a future" and that socialism was gaining strength every day, the Soviets had not made any significant success in the Middle East. As a matter of fact, the Soviet client Syria had lost the 1973 Arab–Israeli War big time, while Egypt in 1976 was securely in the American camp, negotiating with Israel. Furthermore, in Iraq, Saddam Husayn was not a true Soviet client, and in Dhofar, the Marxist forces had lost their war against the government-backed forces. For a commentary of Leonid Brezhnev's remarks, which he made during his speech at the 25th congress of the Communist Party, see: Michael Dobbs, "Afghan Pullout Marks Historic Reversal for Soviets," *The Washington Post*, February 13, 1989, A1.

[13] David B. Ottaway, "Saudi Arabia Cool to US Africa Policy; Saudis Score U.S. Failure to Challenge Cubans," *The Washington Post*, May 15, 1978, A1.

Embassy in Paris, Khalid's main message to the French officials was to express the royal family's concern about the implications of the communist coup in Afghanistan and the internal vulnerability of the Saudi kingdom. The Saudis had also told the French that they had been principally concerned about the smuggling attempt of a shipment of "Czech/Soviet arms" to Saudi Arabia, which their security forces had intercepted. Although there are no archival records available that would show which entity had been behind the smuggling attempt, it is quite likely that the seized weapons were meant for the Qadhafi-sponsored insurgents fighting against the monarchy. It is also possible that the weapons were meant for a planned coup attempt against the Saudi royal family.[14] In fact, a few months earlier—in reference to the Western petroleum interests—British energy officials in London had expressed in their own assessment that if a radical regime similar to Libya's Muammar Qadhafi would succeed in taking over Saudi Arabia, it "would almost certainly lead to limits on [oil] production and a disregard of shared Saudi and Western economic interests."[15] In other words, the assessment declared that preserving the Saudi monarchy was in the Western interests.

With regard to King Khalid's visit to Paris, the French officials were struck by the Saudis' pessimistic analysis of the international political developments. Not only were the Saudis worried about the advance of Soviet influence in the region, but they also seem to have been concerned about becoming "the frontrunners for financial aid in too many areas at once."[16] That is to say, the Saudis were concerned that financing the fight against the Soviet-sponsored communists in Africa was becoming a significant financial burden for them, and therefore it was draining the Saudi treasury. Such a response could indicate that the Saudis expected the French and other Western nations, and especially the United States, to contribute financially to the struggle against communism and thus relieve the possible financial burden on Saudi Arabia. In fact, Ottaway claimed that in 1978, the Saudis were distributing more aid to Africa than the

[14] "France and Saudi Arabia: Visit of King Khalid" (confidential report), J.R. Young (British Embassy, Paris) to Robin A. Kealy (MED, FCO, London), June 7, 1978, no. 18, *FCO 8/3260.*

[15] "Oxe Study on Supply and Demand for Oil in 1985" (confidential report), David Hannay (Energy, Science and Space Department, FCO, London) to Burrows (HM Treasury, London), February 3, 1978, no. 3, *FCO 8/3263.*

[16] "France and Saudi Arabia: Visit of King Khalid," June 7, 1978.

United States.[17] Although it is hard to tell what the actual numbers were, the Saudi financial aid for the militaries fighting the Marxist revolutionaries (for instance, Soviet-backed Cuban fighters), and Libyan-sponsored mercenaries, must have been significant. As the British diplomatic report indicates, the Saudis had told the French officials that they wanted the United States to "adopt a tougher line towards the Russians in Africa."[18] Furthermore, possibly as an indirect threat to the United States, the Saudis had also expressed that they would not be able to hold the oil prices low much longer—perhaps in reference to the revolutionary threat—while indicating that the Americans would need to do more to secure the Saudi interests if they desired the monarchy to continue oil policy favorable to the United States.

The British officials in Paris assessed the details of the Saudi–French meeting and commented that the Saudis seemed to have launched a more in-depth dialogue with the French because they identified the French as "standing up to the Russians" in Africa,[19] unlike the Americans in whose policy they were disappointed.[20] Such comments were in line with an assessment made by anonymous American officials, which was reported by *The Washington Post*. According to these government sources, the Saudi royal family was puzzled and irritated over "[American] passivity toward Soviet and Cuban expansionism [in Africa]."[21] It is possible, although it is not revealed in the official documents, that the major reason for King Khalid's visit to Paris was to negotiate French weapon supplies to the Somali government that was fighting the Soviet-backed Ethiopian forces, and possibly in return, the Saudis provided the French financially more

---

[17] Ottaway, "Saudi Arabia Cool to U.S. Africa Policy."

[18] "France and Saudi Arabia: Visit of King Khalid," June 7, 1978.

[19] The Saudis probably were referring to these French military interventions of varying scale in Djibouti, Chad, Mauritania, Angola, and Zaire during 1977 and 1978. By intervening in the African conflicts, the French government was naturally protecting its own interests. However, the justification given by the French for their activity was to fill "the role abandoned by the United States since the Vietnam War" and therefore to prevent Soviet efforts destabilizing the African continent. See, for instance: Ronald Koven, "France's New Role: Africa's Gendarme," *The Washington Post*, May 9, 1978, A13.

[20] Interestingly, a handwritten comment in the telegram said that "funny, we never got much credit for beating the communists in Dhofar," while another comment added that "true, but we [the British] kept so quiet about it." "France and Saudi Arabia: Visit of King Khalid," June 7, 1978.

[21] Ronald Koven, "Saudi, French Express Anxiety Over Soviets in Africa," *The Washington Post*, June 1, 1978, A14.

148   S. E. WILLNER

favorable long-term oil contracts. However, following the circulation of earlier reports about Saudi supply of French weapons to the Somalis, the French government utterly denied such rumors. It was suggested that the French response came because they thought their forces in Djibouti were highly exposed to Ethiopian attacks.[22]

In mid-June 1978, a few weeks after King Khalid's visit to Paris, the Saudi royal family conveyed, through Minister of Petroleum Yamani, that the aim of the Soviet policy was to "control the petroleum routes and sources, or at least some of the sources."[23] Yamani had assessed that the logic behind such a policy was a long-term Soviet energy strategy, which calculated that the Soviet Union would turn into a net-importer of crude oil sometime in the 1980s, forcing it to look for new sources of oil. As such, the Saudis seemed to have been convinced that the Soviets were eyeing the Saudi oil fields, which they thought was based on such a policy, driven primarily by the Soviet need to secure oil supplies for the coming decades.[24] As it seems, the communist takeover in Afghanistan had worsened the Saudi distrust of Soviet intentions and policy in the Middle East region.[25] Moreover, an assessment in the *Middle East Economic Survey (MEES)* suggested that Yamani's public linkage between the growing Soviet role in Afghanistan and the Horn of Africa, and the potential threat that it posed to the safety of the Persian Gulf oilfields and oil supply routes, "could be read as a warning to the industrial Western powers to act to protect their vital oil interests in the area by facing up to the Soviet challenge."[26] This could suggest that the Saudis wanted to stress the Soviet danger to the Middle East oil more than what they actually believed. In other words, the purpose of such a policy was probably to frighten the Europeans and the Americans, and thus, to make them respond more rigorously into Saudi strategic interests.

---

[22] Koven, "France's New Role: Africa's Gendarme."

[23] Minister of Petroleum Yamani was interviewed by the Saudi daily newspaper *Ukaz*. See: "*Tajmīd as'ār al-bitrūl ḥaqiqa mu'aqqata*" [The freezing of oil prices is temporary], *Ukaz*, June 10, 1978, 1–3; "Oil Minister Says Soviet Union Wants to Control Oil Supplies," *FBIS*, June 12, 1978, C3.

[24] See for instance: "Research Study: The Soviets in the Persian Gulf/Arabian Peninsula—Assets and Prospects" (secret report), CIA Office of Political Research (Langley VA), December 1976, no. PR 7610077, 2.

[25] In addition, during 1978–1979 Saddam Husayn also became deeply worried following the communist *coup d'état* in Afghanistan. Since he considered that communism posed a threat to his regime, he began arresting and killing the Iraqi communists, which led to a diplomatic crisis with the USSR.

[26] "Yamani Warns Against Soviet Designs on Middle East Oil." *MEES*, June 19, 1978.

CHAPTER 11

The 1978–1979 Islamic Revolution in Iran

THE REVOLUTION

The fall of Muhammad Riza Shah Pahlavi's monarchy in Iran in February 1979 was one of the major political events of modern history. The Islamic Revolution (or the 1978–1979 Revolution), which overthrew the Shah, was led by Ayatollah Ruhollah Khomeini, who had been exiled from Iran in 1964 due to his opposition to Shah's reforms and to the grant of capitulations to US personnel serving in Iran. Said Amir Arjomand has assessed that most observers and participants in the demonstrations against the Shah (January 1978–January 1979) "did not make much headway in comprehending the unfolding revolution," which was neither "bourgeois" nor "proletarian," and "whose slogans emphasized neither democracy nor progress."[1] Instead, it was led by Shi'a clergymen in attempt to turn the nation into an authoritarian, theocratic Islamic Republic.

The revolution was, no doubt, caused by the Pahlavi regime's internal weaknesses and vulnerabilities, and was coordinated by the social groups and individuals opposing it. The revolution itself was a consequence of a series of issues and events, which commenced from relatively minor demonstrations in October 1977, and which eventually culminated into

---

[1] Said Amir Arjomand, *The Turban for the Crown: The Islamic Revolution in Iran,* New York, NY: Oxford University Press, 1988, 4.

© The Author(s), under exclusive license to Springer Nature
Switzerland AG 2023
S. E. Willner, *Preserving the Saudi Monarchy,*
https://doi.org/10.1007/978-3-031-30006-6_11

149

150   S. E. WILLNER

massive demonstrations and civil unrest during later 1978, and finally leading to the downfall of the regime in early 1979.[2] From the Saudi point of view, it is imperative to pinpoint that the United States was a central foreign actor in Iran's domestic politics, specifically from the coup of August 1953 until the revolution in 1979. Securing Western access to the Middle East oil was a top priority for the Americans. This was a policy that was enforced by supporting the Western-oriented regimes, such as the Shah of Iran and the Al Saud of Saudi Arabia, and supplying them with modern weapon systems. Following the death of Joseph Stalin, the general secretary of the Communist Party of the Soviet Union (1922–1952), in March 1953, the Americans became increasingly worried about the future course of the Soviet foreign policy. Mainly, the United States was worried that the communist Tudeh Party of Iran—which had been established in 1942[3]—would push the country into the Soviet camp, which in turn could have threatened the Western interests in the Middle East's oil production regions. Therefore, the "geopolitical anxieties conditioned by the Cold War," as Maziar Behrooz put it, "were the prime concern to the perpetrators of the plot" to depose Muhammad Musaddiq, the relatively popular, but politically weak, democratically elected prime minister of Iran (1951–1953). From the American

---

[2] Several books have been written about the collapse of Iran's political order. For instance, the following books provide highly important historical perspective, which can help to understand both the causes and the consequences of this revolution: Arjomand, *The Turban for the Crown*; Gary Sick, *All Fall Down: America's Tragic Encounter with Iran*, New York, NY: Random House, 1985; Marvin Zonis, *Majestic Failure: The Fall of the Shah*, Chicago, IL: The University of Chicago Press, 1991; Gary Sick, *October Surprise: America's Hostages in Iran and the Election of Ronald Reagan*, London: I.B. Tauris, 1991; Barry Rubin, *Paved with Good Intentions: The American Experience and Iran*, New York, NY: Oxford University Press, 1980; William Shawcross, *The Shah's Last Ride: The Fate of an Ally*, New York, NY: Simon and Schuster, 1988; Amir Taheri, *The Persian Night: Iran under the Khomeinist Revolution*, New York, NY: Encounter Books, 2010; Shaul Bakhash, *The Politics of Oil and Revolution in Iran*, Washington, D.C.: The Brookings Institute, 1982; Shaul Bakhash, *The Reign of the Ayatollahs: Iran and the Islamic Revolution*, New York, NY: Basic Books, 1984, Nikki Keddie, *Modern Iran: Roots and Results of Revolution*, New Haven, CT: Yale University Press, 2003.

[3] The early members of the Tudeh Party were from a group of 53 leading members of the Iranian Communist Party, who were arrested in 1937. They were released in two waves, the first one being at the end of September 1941, and the second in February 1942, after which the *Hizb-is Tudah-yi* Iran was formally established.

11 THE 1978–1979 ISLAMIC REVOLUTION IN IRAN 151

perspective, this was the main reason for Operation TP-AJAX of August 1953.[4] Moreover, that operation assisted the Shah to replace Musaddiq. For the Shah, it was important that the prime ministers were yes men and loyal to him.[5] Almost three decades later, in 1978–1979, when the fatal events that preceded the fall of the Shah's regime were taking place, the Saudis seemed to have been anxious to press the Carter Administration to intervene in Iran in similar fashion as it had done in 1953, but the United States failed to do so.

SAUDI REACTIONS BEFORE THE SHAH'S FALL

The fall of the Pahlavi dynasty in Iran in February 1979 had a great impact on the self-confidence of the Saudi monarchy, and, as a result, the royal family even questioned whether it could trust the United States to safeguard it from potential threats.[6] For the Saudis, the crisis in Iran was seen as a test of the US ability and willingness to help its friends and allies.[7]

In November 1978, when Iran's slide to chaos had become even more evident, Prince Saud al-Faysal, the Saudi minister of foreign affairs, expressed the kingdom's support for the Pahlavi regime and hoped that "the situation in Iran [would] calm down so that it [could] resume its important role in the area." According to Saud al-Faysal, the royal family

---

[4] Behrooz quoted Donald N. Wilber's report *Overthrow of Premier Mosaddeq of Iran: November 1952–August 1953.* Wilber served as a CIA analyst. See: Maziar Behrooz, "The 1953 Coup in Iran and the Legacy of the Tudeh," in Mark Gasiorowski and Malcolm Byrne, eds. *Mohammad Mosaddeq and the 1953 Coup in Iran,* Syracuse, NY: Syracuse University Press, 2004, 102. See also: Stephen Kinzer, *All the Shah's Men: An American Coup and the Roots of Middle East Terror,* Hoboken, NJ: John Wiley & Sons, 2008.

[5] The UK Secret Intelligence Service (MI6) was also closely involved in the planning of the operation. The British were eager to replace Musaddiq following the decision of the Iranian parliament in March 1951 to nationalize the British-owned Anglo-Iranian Oil Company (AIOC), a decision which was initiated and pushed forward by Muṣaddiq.

[6] "Country Assessment Paper: Saudi Arabia" (confidential report), Christopher M.J. Segar (MED, FCO, London) to FCO (London), August 31, 1979, no. 4, *FCO 8/3417.*

[7] Interestingly, the seriousness of the Islamic Revolution, and its repercussions on the Saudi monarchy can be observed when the Jeddah daily newspaper *Ukaz* stopped publishing any pictures of women in its news stories right at the beginning of January 1979. In fact, it appears that almost every issue of *Ukaz* throughout 1978 had a page dedicated for women readers. As such, nearly every issue of the newspaper had fashion photos and advertisement, in which women posed in Western clothes (and without any head covering). The decision to stop publishing photos of women could indicate that the Saudis had calculated that they needed to portray themselves as more religious to prolong their monarchy.

152 S. E. WILLNER

believed that the Shah's government "should remain in the country because his achievements [... were] an example for the development of any state."[8] In January 1979, Deputy Prime Minister Fahd expressed similar sentiments. These Saudi statements indicate that the Saudi monarchy had calculated that it was in its best interest that the Shah's secular, pro-American regime stayed in power instead of letting Ayatollah Khomeini, who was known to be a Shi'i fanatical, religious fundamentalist and anti-American, take over the country. Therefore, based on such calculations, Fahd publicly expressed his strong support for the Pahlavi dynasty on the grounds that it was a legitimate regime and that the Shah staying in power was good for the regional stability.[9] At the time, some sources claimed that the Saudis were suspecting that the Soviets had been behind the Iranian instability. For instance, the Jeddah daily newspaper *Ukaz* blamed the Soviet Union for the wave of violence and tension in the region.[10] In an interview on January 6, 1979, Fahd iterated that "for [this] reason and without any doubt we support its [Shah's regime] survival."[11]

It is possible that, in addition to Saudi monarchy's natural fear of Khomeini and of his revolution, Fahd's remarks were also a response to President Carter's earlier statements, in which he casted doubts on the possibility that the Shah would survive the demonstrations, which were pushing Iran towards the revolution. Accordingly, on December 7, 1978, President Carter was asked at a news conference whether he expected the Shah to survive the revolution, to which he answered that "I don't know, I hope so. This is something in the hands of the people of Iran."[12] For instance, Gary Sick, who served on the staff of President Carter's National Security Council (1976–1981), wrote that although Carter's comments were "an honest reading of the president's mind [...], it was the wrong

---

[8] The *Qatar News Agency* (QNA) quoted Foreign Minister Saud al-Faysal's interview with the Saudi newspaper *Al-Madīnah Al-Munawwarah*, November 20, 1978. For the English translation, see: "Interview of Prince Saud al-Faisal," *FBIS*, November 20, 1978, C3.

[9] "*Kalimat 'Ukāẓ*" [Editorial of *Ukaz*], *Ukaz*, January 7, 1979, 1.

[10] "*Kalimat 'Ukāẓ*" [Editorial of *Ukaz*], *Ukaz*, January 3, 1979, 1; "*Kalimat 'Ukāẓ*" [Editorial of *Ukaz*], February 3, 1979, 1; "*Ukaz* Blames Soviet Union for Violence in Area," *FBIS*, January 12, 1979, C2; *Ukaz* Scores Communist Encroachment in Iran," *FBIS*, February 8, 1979, C5-C6.

[11] Fahd's interview was aired on Saudi radio news (SPA) on January 6, 1979. He gave the interview to the Saudi newspaper *Al-Jazirah* on the same day: "Crown Prince Expresses Support for Shah," *FBIS*, January 8, 1979, C1.

[12] Carter's comments were printed on page A14 of *The New York Times* on December 8, 1978; Zonis, *Majestic Failure*, 257.

11 THE 1978–1979 ISLAMIC REVOLUTION IN IRAN   153

signal for the president to send at that critical moment."[13] In addition, some of the policy statements that had come from the Carter Administration were confusing. For instance, after the demonstrations erupted against the Shah, Cyrus Vance, the US secretary of state (1977–1980), had argued that the Shah should institute a series of reforms to appease the demonstrators, while Zbigniew Brzezinski, who served as President Carter's National Security Advisor (1977–1981), had argued in favor of a crackdown on the violent demonstrators. Therefore, instead of helping to calm down the situation, the Carter Administration had only confused the Shah, and with mixed messages the Americans had contributed to the Shah's indecision concerning how to resolutely deal with the instability in the country.

Surely, the Saudis were not blind or *naïve* about where the political situation in Iran was heading. However, it appears that Fahd's message of support for the Shah was meant for the United States as a last-minute appeal to try to change the course of the events. The Saudis might have hoped that the United States would have supported the Shah in similar fashion as it had helped him to replace Prime Minister Musaddiq in 1953.

Interestingly, at the beginning of February 1979, some editorials in the Saudi press commented that it was difficult to analyze the political situation in Iran. In fact, after Ayatollah Khomeini's return to Iran, the Jeddah daily newspaper *Ukaz* commented that it was "extremely difficult to visualize" the future developments in Iran.[14] Although the Saudis were afraid of communists supported by the Soviet Union, and although the Saudis thought that the communist threat was less urgent than Khomeini's ideology,[15] it is possible that the Saudis were not completely sure where things would go in Iran, and therefore they might have hoped they could still somehow manage good relations with Tehran.

---

[13] Sick, *All Fall Down*, 110.

[14] "*Kalimat 'Ukāz*" [Editorial of *Ukaz*], *Ukaz*, February 1, 1979, 1.

[15] As a senior religious Shi'ite figure, Ayatollah Khomeini had followers not only in Iran, but throughout the Persian Gulf, mainly among the Shi'a population. Furthermore, it is likely that the Saudis were concerned about the rapid spread of Khomeini's cassette tapes, which contained his teachings. Since these cassette tapes had spread fast in Iran, the Al Saud might have been concerned that those tapes could also spread into Saudi Arabia. Furthermore, the Saudis might have also been concerned that Khomeini's revolution could spread not only among the Shi'a population of the Eastern Province but also among some of the Saudi Sunnis. For instance, the Egyptian Muslim Brothers had been supportive of Khomeini.

In reference to Fahd's earlier statements, in which he supported the Shah's regime, the Crown Prince's message was clear: the Saudis were deeply concerned about the impact of Iran's unstable situation on their monarchy's survival.[16] However, on January 8, 1979, only two days after Fahd's latest press statements in support for the Shah, *The New York Times* reported (on the basis of a leak) that the Carter Administration had advised the Shah to leave the country temporarily.[17] Then, on January 11, 1979, Secretary of State Vance announced publicly that the Carter Administration endorsed the Shah's decision to leave for exile.[18] Five days later, on January 16, 1979, the Shah and his family left Iran for exile, while on February 1, 1979, two weeks later, Ayatollah Khomeini returned to Iran from his more that 14-year-long exile.

SAUDI REACTIONS AFTER THE SHAH'S FALL

Through various newspaper editorials, which were published in the Saudi Arabian press, the Saudi monarchy conveyed that it was dissatisfied with the American Middle East policy. As the CIA assessed, the Saudi newspapers had been exceptionally critical of US foreign policy following the communist coup d'état in Afghanistan and the revolution in Iran, in 1978 and 1979, respectively. Also, British diplomatic reports revealed that the Saudis believed that the Americans should not have allowed these events in Afghanistan and Iran to take place.[19] The CIA also assessed that an editor-in-chief of a leading Saudi newspaper[20] had unprecedentedly attacked American foreign policy in the Middle East in general and President Carter in particular. The CIA reported that the editor's views were very harsh by Saudi standards, which usually avoid direct attacks on

[16] Unlike Crown Prince Fahd, President Carter had avoided making public statements on Iran; see: "US/Saudi Relations" (report) (restricted telegram), Peter Jay (Ambassador, British Embassy, Washington) to FCO (London), January 16, 1979, *FCO 8/3420.*
[17] Bernard Gwertzman, "Stresses a Trip Would Be Temporary, but Return Is Viewed as Difficult," *The New York Times,* January 9, 1979, 1. However, the American intelligence analysts were concerned that "Iranian military officers were positioning themselves to seize power if Prime Minister Shapur Bakhtiyar fails to form a government friendly to the military establishment." Jim Hoagland, "Prospect of Coup by Iran Military Concerns Experts," *The Washington Post,* January 11, 1979, A1.
[18] "US/Saudi Relations," January 16, 1979.
[19] "US Foreign Policy" (confidential report), John Wilton (Ambassador, British Embassy, Jeddah) to John Leahy (FCO, London), April 21, 1979, no. 22A, *FCO 8/3420.*
[20] The name of the newspaper is not specified.

leaders of friendly countries.[21] Such remarks were a clear indication of how deeply disappointed the Saudis were of President Carter's Middle East policy. Crown Prince Fahd's interview published a few months later (April 1979) repeats the Saudi frustration towards the Americans. Fahd said that "power vacuums, especially in the world's most strategic area, are always dangerous [...] There is no need for the US to respond so egocentrically to every movement. [...] We must respond in unison [to Middle East security]."[22] In other words, Fahd wanted to convey that Shah's removal, on the one hand, and President Carter's ineffectiveness in his Iran policy, on the other hand, were the primary reasons, which enabled the religious, anti-Saudi, anti-American regime taking over in Tehran.[23]

When the Shah was still in Iran, Kamal Adham[24] had told that Saudi Arabia was in no position to do anything but wait and see what would happen in Iran.[25] Nevertheless, it seemed obvious that Carter's decision to let the Shah to leave Iran was not only a shock but also a great embarrassment to Saudi Arabia. Furthermore, it was a slap in the face of Deputy Prime Minister Fahd, who had declared his public support for the Shah just days earlier. According to the CIA, the Saudis were "bitterly unhappy" over what they saw as a "very inadequate US response to the Iranian

[21] "The Impact of Iran on Saudi Arabia: Security Concerns and Internal Reaction" (secret report), CIA, January 26, 1979, no. 181, *FRUS, vol.* XXXVIII, *Middle East Region; Arabian Peninsula*, 591.

[22] Arnaud de Borchgrave, "The Saudis Play their Hand," *Newsweek*, April 7, 1979, 37.

[23] In addition to Carter's Iran policy, there were several other instances, which contributed to the impression that President Carter's foreign policy was ineffective and indecisive. Perhaps one of Carter's most significant failures was his inability to free the hostages taken from the US Embassy in Tehran (November 1979). As the hostage crisis prolonged, the American public grew impatient with the ostensibly indecisive president who could not win the hostages' release. Another example of Carter's weak policies was related to the Soviet invasion of Afghanistan (December 1979). In retaliation to the Soviet invasion, Carter cut off grain sales to the Soviet Union and issued a boycott of the 1980 Moscow Summer Olympics by the US athletes. Robert A. Strong has argued that "because much of the public considered this to be more punitive towards American swimmers and runners than Soviet leaders, Carter's response only reinforced his weak image." Robert A. Strong, "Jimmy Carter: Foreign Affairs," Miller Center, University of Virginia. https://millercenter.org/president/carter/foreign-affairs. Accessed April 22, 2020.

[24] At the time, Adham still served as the head of the General Intelligence Directorate.

[25] Kamal Adham had had a discussion with the British diplomats in Jeddah on January 10, 1979. "Saudi Arabia/Iran" (confidential report), Tim P. Hollaway (British Embassy, Jeddah) to Anthony Layden (MED, FCO, London), January 23, 1979, no. 2A, *FCO 8/3421.*

156   S. E. WILLNER

crisis."[26] In other words, the Saudis were very critical of Carter Administration's undesirability to help the Shah to remain in power. There are several examples of such sentiments. For instance, on January 15, 1979, the Saudi deputy foreign minister for economic affairs[27] spoke critically of the American action in "pulling the rug from under their friends"[28] in the matter of support for Iran. The Saudis were concerned that the downfall of the Shah's monarchy, and a successful republic in Iran, could become an inspiration for revolutionaries in other Gulf countries.[29]

As reported by John Wilton, the British ambassador to Saudi Arabia (1976–1979), privately the Saudis were also critical of what it saw as American "ditching" of Taiwan.[30] These remarks were made in reference to United States' decision to move its diplomatic recognition from Taipei (Taiwan) to Beijing in January 1979 and establish diplomatic relations with the communist People's Republic of China in March 1979. What makes the "ditching of Taiwan" truly relevant to the Saudis is because the event coincided with the US decision to withdraw support from the Shah. Furthermore, what seemed to have worried the Saudis was the geopolitical implications of such a decision. Although Saudi Arabia's official position, at the time, in relation to Taiwan, is unknown, the Saudis might have contemplated that the improved US diplomatic relations with China were made at the expense of Taiwan.[31] The Saudis had told Wilton that they

---

[26] "The Impact of Iran on Saudi Arabia," 588–589.

[27] The report only mentions his first name Abd Allah.

[28] "Saudi/American Relations" (confidential telegram), Wilton to FCO (London), January 16, 1979, no. 4, FCO 8/3420.

[29] It is possible that Carter had naively envisioned that the demonstrations could bring an end to the Shah's undemocratic monarchy, and, instead, establish a democratic republic. However, the reality turned different, and the authoritarian and theocratic republic of Ayatollah Khomeini emerged. Furthermore, there exists a belief that the United States enabled the Shah's fall as a revenge for the Shah's quadrupling of oil prices (1973–1974) and for his growing involvement in world politics to the level of criticizing the world's main leaders and countries quite harshly. As such, it is possible that the United States might have hinted the Saudis that if they would join another oil embargo against the US interests, then the case of the Shah should be a warning to it. Although it is difficult to contribute this kind of conspiratorial theory to Carter Administration, it could have well fitted into the period of Nixon Administration (and to the mindset of Henry Kissinger). Nevertheless, no evidence exists that could help to elaborate such conspiratorial theories.

[30] "US Foreign Policy," April 21, 1979.

[31] Furthermore, it is useful to note that the People's Republic of China has claimed sovereignty over Taiwan ever since its communist revolution in 1949 (especially because the overthrown government had exiled to Taiwan).

"wondered who might be ditched next and, indeed, whether they might not themselves be ditched at some stage in order to satisfy some purely American need."[32] These Saudi remarks raise the 'ineffectiveness' and 'indecisiveness' issue of Carter's foreign policy. While the Saudis had accused that Carter's foreign policy was harming the interests (and the survival) of the US allies, the US Republicans, in turn, argued that Carter was undermining the US strategic interests, for instance in Panama and Iran.[33] Based on his discussions with some of the Saudi royals, Ambassador Wilton argued that the American unwillingness to help the Shah may even have led the royal family to ask whether the time might come for the Saudi monarchy to leave for exile too.[34]

Although the Islamic Revolution had increased the regional instability, and although the Saudis had been worried about Khomeini's ideology, it is possible that the Saudis had exaggerated the Iranian threat because they wanted the Americans (and the Europeans) to pay more attention to the Saudi needs. Most importantly, the Saudis wanted the Western powers to understand that the Saudi monarchy's overthrow would lead to disruptions in Saudi oil production (as had happened in Iran a few months earlier), which, in turn, would have catastrophic effects on the world economy. However, as Wilton put it, there was a lack of clarity regarding what the Saudis wanted the Americans to do. He added that "if challenged on this, the Saudis evade the question by saying that it is not for them to tell a superpower how to conduct its relations."[35] The CIA drew similar conclusions.[36] Interestingly, such logic of operation was much in line with the Saudi way of conveying messages to foreign governments. Usually, the Saudis would first present the less-concerning issues, perhaps even overemphasizing their importance, and only in the sidelines would they present the most important issues. By acting this way, the Saudis wanted to avoid showing sign of weakness. When the Saudis wanted to make a point, they often tended to show concern for other nations' problems, while indicating that they were worried about the survival of their monarchy.

---

[32] "US Foreign Policy," April 21, 1979.

[33] Strong, "Jimmy Carter: Foreign Affairs."

[34] "Saudi Arabia: Annual Review for 1978" (confidential report), Wilton to Secretary of State for Foreign and Commonwealth Affairs (FCO, London), January 15, 1979, no. 1, FCO 8/3416.

[35] "US Foreign Policy," April 21, 1979.

[36] "The Impact of Iran on Saudi Arabia: Security Concerns and Internal Reaction," 588–589.

158   S. E. WILLNER

In conclusion, due to Carter's foreign policy focus, which culminated in his lack of responding resolutely to the crisis in Iran, the Saudis had realized that there was very little the United States could have done to save the Shah's monarchy. As such, the Saudis most likely understood that Carter could not send the US Navy to help the Shah. Instead, the Saudis could have suggested Carter to allow the Shah to use heavy firepower against the revolutionaries. However, the royal family probably were unwilling to suggest such an action because saying so would not have helped them and because saying so would not have been 'nice' according to of Carter's human rights-focused foreign policy. In terms of the Unites States' policy towards Saudi Arabia, Ambassador Wilton iterated that "the Americans manage the Saudis badly. They too often take their support for granted and lose patience when the Saudis are not prepared to ignore their other interests and fall into line behind the Americans."[37] In other words, the Saudis had concluded that President Carter expected Saudi Arabia to stabilize the oil markets without seriously responding to their strategic interests.

PROTESTING CARTER'S POLICIES

"He who ignores you, hates you" [*illī biyijhalak biyikrahak*], declares an ancient Bedouin proverb as recorded by Bailey.[38] After the Saudis had multiple times articulated their dissatisfaction towards Carter's Middle East policy, the Americans were reported to have concluded that they needed to improve their relations with the Saudi monarchy.[39] As part of this American conclusion, the Carter Administration had extended an invitation to Crown Prince Fahd to visit Washington. Secretary of State Cyrus Vance communicated that the White House regarded Fahd's visit to Washington as an important point in relations between the two countries. Vance described the planned visit as "a time for extensive consultations on the range of major issues, which impact upon our common interests."[40]

---

[37] "US Foreign Policy," April 21, 1979.

[38] Bailey, *A Culture of Desert Survival*, 187.

[39] See for instance: Jim Hoagland, "U.S. Moving to Repair Saudi Ties," *The Washington Post*, June 12, 1979, A1.

[40] "Meeting with Crown Prince Fahd: Oil Matters" (confidential letter), Cyrus Vance (US Secretary of State, Washington) to John West (Ambassador, US Embassy, Jeddah), February 9, 1979, no. 188, *FRUS*, vol. XXXVII, *Energy Crisis*, 601–602.

The Americans had tried to get Fahd to Washington ever since Camp David accords were signed on September 17, 1978, but Fahd had "put them off with one excuse after another."[41] Fahd might have thought that a public visit to the United States would have put Saudi Arabia too much into the spotlights as he was already being accused of being an agent of the West by the radical Arabs.[42] It is also possible that Fahd's earlier unwillingness to meet President Carter in Washington was because he had become disappointed in Carter's foreign policy soon after he had entered the White House in January 1977. However, when the meeting was finally set to take place in March 1979, the Saudis decided to cancel Fahd's visit.

Officially, the Saudis told at first that the cancellation of the trip was due to Fahd's health problems.[43] However, David Tatham, a staff member at the FCO Middle East Department, assessed that "we know that Fahd decided not to go to Washington for political reasons and his 'medical treatment' was therefore diplomatic."[44] In addition to Tatham's assessment, US intelligence reports suggested that there was new fragility and unsteadiness within the Saudi royal family.[45] In fact, it was also rumored that Fahd was in hiding and perhaps in disfavor with King Khalid and other senior princes.[46] Furthermore, according to Jim Hoagland of *The Washington Post*, the American analysts had been observing suggestions of serious splits between Fahd and the rest of the royal family over Saudi policy towards the United States and the Arab world since November 1977 when President Anwar al-Sadat of Egypt made his historic trip to Jerusalem.[47] However, several senior Saudi officials denied any rumors of

---

[41] "Crown Prince Fahd" (confidential telegram), Wilton to MED (FCO, London), February 27, 1979, no. 17B, *FCO 8/3420*.

[42] Abir, *Saudi Arabia: Government, Society*, 75.

[43] For instance, Jim Hoagland wrote that "the Saudis indicated the visit [...] was canceled for political reasons, while the White House insisted that Fahd was ill; see Jim Hoagland, "U.S. Gives Saudi Leaders Reassurances of Support," *The Washington Post*, April 27, 1979, A2.

[44] "Prince Fahd" (confidential report), David Tatham (MED, FCO, London) to Alan Munro (FCO, London), February 27, 1979, no. 19, *FCO 8/3420*.

[45] Jim Hoagland, "US Uneasy that Saudi Crown Prince's Power is Slipping," *The Guardian*, April 17, 1979, *FCO 8/3414*.

[46] Hoagland, "US Uneasy that Saudi Crown Prince's Power is Slipping."

[47] Ibid.

160   S. E. WILLNER

disagreements within the royal family.[48] It is also possible that the rumors of disagreements might have been purposefully disseminated by the Saudis in order to provide the royal family more leeway in its decision-making. In other words, the royal family might have been contemplating whether to side with Iraq in condemning the Egypt-Israel Peace Agreement that was signed in March 1979.

Nonetheless, the Saudis seemed to have realized quite quickly that these stories of sick Fahd—even if the sickness was only a diplomatic bout of flu—portrayed an image of a weak monarchy. An ailing leader was certainly not a strong leader. Indeed, the American diplomatic reports suggested that Fahd's health condition was not good. According to Gary Sick, Crown Prince Fahd was a diabetic. His report contemplated that "we have had considerable evidence recently that his condition is worsening. He has gained weight and appears puffy and unhealthy. [...] His concentration is said to be poor, and he is meeting with very few people, in contrast with his rather vigorous schedule of a year ago."[49] It is useful to note here that Sick's report was prepared more than two decades before Fahd died.

Returning to Fahd's cancelled visit to the United States, Richard Muir reported that the Saudi Embassy in Washington, on instructions from "high officials" in Riyadh, "very quickly told American reporters that Fahd was in perfect health."[50] Instead, they said that Fahd's visit had been "postponed through mutual agreement" in order to "provide [the] time needed for a comprehensive study of the issues of mutual concern."[51] David Tatham wrote in response to Muir's telegram that Fahd "[tended]

[48] For instance, Prince Abd Allah told the *Gulf Press Agency* on April 23, 1979, that he utterly denies such rumors. ("Saudi Arabia," *MEES*, April 30, 1979, 1–5) Similarly, in an interview published in the London newspaper *Asharq Al-Awsat*, 'Abdū Yamani, the Saudi Minister of Information (1975–1982), reiterated, that "we attach no importance to such matters." "Interview Granted by Saudi Minister of Information Dr. Muhammad Abdu Yamani to Abd Allah Jafari in Jeddah," *Asharq Al-Awsat*, August 6, 1979, 3, 7; "Minister Discusses Threats to Oil Fields, Energy Issues," *FBIS*, August 10, 1979, C4-C6.

[49] "Cracks in Saudi Façade" (secret report), Gary Sick (Member, US National Security Council Staff for MENA) to Zbigniew Brzezinski (President's National Security Advisor, Washington), December 22, 1978, no. 175, *FRUS*, vol. XXVIII, *Middle East Region; Arabian Peninsula*, 560.

[50] "Prince Fahd's Visit to the US" (confidential telegram), Richard J.S. Muir (Staff Member, British Embassy, Washington) to David C. Beaumont (Staff Member, MED, FCO, London), February 27, 1979, no. 18, *FCO 8/3420.*

[51] Ibid.

11 THE 1978-1979 ISLAMIC REVOLUTION IN IRAN **161**

to shun straight answers and to give everyone he meets the impression that he agrees with them. Now he has strong reasons for flannelling[52] with the Americans."[53] Nonetheless, in conclusion one could say that Fahd's decision not to travel to the United States in March 1979 was continuation of Saudi logic of operation. It was a strong but indirect way of conveying that the Saudis were disappointed in President Carter's foreign policy. As will be revealed next, the situation only got worse from the Saudi perspective.

THE REPERCUSSIONS OF THE YEMENITE WAR (FEBRUARY– MARCH 1979)

At the end of February 1979, coinciding less than one month since Ayatollah Khomeini's arrival to Iran following the victory of the Islamic Revolution, serious border fighting broke out on Saudi Arabia's southern flank between its two rival neighboring states, South Yemen (PDRY) and North Yemen (YAR).[54] The three-week long conflict between the two Yemens was a consequence of two coup d'états that had shaken the governments in each state earlier in 1978. These violent developments in Yemen were continuation to perennial political instability, which first escalated into small-scale border skirmishes, and then led to a full-scale war. Although the revolution in Iran and the war in Yemen were not directly connected to one another, the Saudis seemed to have concluded that the war in Yemen might spill "beyond the limits of the Arab nation," and, as such, the security situation along its borders was becoming intolerable.[55] On February 28, 1979, the royal family communicated that it was "gravely concerned" by the fighting in the Yemen, while at the same time it even

[52] 'Flannelling' refers to "meaningless talk intended to hide one's ignorance or true intentions." Robert Allen, ed., *Chambers Encyclopedic English Dictionary*, Edinburgh: Chambers, 1994, 468.

[53] "Prince Fahd" (confidential report), Tatham to Munro, February 27, 1979, no. 19, *FCO 8/3420*.

[54] Saudi Arabia and its allies—including the United States, Jordan, Iraq, and Egypt—supported the YAR while the PDRY was supported by the Soviet Union, Libya, and Syria.

[55] Don Oberdorfer and Thomas W. Lippman, "Yemeni Border War Prompts U.S. to Speed Weapon Deliveries," *The Washington Post*, March 1, 1979, A14.

162   S. E. WILLNER

decided to mobilize its military and concentrate its forces on the border region of Asir near Yemen.[56]

In addition to mobilizing its military forces, the Saudis had secretly requested King Husayn of Jordan to place his military on stand-by to be ready to assist the Saudi armed forces had the conflict uncontrollably spread into Saudi Arabia and had the kingdom been unable to contain the situation. Based on information obtained by the British Embassy in Washington, the Jordanians responded positively to the Saudi request and informed the Americans, "primarily with a view to securing American assistance with any large scale transport of troops and equipment, which might be required if they were to fulfill this commitment."[57] According to the British, however, "the Saudis back-pedaled fast" after the conflict was over at the end of March 1979.[58] Such a response could indicate that the Saudis had felt that a substantial foreign military presence in the kingdom could pose a serious threat to its territorial integrity and undermine its regime. Furthermore, the Saudis might have considered that once a foreign military had entered and settled in the kingdom, it would have been difficult to get rid of it. This had happened with the Iranian commando forces in Oman, who had overstayed several years after they had successfully assisted Sultan Qabus' army to beat the communist-backed rebel forces in Dhofar.[59]

While talking to the Jordanians for possible military assistance, the Saudis seem to have requested the Americans for a show of force. In response, President Carter ordered aircraft carrier Constellation into the Arabian Sea to show support for Saudi Arabia, and to warn the Soviets of the risks involved in their backing of the incursion in Yemen. However, according to *The New York Times*, officials in Carter Administration had said that "Saudi Arabia had not specifically requested a carrier but that [… the Saudis] had asked for a show of American concern over the conflict in

---

[56] Christopher S. Wren, "Saudis Alert Their Army in Response to Yemeni War," *The New York Times*, March 1, 1979, 3.

[57] "US/Jordan/Saudi Arabia" (secret report), Adrian Fortescue (British Embassy, Washington) to Roger Tomkys (Head, Near East and North Africa Department, FCO, London), February 12, 1980, *FCO 8/3745*.

[58] Ibid.

[59] Jordanian commando forces had also been present in Oman, and they left after the insurrection was put down.

Yemen."[60] Perhaps the most significant contribution that the Saudis made in assisting the YAR forces was their decision to subsidize the American emergency infusion of arms. While President Carter announced (March 7, 1979) his decision to sell YAR $390 million worth of arms, it was estimated that the Saudis had paid up to $200 million of this sum.[61]

Although it has been claimed that the Carter Administration had "seized on the Yemen fighting to prove its determination to protect the Saudis,"[62] and although the conflict did not end up spreading into Saudi Arabia, the facts on the ground seem to point out that the US actions did not impress the Saudis of Carter Administration's willingness and ability to safeguard the Saudi regime. Quite the contrary, Carter's reputation was further tarnished in the Saudi eyes. Perhaps one of the most embarrassing failures in the conflict occurred when a top-secret paramilitary operation against PDRY—that was set up by the CIA following a request by National Security Advisor Brzezinski—had utterly failed while ending tragically with capture and confession of the CIA-sponsored operatives.[63] Although it is quite likely that the news of the operation's failure eventually reached Riyadh, there is no direct evidence that would indicate how the Saudis reacted to this unsuccessful operation. However, based on the earlier reports, the Saudis must have been very frustrated about the situation.

[60] Richard Burt, "U.S. Sends Ships to Arabian Sea in Yemen Crisis," *The New York Times*, March 7, 1979, 1.

[61] Yodfat, *The Soviet Union and the Arabian Peninsula*, 106–107; Steven V. Roberts, Stephen Engelberg and Jeff Gerth, "Prop for U.S. Policy: Secret Saudi Funds," *The New York Times*, June 21, 1987, 1; Arthur Schlesinger Jr., "Arms for Yemen. Qualms for Us," *The New York Times*, April 9, 1979, 19.

[62] Jonathan C. Randal, "The Yemens: A Legacy of Hostility and Division," *The Washington Post*, March 28, 1979, A25.

[63] The details of the failed CIA operation were leaked to the press more than six years after the events had occurred. Bob Woodward, "Carlucci Launched CIA Operation in Yemen That Collapsed," *The Washington Post*, December 4, 1986, A1.

CHAPTER 12

Inspired by the Islamic Revolution: Rebellions, Uprisings, and Coup Attempts

The Ramifications of the Alleged Military Coup (August 1979)

Since the emergence of pan-Arab ideology in the 1950s, and especially after Muammar Qadhafi's rise to power in Libya (September 1969), there had been frequent sabotage activity against the Saudi kingdom. In addition, the Saudis had foiled several coup attempts against the monarchy. As I have discussed previously, prior to mid-1970s, also Iraq had sponsored socialist Ba'ath revolutionary activity against the Saudi monarchy. Perhaps more often, it had threatened to use subversive forces against Saudi Arabia, especially when the two states had had disagreements over oil policy. However, following the Shah's fall, the government in Baghdad changed its focus to dealing with a new threat, which it shared with the Saudis, and which had surfaced in Iran [1]

In terms of Libyan foreign policy, one can always hypothesize about what was going on in Muammar Qadhafi's somewhat 'enigmatic' mindset when he decided to back various radical-Arab guerrilla groups, such as

---

[1] Whatever was the Iraqi Ba'athi ideological way of explaining its nonrevolutionary foreign policy before Khomeini's rise to power, however, since April 1979, important Iraqi sources explained it in terms of political pragmatism and Arab anti-Persian solidarity. Amatzia Baram, "Qawmiyya and Wataniyya in Ba'thi Iraq: The Search for a New Balance", *Middle Eastern Studies*, 19, 2, April 1983, 195, 200. Based on Baghdad's *Al-Thawra, al-Jumhuriyya*, July 18, 1975.

© The Author(s), under exclusive license to Springer Nature Switzerland AG 2023
S. E. Willner, *Preserving the Saudi Monarchy*, https://doi.org/10.1007/978-3-031-30006-6_12

165

the Black September Organization [*Munazzamat Aylūl al-Aswad*], to attack Saudi Arabia.[2] It appears that Qadhafi was a generous supporter of the anti-Saudi militant groups that targeted the kingdom. Nevertheless, the royal family was convinced that Carter's weak foreign policy in the Middle East (especially after the Shah's fall) had inspired and increased such activities. One of these alleged and very little-known Qadhafi-sponsored attempts to overthrow the Saudi royal family took place in the beginning of August 1979. Unfortunately, it is not known how many people had participated in the coup attempt or whether there had been foreigners involved, but that most of the conspirers had been members of the Saudi military forces, and that it had been planned by the Libyan intelligence.[3]

Interestingly, as it was reported, the main perpetrators of the coup attempt managed to flee to Tripoli (Libya) while several the conspirators were arrested by the Saudi authorities. Some of the latter had revealed that the purpose of the coup was 'for the country' and that it was "high time for the country to be ruled by the young and educated, rather than by people who were old and illiterate."[4] Those arrested also stated that they objected to the extensive American presence in the Saudi armed forces.[5] This comment was probably made in reference to the relatively extensive US training and advisory mission that was stationed in the kingdom, and whose task was to modernize the Saudi military and the National Guard. These developments and statements are quite like the events and claims of some of the revolutionaries in Iran. Although the coup seems to have been sponsored by Libya, it is possible that the Iranian revolution had affected, and even formed a model for the conspirators in Saudi Arabia.

According to an anonymous intelligence source, the Saudis had been able to prevent the above-mentioned coup attempt because Prince Turki al-Faysal, the Director of General Intelligence (1979–2001) had received information about the attempt from an "outside source," revealed to be a member of the Egyptian intelligence. It appears that the information

---

[2] There is no documentation available that could indicate which radical-Arab groups the Libyans had sponsored to attack the Saudis. However, in March 1973, the Libyans ordered the Palestinian Black September Organization, which was the secret arm of *Al-Fatah*, to attack the Saudi Embassy in Khartoum.

[3] "Khalid Flees August Coup D'état."

[4] Ibid.

[5] Ibid.

12 INSPIRED BY THE ISLAMIC REVOLUTION: REBELLIONS, UPRISINGS... 167

provided to the Saudis took the royal family by almost complete surprise as the authorities had no clue about the "extent and of the imminence of the coup." According to the news report in the *Afro-Asian Affairs*, the monarchy had survived the coup attempt "only by sheer luck."[6]

Following the press reports of the above-mentioned coup attempt, the Foreign Office (FCO) began to assess the validity of such information. The Foreign Office was convinced that such rumors about a coup in Saudi Arabia were untrue or "at least [there was] a fair degree of journalistic exaggeration in the report."[7] One of the arguments why the British rejected the report in *Afro-Asian Affairs* was because it was edited by Jon Kimche, a journalist and historian, who was known to be friendly toward Israel. Moreover, Jon Kimche's younger brother, David Kimche served as the Deputy Director of Mossad (unknown–1979), Israel's secret intelligence agency. However, it is unlikely that the Israeli intelligence would have been behind the report. Instead, it could be that the CIA had leaked the information to Jon Kimche knowing that he would publish it, and possibly also making it look as if Israel had been behind it.

In response to an inquiry from H.M. Treasury regarding the claims that mutiny had taken place in two airbases, David Hannay, an official at the Foreign Office, wrote that several the names in the report were quite wrong and there were no airbases at Sharqa or at Kharj. Instead, there was a runway in Kharj for emergency landings by aircraft from the King Faysal's Academy. Furthermore, Hannay wrote that "we would have heard from our RAF Advisory Team or from the British Military Mission to the [Saudi] National Guard if any of these alleged events had taken place."[8] In response to a claim that the fighter jets controlled by the perpetrators of this failed military coup had managed to bomb and damage some of the Saudi royal palaces, the British Defense Attaché in Jeddah commented that "all palaces are believed to still be intact."[9] In turn, Robin D. Lamb,

---

[6] "Khalid Flees August Coup D'état."

[7] "Saudi Internal" (restricted telegram), Tatham to Robin Lamb (Staff Member, British Embassy, Jeddah), November 1, 1979, no. 37, *FCO 8/3414.*

[8] "Stability in the Middle East" (restricted letter), Hannay to David Peretz (H.M. Treasury, London), November 12, 1979, no. 40, *FCO 8/3414.*

[9] "Dollar Crisis" (confidential telegram), M.P. de Klee (Colonel, Defense Attaché, British Embassy, Jeddah) to Christopher Segar (MED, FCO, London), December 17, 1979, no. 48, *FCO 8/3414.*

168 S. E. WILLNER

a British diplomat stationed in Jeddah assessed that "we have no trace of any of the names quoted in the report."[10]

Although the British foreign officials had dismissed the rumors of the alleged August 1979 coup attempt, the press reports of Saudis purchasing $3.2 billion worth of gold between mid-July 1979 and September 1979 could indicate that these gold purchases had been triggered, at least partly, by the supposed coup attempt.[11] In addition, less than a week after the failed coup attempt, Abdu Yamani, the Saudi Minister of Information (1975–1982), responded to the rumors of serious royal family disagreements, which had been circulating in the press.[12] According to an interview that was published on August 6, 1979, and in reference to earlier statements made by senior members of the royal family, Abdu Yamani stated that "those who spread such tendentious reports have no idea of the structure of the Saudi family. … There was not one single incident that warranted such rumors and reports."[13] Whether or not his remarks were made in response to the alleged coup attempt, it is quite possible that the royal family had requested Abdu Yamani to give a statement concerning rumors, which claimed that the Saudi royal family was unstable and may even be on the verge of collapse.

Several important questions remain unanswered, some which are related to the above-mentioned inaccuracies. Most significantly, why would such a report, which otherwise seems credible, be published with such simple mistakes (e.g., the locations of Saudi Air Force bases in places that do not have such bases) that could have easily been checked and corrected had the report not been authentic as the FCO suggests? It is quite likely that the 'wrong names', as Lamb indicated, were cryptonyms for actual military bases or persons, and that they had been established to protect the original intelligence gathering method or the source, which had provided the information. Furthermore, it is also possible that the information about the coup attempt was released by the CIA with the aim to convey a message to President Carter saying that Saudi Arabia was seriously vulnerable to revolutionary threat. If such assessment is accurate, it

[10] "Following for D.E. Tatham" (confidential telegram), Robin D. Lamb (British Embassy, Jeddah) to David Tatham (MED, FCO, London), November 7, 1979, no. 39, *FCO 8/3414*.

[11] "Khalid Flees August Coup D'état," 4.

[12] It is unknown which press report Abdu Yamani was referring.

[13] Abdu Yamani's interview was published in the London newspaper *Asharq Al-Awsat*, on August 6, 1979, on pages 3 and 7: "Minister Discusses Threats to Oil Fields, Energy Issues," *FBIS*, August 10, 1979, C4-C6.

12 INSPIRED BY THE ISLAMIC REVOLUTION: REBELLIONS, UPRISINGS... **169**

could further confirm that Carter had repeatedly neglected CIA's warnings about the Saudi vulnerability. In addition, it could confirm that Carter had dismissed CIA's advice that the President should show more support for the Saudis. I will return to this subject in the following chapters. However, it appears that the CIA had repeatedly used the press to convey messages to President Carter.

Finally, in conclusion to the described plot, one could say that perhaps what is more important is not necessarily the details of this purported coup attempt itself, but rather the indication that the Saudis were very worried about the implications of the revolution in Iran.

The Mecca Rebellion (November 1979)

The seizure of the Grand Mosque—Islam's holiest shrine—in Mecca was both a dramatic and tragic event. In the early morning hours of November 20, 1979, a band of organized and seemingly well-trained armed men stormed the mosque compound and quickly seized it. After the attackers had gained control of the compound, they declared one of their leaders, Muhammad ibn Abd Allah al-Qahtani, as the *mahdi*[14] (the guided one). The event came to be known as the 'Mecca rebellion' and was at first mistakenly attributed as having been a result of "a radicalizing influence" of the Islamic Revolution in Iran. It was even claimed that the attack had been part of a "people's revolution" aimed at establishing a republic in Saudi Arabia.[15] However, it is important to note that the attackers were not led by the Shi'a, but rather the entire incident was organized by Sunni zealots to undermine the Saudi rule. Moreover, the rebels were Sunni Islamists who subscribed to Salafi doctrines. The seizure had been a major operation and it took several weeks for the insurgents to prepare for purchasing and smuggling all the weapons, ammunition, and other supplies to the mosque compound. After two weeks of fighting, which resulted in

---

[14] The root of the word *mahdi* derives from the word *mahhada*, which means: to facilitate; to make ready; to prepare the way. *Mahdi* is an eschatological redeemer of Islam before the Day of Judgment or the Day of the Resurrection [*yawm al-qiyāmah*].

[15] Thomas Hegghammer and Stephane Lacroix quoted Nasir al-Said, the historic leader of the Arabian Peninsula People's Union, which was a Nasserist underground political party in Saudi Arabia: Thomas Hegghammer and Stephane Lacroix, *The Meccan Rebellion: The Story of Juhayman Al- Utaibi Revisited*, Bristol: Amal Press, 2011, 23–24.

170 S. E. WILLNER

heavy casualties, the mosque seizure ended.[16] Following the incident, several strange details began to emerge about the possibility that the Saudi authorities might have had prior knowledge of the attackers' plans to take over the mosque compound.

After the violent takeover of the mosque, several rumors began circulating among diplomats and foreign journalists in reference to who was behind the attack and what could have been the attackers' motive. Some of these stories mistakenly went to say that Iranians had been behind the attack,[17] while Shaikh Rumaih,[18] the Saudi Ambassador to Abu Dhabi, claimed that the attackers had been "a mixture of the *al-Khawarij* and other religious lunatics."[19] By making such a statement, Shaikh Rumaih wanted to point out that the attackers had been Muslim extremists fighting for religious purity. Moreover, Hegghammer and Lacroix, who have extensively analyzed this event, conclude that "the Mecca rebellion was the work of an apocalyptic, charismatic sect with a very peculiar ideology" and that the leaders of the rebel group genuinely believed that Al-Qahtani was the *mahdi*.[20]

The Mecca rebellion was organized by Juhayman al-Utaibi, who led an offshoot *ikhwān* (brotherhood) group of a less radical Salafi organization

---

[16] The use of force and fighting inside the mosque was one of the main issues that prolonged taking down the attackers. However, in the final show of force, the Saudi security units, together with Pakistani and French commandos, stormed the premises of the Grand Mosque, crushing the insurgents and taking control of the compound. In reference to the allegations that French commandos had been assisting the Saudis to overpower the rebels, Saud al-Faysal told *Der Spiegel* that "it is absolutely untrue." "*Der Spiegel* Interviews Saudi Foreign Minister," *FBIS*, April 17, 1980, C5.

[17] Philip Taubman, "Mecca Mosque Seized by Gunmen Believed to Be Militants from Iran," *The New York Times*, November 21, 1979, A1.

[18] Shaikh Rumaih's first name is not known.

[19] *Al-Khawarij* (the dissidents, the rebels) is the oldest religious sect of Islam. Its roots are in the first century of Islam. The origin of the school of thought of *al-Khawarij* lies in the struggle for political supremacy over the Muslim community in the years following the death of Prophet Muhammad in 632 AD. "Kharijite," *Encyclopaedia Britannica- online version*, www.britannica.com/topic/Kharijite, accessed June 20, 2018. Shaykh Rumaih's remarks were recorded in: "Mecca Incident" (confidential telegram), David Roberts (Ambassador, British Embassy, Abu Dhabi) to FCO, London, January 14, 1980, no. 7, *FCO 8/3734.*

[20] Hegghammer and Lacroix, *The Meccan Rebellion*, x.

called *Al-Jama'a Al-Salafiyah Al-Muhtasibah*.[21] Before joining the Salafi organization (and later splintering to his own brotherhood group), Juhayman had served in the Saudi National Guard. Hegghammer and Lacroix write that Juhayman was a charismatic leader and his *ikhwān* group had "the many traits of a personality cult." Furthermore, most of the members in Juhaiman's brotherhood were young unmarried men, who came from politically and economically marginalized or discriminated backgrounds. Many of the members were young and recently urbanized *badawī* men. In addition, Juhayman's *ikhwān* had members from foreign origin, mostly from Yemen. In terms of funding, Hegghammer and Lacroix indicate that Juhayman's activities, such as the weapons purchases, were financed by wealthier members of his group.[22]

Interestingly, however, several weeks after the incident, Deputy Prime Minister Fahd said in an interview that Juhayman al-Utaibi, the militant leader behind the seizure, "was exploited by other people, who perhaps have not been discovered. They might be in Kuwait or in any other place."[23] Fahd's remarks seem quite cryptic as it was quite clear that the leaders of the rebellion had been Saudi citizens. However, it is possible that Fahd wanted, without mentioning anyone specifically, to put the blame either on the Iranians, the Soviets, or the Palestinians.

According to Robert Moss of *The New York Times*, anonymous Western intelligence sources had disclosed that several the attackers had been trained by Cuban and East German instructors in South Yemen. The source added that the Popular Front for the Liberation of Palestine [*Al-Jabhah al-Sha'biyah li-Tahrīr al-Filastīn*]—a Marxist (but also a pan-Arabist) guerrilla organization—had also used the same training camps to train its own recruits.[24] Such remarks raise the question whether Marxist

---

[21] *Al-Jama'a al-Salafiyah al-Muhtasibah* was a revivalist Sunni movement in Saudi Arabia that was formed in mid-1960s. The movement was driven by a general conviction that "mainstream school and tendencies in the Muslim world at the time needed to be purified of innovations and misperception." Hegghammer and Lacroix, *The Meccan Rebellion*, 7.

[22] Hegghammer and Lacroix, *The Meccan Rebellion*, 13, 19; see also: "Saudi Arabia Internal" (confidential telegram), Craig to FCO, London, January 2, 1980, no. 1, *FCO 8/3734.*

[23] *"Hiwār shāmil baina as-Safir wa-al-'amīr Fahd"* [Comprehensive Discussion between *As-Safir* and Amir Fahd], *As-Safir*, January 9, 1980, 1, 8–10; "The Mecca Incident" (confidential telegram), J.W.D. Grey (British Embassy, Jeddah) to Tatham, January 19, 1980, no. 5, *FCO 8/3734.*

[24] Moss, "Terror: A Soviet Export."

172   S. E. WILLNER

elements had infiltrated Juhayman al-Utaibi's brotherhood group. If this is true, it could explain why the group had been relatively well-trained.

In February 1980, some two months after the Mecca rebellion, Kamal Adham said, in a private conversation with the British diplomats in Jeddah, that the radical Arabs and Iranians might use the religious extremists—who according to him were often "simple men of little education"—as a "cover" in their operations against the Saudi monarchy. According to his view, and in a possible reference to the perceived Soviet threat, he said that the "Marxists radicals" were manipulating these "simple men" into extremist activity by providing them with training and by "[helping] them to get organized by introducing them Marxist techniques."[25] Such a statement seemed to be in line with other Saudi concerns, according to which the Soviets were sponsoring Pakistani Baluchis to study at the Patrice Lumumba University in Moscow in order to turn them into Soviet agents.[26] That university was founded in 1960 with its official purpose being to help developing nations. However, the university seems to have been a focal point in providing a center for the recruitment of intelligence agents and saboteurs for the Soviets from third-world countries.[27] Nonetheless, it seems highly unlikely that the Soviets had been behind the Mecca rebellion. In fact, several studies, which have been published since the rebellion, agree that Juhayman al-Utaibi acted according to his own plans.[28] However, perhaps a more important question is not who perpetrated the attack, but rather, if the Saudis had prior knowledge of the attacks, and if they did, then why did they allow the Mecca rebellion to take place?

According to King Husayn of Jordan, Saudi Arabian security authorities had known about the intention to occupy the Grand Mosque in Mecca

---

[25] "Call on Shaikh Kamal Adham" (confidential report), Craig to FCO, London, February 21, 1980, no. 23, *FCO 8/3734.*

[26] Baluchistan is a province in southwest Pakistan, which has attempted on numerous occasions to gain autonomy from Pakistan and from Iran. In a speech delivered at the King Abd al-Aziz University in Jeddah on April 16, 1980, Ahmad Zaki Yamani stated that large numbers of Baluchi students were studying in Patrice Lumumba University in Moscow. According to Yamani, the Saudis suspected that the Baluchis were studying in Moscow to encourage Baluchi nationalism so that the Baluchis would start demanding autonomy from Pakistan and Iran. "If Baluchistan became independent, it would fall like an apple into Brezhnev's hands," said Yamani. "The Impact of Oil in International Politics," *MEES*, May 5, 1980, 4.

[27] Moss, "Terror: A Soviet Export."

[28] Hegghammer and Lacroix, *The Meccan Rebellion*, viii–xi.

two months[29] before the rebellion took place. Husayn's view was that the Saudi authorities "had failed to take any effective counteraction."[30] Moreover, a British diplomatic report prepared in London responded to King Husayn's remarks and revealed that this was not the first time that the Jordanian King had expressed his concerns about the stability and future prospects of the Saudi royal family.[31] The report continued that "for at least the last two years, and probably longer, King Husayn has taken a critical view of the situation in Saudi Arabia and he has talked of the danger of collapse there." King Husayn's remarks could point out that he was more worried about the impact of the revolutionary forces on the stability of his own kingdom. As such it is quite possible that Husayn had been concerned about the impact of the same forces on his kingdom that had been tormenting the Saudis. He argued that "too often the Saudis take the easy course of deciding to do nothing."[32]

In the light of the diplomatic correspondence, there is no reason to question the truthfulness of King Husayn's remarks according to which the Saudis had been warned in advance about the imminent attacks.[33] In fact, it is even possible that King Husayn himself had provided such vital

[29] Prince Nayif, the Minister of Interior, told in a press conference on January 13, 1980, the official Saudi line that the decision to seize the Grand Mosque in Mecca was "taken only two weeks in advance." The British Embassy in Jeddah commented on the press conference by saying that "Nayif's performance was unconvincing" while a British journalist who was present at the event "described it as lamentable." "The Mecca Incident" (confidential telegram), Grey to Tatham, January 19, 1980, no. 5, *FCO 8/3734.*

[30] King Husayn of Jordan met with British Prime Minister Margaret Thatcher (1979–1990) and Foreign Minister Peter Carrington (1979–1982) in London in January 1980: "Record of Conversation between the Prime Minister and King Husayn of Jordan at 10 Downing Street" (secret memo), January 24, 1980, no. 13A, *FCO 8/3734.*

[31] "Saudi Arabia" (confidential report), John C. Moberly (Assistant Under-Secretary, Middle East Affairs, FCO, London) to David Miers (Head, MED, FCO, London), January 18, 1980, no. W9, *FCO 8/3734.*

[32] Ibid.

[33] The British reports indicate that the Jordanians had access to relatively accurate intelligence in Saudi Arabia. In the 1970s and 1980s, many Jordanian school teachers were employed in Saudi Arabia. These teachers were mostly from Bedouin families as it was easier for the Saudis to trust them unlike the Palestinians who compose most of the Jordanian population. Jordanian intelligence was using these teachers to spy on the Saudis and to report back to their government on the conditions in Saudi Arabia. Some of them had private tutoring jobs in the upper-class homes, including a good number of households of senior officers who served in the Saudi Armed Forces. See: "Saudi Arabia: Internal" (report) (confidential telegram), Oliver Miles (NENA, FCO, London) to Segar, May 21, 1982, no. 17, *FCO 8/4770.*

174   S. E. WILLNER

information to the Saudis.[34] Anyway, if such information is true, it would seem more likely that the Saudi intelligence had closely monitored Juhaiman's group. In accordance with King Husayn's remarks, Ali Riza[35] revealed that Juhayman had planned similar attacks also for Medina and other locations but the security authorities in the kingdom had been able to prevent these attacks. Ali Riza added that the reason the Saudis had been able to prevent the attack in Medina was because "the prayer times in Mecca were 10 minutes ahead of Medina and the Governor [of Mecca] had been able to send a warning to Medina."[36]

Considering the confusion and chaos that followed the seizure of the Grand Mosque in Mecca, it was quite unlikely that the Saudis would have been able to group their security forces in Medina in just ten minutes after the attack had taken place in Mecca, unless of course they had had prior information about the attacks. In pointing toward such a conclusion, the British Ambassador James Craig (1979–1984) commented Ali Riza's remarks by writing that "the explanation why the Saudis [had] failed [preventing the attack in Mecca] does not hold water. Given the confusion, which reigned when the attempt began in Mecca, ten minutes would have been quite inadequate amount of time for warning to have been passed to Medina."[37] Furthermore, it would seem utterly strange that the Saudis would have dismissed such important information about the Mecca rebellion, but had been able to prevent the other attacks that had been planned to occur at the same day and within minutes from each other.

If the Saudis had known about Juhaiman's plans to attack several key locations in Saudi Arabia, including Medina,[38] and if they had decided to prevent all the other attacks except the seizure of the Grand Mosque in Mecca, then what could have been their motivation for acting in such a way?

It is possible that the Saudis had intentionally allowed the Mecca rebellion to proceed in a more limited scale but had underestimated the combat

---

[34] King Husayn had also warned the Israeli leaders on multiple occasions during 1973 of the imminent danger of Egyptian and Syrian war plans against Israel. See for instance: Bar-Joseph, *Watchman Fell Asleep*, 89–90.

[35] It is not mentioned in which position Shaikh Ali Riza served at the time. However, it is quite likely that the document was quoting either Muhammad Ali Riza, the former Minister of Commerce, or his son, Abd Allah Ali Riza, who served as the Deputy Minister of Foreign Affairs for Economic and Cultural Affairs.

[36] Untitled letter, Craig to MED (FCO, London), February 7, 1980, *FCO 8/3734*.

[37] Ibid.

[38] The exact locations have not been revealed in the diplomatic correspondence.

capabilities of the attackers—and might have even labeled their leader as crazy—thus failing to contain it. Eventually, it took two long weeks for the Saudi authorities to retake the mosque and to crush the rebellion. By spreading disinformation and saying that one of their leaders had claimed to be the expected *mahdi* of the Shiʻa branch of Islam, the Saudis might have wanted to put the blame on Iran. Therefore, the Saudis might have also calculated that by allowing the Mecca rebellion to take place, they wanted to demonstrate to President Carter that the revolution in Iran was already undermining the Saudi legitimacy to rule the kingdom. In other words, the message was that Khomeini's revolution was now threatening the world's most prominent petroleum exporter, Saudi Arabia. In addition, the Saudi intent could have also been to gain leverage against its main enemies, and thus to legitimize tighter policy against the Iranians. The royal family was especially concerned about the Iranian pilgrims, among which they suspected were Iranian agents, who were spreading subversion in the kingdom. As a result, the number of Iranian pilgrims that were allowed to enter Saudi Arabia decreased dramatically. In reference to tightened Saudi policy, Abd al-Muhsin ibn Abd Allah al-Jiluwi, the Governor of the Eastern Province (1967–1985), confirmed that, since the beginning of the year until October 1980, "there had been six [Iranian] individuals only … whereas in ordinary years 10,000 Iranians would have passed [the oil-rich Eastern Province]".[39] However, a few days after the start of the Mecca rebellion, serious unrest broke out in the Eastern Province.

THE QATIF UPRISING (NOVEMBER 1979)

The popular demonstrations in the Eastern Province of Saudi Arabia, which came to be known as the 'Qatif uprising' or the '*Intifaḍah* of Muharram 1400', commenced on November 25, 1979 (or 5th of Muharram, 1400,[40] according to the Islamic calendar). Thousands of people participated in the demonstrations demanding that Saudi Arabia would

---

[39] "Saudi Internal" (confidential telegram), Craig to FCO, London, October 10, 1980, no. 68, *FCO 8/3735*.

[40] The events commemorated by the Shiʻa Muslims on the first month of the Islamic calendar, Muharram, mark the anniversary of the Battle of Karbala. During this historic battle, Husayn ibn Ali was killed. Husayn ibn Ali was the grandson of Prophet Muhammad and the second son of Imam Ali, the first Shiʻi imam. Furthermore, for Shiʻa Muslims, Husayn ibn Ali was the Third Imam.

176 S. E. WILLNER

halt its oil exports to the United States and that the kingdom would support the Islamic Revolution in Iran. News reports showed photos and videos of demonstrators carrying posters of Ayatollah Khomeini and placards denouncing the Saudi monarchy and American imperialists.[41]

Laurence Louer has argued that the Qatif uprising "constituted a watershed in the political mobilization of Saudi Shi'as."[42] For the Saudis, however, the eventuality was another confirmation that political agents sponsored by Iran were a major threat to the monarchy. The fact that the uprising happened in the kingdom's oil production areas was a serious reminder that the Shi'a population in the Eastern Province, which constituted a notable minority in the kingdom and a majority in the region, could become an ideal recruitment ground for Iranian sponsored insurgents and sympathizers of the Islamic Revolution. The uprising lasted for several days and was finally put down by the Saudi security forces. The Saudis took the uprising very seriously. In accordance with such a view, Louer writes that the "violence quickly calmed down," which according to her "was probably thanks to a significant shift in Saudi public policy towards the Eastern region."[43] The Saudis seemed to have realized that, in great part, the violence stemmed from the fact that the Saudi government had neglected the country's Shi'a population. In response, the Saudis decided to make significant investments to develop the infrastructure in the Eastern Province. This Saudi initiative was largely successful as the government action began to fill the socioeconomic gap between the Shi'a areas of the Eastern Province and the rest of the country.

THE SOVIET INVASION OF AFGHANISTAN (DECEMBER 1979)

At dawn of December 24, 1979, thousands of Soviet airborne troops and mechanized divisions were brought to Kabul and other central cities in Afghanistan to take over strategic points around the country. Although the Russian decision to invade Afghanistan has often been attributed as being a consequence of its (historic) intention to expand southward toward the Indian Ocean, the consensus among American experts was that

---

[41] Laurence Louer, *Transnational Shia Politics: Religious and Political Networks in the Gulf*, New York, NY: Columbia University Press, 2008, 161; Abir, *Saudi Arabia: Government, Society*, 86; "Saudis Are Said to Deploy Forces in Oil Region of East after Riots," *The New York Times*, December 4, 1979, A1.

[42] Louer, *Transnational Shia Politics*, 162.

[43] Ibid. 166.

the aim of the Soviet operation was to prop up its new client state, and thus, support the Afghan communist government.[44] Another important Soviet aim was to prevent the Islamic Republic of Iran from taking over Afghanistan where there is a Shi'a-minority. However, from the Russian point of view, Alexei Vassiliev has argued that the decision was not taken by the entire Soviet politburo but only by a few within its top leadership. Furthermore, Vassiliev has also argued that, by itself, Afghanistan was not important for the Russians, and that the Soviet leadership in Kremlin had made no prior calculations as how matters might develop in the country. In addition, as Vassiliev puts it, the Soviets had failed to foresee the reactions in the West, in the Muslim world and in China, all of whom condemned the invasion.[45]

Numerous press statements and interviews of Saudi officials indicate that the Soviet invasion was a major shock for its royal family. Accordingly, Deputy Prime Minister Fahd expressed his concerns that the USSR had long-term goals in the region.[46] As such, the Saudis were convinced that Moscow had more extensive military plans, which they thought could reach further south beyond the borders of Afghanistan. The Saudis not only condemned the Soviet move but also warned that the long-term Soviet aim was to control the Middle East oil production areas.[47] For instance, Minister of Petroleum Yamani had argued that "the main motive for the Soviet military intervention in Afghanistan was long-range energy strategy."[48] In March 1980, Saudi Intelligence Chief Turki al-Faysal raised

[44] Don Oberdorfer, "The Making of a Soviet Coup," *The Washington Post*, January 2, 1980, A1; Michael Dobbs, "Afghan Pullout Marks Historic Reversal for Soviets," *The Washington Post*, February 13, 1989, A1.

[45] Vassiliev, *Russian Policy in the Middle East*, 256, 264.

[46] See for instance, Deputy Prime Minister Fahd's interview with the French newspaper *Le Figaro*, as published by the *Saudi Press Agency* on February 23, 1980: "Prince Fahd Makes a Statement on Afghanistan, Palestine, Oil," *FBIS*, February 25, 1980, C2-C4.

[47] "*Kalimat 'Ukāz*" [Editorial of *Ukaz*], *Ukaz*, January 8, 1980, 1.

[48] As discussed earlier, the Saudis had warned already in June 1978 that the aim of the Soviet policy in Afghanistan and in the Middle East was to control the petroleum routes and sources. The Saudis had argued that the logic behind the long-term Soviet energy strategy was based on a calculation that the USSR would turn into a net-importer of oil sometime in the 1980s, forcing it to look for new sources of oil. As such, the Saudis seemed to have been convinced that the Soviets were eyeing their oil fields, which they thought was based on such a policy, driven primarily by the Soviet need to secure oil supplies for the coming decades. Yamani's statements were reported from Davos, Switzerland on February 7, 1980, by the *Reuter* news service. See: "Yamani: USSR Invasion of Oilfields would Cause War," *FBIS*, February 8, 1980, C2.

178   S. E. WILLNER

similar concerns. He said in an interview with *Fortune* magazine (March 1980): "[W]hat is the Soviet goal in the Middle East[?] ... The answer is simple: Our oil. Iran has too many domestic problems and its oil reserves are being quickly depleted. ... At this moment, we do not expect an invasion but we do expect the Soviets to use their power to maneuver themselves into a position to make arrangements for a guaranteed oil supply."[49] In the beginning of January 1980, Foreign Minister Saud al-Faysal told the press that "the serious situation in Afghanistan had meant that the strong could do what they wanted with the weak,"[50] while in another press statement he described the Soviet invasion as "extremely dangerous".[51]

Interestingly, the American response to the Soviet invasion of Afghanistan—also known as the Carter Doctrine, was only issued around one month after, on January 23, 1980. During his State of the Union Address, President Carter declared that, if necessary, the United States would use military force to defend its national interests in the Persian Gulf.[52] The Carter Doctrine was drafted to deter the Soviets from seeking dominion in the Persian Gulf. Furthermore, the doctrine was based on the US concern that after invading Afghanistan, the Soviets were aiming at the Persian Gulf oil production region. A few weeks later on February 7, 1980, in an obvious reference to Carter's address, Minister of Petroleum Yamani reassured that the kingdom "would be defended by the United States, Western Europe and Japan in the event of a Soviet invasion [in Saudi Arabia]."[53] He also warned that if the Soviet Union decided to march into Saudi oil fields it would ignite a third World War. He added that "the heat is coming nearer to the oil fields, and heat is dangerous near oil." In conclusion one could say that since the Saudis had increased their

---

[49] Quoted in: Mazher A. Hameed, *Saudi Arabia, the West and the Security of the Gulf*, London: Croom Helm, 1986, 37.

[50] Saud al-Faysal made his statement to the press on January 7, 1980. See: "Afghanistan: Saudi Official and Press Statements" (restricted telegram), Craig to FCO (London), January 12, 1980, no. 5, *FCO 8/3745*.

[51] Foreign Minister Saud al-Faysal spoke at a press conference in Riyadh on January 16, 1980. See: "Foreign Minister Saud/Afghanistan" (restricted telegram), US Embassy (Jeddah) to Department of State, January 16, 1980, *FCO 8/3734*.

[52] During his State of the Union Address, President Carter declared that "let our position be absolutely clear: An attempt by any outside force to gain control of the Persian Gulf region will be regarded as an assault on the vital interests of the United States of America, and such an assault will be repelled by any means necessary, including military force."

[53] The *Reuter* news service reported from Davos, Switzerland on February 7, 1980. See: "Yamani: USSR Invasion of Oilfields would Cause War," *FBIS*, February 8, 1980, C2.

investments in safe assets—such as gold, in response to these destabilizing political events (in 1978 and 1979)—the royal family did not believe in the US ability and willingness to secure its survival. Furthermore, as Ian Skeet has argued, the Saudis were publicly embarrassed by the Carter Doctrine for defending the Middle East.[54] Skeet's conclusion is in line with the earlier Saudi statements. Accordingly, the Saudis seem to have concluded that because of Carter's past foreign policy failures (which in most part were due to the ideological foundations of his foreign policy, most importantly, with reference to the Shah's fall), the Carter Doctrine had little credibility in the Saudi eyes concerning the stability in the Middle East. In other words, it was not that the Saudis did not want the United States to defend Saudi Arabia, quite the contrary. Instead, because of Carter's human rights-focused foreign policy, the Saudis didn't feel confident that the Carter Administration would be able, or even willing, to help the kingdom in the way that the United States had been committed in the past (in accordance with the earlier American foreign policy and defense doctrines).

Significant Amount of Financial Assets Leaves Saudi Arabia

In general, the oil and gold price fluctuations are useful indicators of political and economic turmoil and instability. Since the early 1970s, and especially following the 1973 Arab oil embargo, the Saudis accumulated substantial financial assets. These funds were primarily managed by the Saudi Arabian Monetary Authority (SAMA) [*Mu'assah an-Naqd al-'Arabī al-Sa'udī*], which is also known as the central bank of Saudi Arabia. Even though the Saudis have been quite secretive when it comes to their finances, and while it has been challenging to produce exact numbers for the multi-billion-dollar Saudi assets, it is useful to note that government money and Saudi private assets were often mixed.

As will be further elaborated, the Saudis purchased large deposits of gold in the late 1970s. Although it is difficult to say how much Jimmy Carter's victory in the November 1976 US Presidential Elections contributed to the increase of gold prices, one can undoubtedly notice that the price of gold began a steady rise following the elections. This gold price

---

[54] Skeet, *OPEC: Twenty-Five Years*, 176.

180   S. E. WILLNER

increase was a three-year lengthy process, which culminated in the events of the Soviet invasion of Afghanistan (December 1979). While in August 1976 the price of gold had been around $110 per ounce, a few years later, in January 1980, the price of gold had climbed to a record-high of $850 per ounce. At this point it is useful to note that the governments, which had most surplus assets, were the rich Arab states, while the Western economies were struggling in the aftermath of the global recession brought by the oil embargo of 1973. Although there are no records available that could indicate how much gold the Saudis had bought exactly, it is possible that the Arab states were the ones that mainly had contributed to the rapid increase of the gold prices in 1978 and 1979. At the same time, the price of oil had increased from $12 per barrel (August 1976) to around $16 per barrel (February 1979) and to around $40 per barrel (April 1980).

Prior to 1979, Iran was the second largest petroleum exporter after Saudi Arabia. Before the revolution, Iran exported some 4.5 million bpd. However, by early November 1978 Iran's oil production had fallen below one million bpd and by the end of 1978, Iran's oil exports had ceased altogether due to the 1978–1979 revolution. At the same time, the daily average oil production in Saudi Arabia had increased from 8.3 million bpd (1978) to 9.5 million bpd (1979) and to 9.9 million bpd (1980). The political instability, and the subsequent reduction in Iranian oil supply, helped to create turbulence in the oil markets, which, in turn, led to sharp rise in the oil prices. Although Iran had supplied some 4–5 percent of the global oil exports, it was the panic in the oil markets that primarily led to the sharp rise in the oil prices.[55]

As has been contemplated earlier, the Saudis blamed that President Carter's weak Middle East policy had encouraged regional instability. It is quite possible that the royal family decided to invest in gold holdings because it was preparing new safe heavens had the political situation significantly worsened within its borders—and perhaps most significantly, had the Islamic revolution spread from Iran to the oil-rich Eastern Province, which had a sizeable Shi'a population.

At the end of 1979, Western bankers and monetary officials were puzzled by a strange dilemma: The Saudi government was growing poorer despite the significant oil price hikes that had followed the Islamic

---

[55] For more about the impact of the Islamic Revolution on the oil markets, read for instance: Daniel Yergin, *The Prize: The Epic Quest for Oil, Money & Power*, London: Simon & Schuster, 2008, 656–680.

Revolution in Iran.[56] During 1979, several newspapers published reports about the increasing weakness and the vulnerability of Saudi Arabia and that as a result, massive amounts of private and public funds were leaving the kingdom for personal survival.[57] Furthermore, it was also reported that wealthy Middle Eastern investors had been transferring their fortunes into safe assets, such as gold, following the Islamic Revolution and due to "the continuing strength of fundamentalist Muslim movement."[58] Subsequently, Andre Sharon, an analyst at the New York-based brokerage firm Drexel, Burnham, Lambert Inc.,[59] explained that the Saudis were buying physical gold (instead of making deposits in foreign banks) because owing gold was anonymous.[60] In the late-1970s, buying gold was also an attractive investment due to increasing gold prices. In general, however, gold was considered a safe asset. Moreover, gold holdings were relatively easy to transport anywhere in the world and converting such holdings to any foreign currency was also quite easy.[61] However, it is important to point out here that some of the sources suggest that the Saudis began investing in gold holdings much before the collapse of the Shah's regime. This noticeable change in Saudi investment behavior had aroused the suspicions and concerns of the foreign banking and intelligence officials.[62]

In response to enquiries from the British diplomatic officials in Jeddah (February 1980), Umer Chapra, an Economic Advisor at SAMA

[56] Paul Lewis, "Saudis' Money Reserves Decline, Puzzling West," *The New York Times*, December 12, 1979, D1.

[57] James L. Rowe Jr., "Panicky Investors Push Gold to Record $575.50," *The Washington Post*, January 3, 1980, A1.

[58] Ibid.

[59] Drexel Burnham Lambert Inc. was a private American investment bank. In the late 1970s and early 1980s, it was one of the United States' most profitable investment banks. See, for instance: Kurt Eichenwald, "The Collapse of Drexel Burnham Lambert; Drexel, Symbol of Wall St. Era, Is Dismantling; Bankruptcy Filed", *The New York Times*, February 14, 1990, A1.

[60] Since these Saudi gold holdings were anonymously deposited in the Swiss banks, it was much harder for anyone to confiscate the gold. The Saudis were probably concerned because, following the fall of the Shah's regime, the new government in Iran had requested that the United States government would confiscate Shah's assets and, instead, return the funds to Iran.

[61] Rowe, "Panicky Investors Push Gold."

[62] See, for instance: Untitled Letter, Peter Edgley (Overseas Department, Bank of England, London) to David Peretz (Deputy Director, International Finance, H.M. Treasury, London), October 31, 1979, no. 35, *FCO 8/3414*.

182   S. E. WILLNER

(1965–1999), told that "the amount of private capital leaving the country was increasing all the time." Moreover, in commenting Chapra's remarks, Tim Hollaway of the British Embassy reported that he had heard stories from "very-well-placed sources" that money was leaving Saudi Arabia for "political reasons"[63] caused by growing doubts over the political stability of the Persian Gulf region, which Iran's Islamic Revolution had intensified. Hollaway added that, for instance, "Citibank had made $8 million in commission on fleeing capital."[64]

The Saudi decision to make significant changes in the composition of the kingdom's financial assets was a calculated and well-planned move. It appears that the first major trigger for the stream of financial transfers out of Saudi Arabia was the communist coup in Afghanistan (April 1978). However, the capital flight further intensified following these five significant events, which occurred in 1979, namely: the victory of the Islamic Revolution in Iran (February 1979); the failed military coup against the Saudi monarchy (early August 1979); the Mecca rebellion (mid-November 1979); the subsequent Shi'a uprising in the Eastern Province (mid-November 1979); and the Soviet occupation of Afghanistan (December 1979).

Throughout 1978 and 1979, billions of dollars' worth of financial assets were transferred by the royal family from the kingdom to abroad—mostly to the United States and Western Europe. The *Afro-Asian Affairs* claimed that the amount, which was missing from SAMA resources, amounted to $13.4 billion. Furthermore, the same newsletter reported, based on anonymous intelligence sources,[65] that Saudi government funds had been "embezzled by certain minor officials [...that were] almost certainly little more than front men or scapegoats for the real culprits," and which "could not possibly have manipulated an operation on this scale,

---

[63] "Saudi Arabia: Reserves" (confidential letter), Hollaway to Edgley, February 27, 1980, no. 4, *FCO 8/3759*.

[64] Ibid.

[65] It is not specified which intelligence service had provided this information. However, it is quite likely that the CIA had been the source. As such, it is possible that the CIA wanted to message President Carter that the Al Saud was vulnerable to the revolutionary threats and that the President should change his policy toward the Al Saud.

without the authority of one or more very senior Saudi princes or members of the government."[66]

In reference to these reported amounts that were missing from the Saudi reserves, Paul Lewis of *The New York Times* quoted anonymous sources in the International Monetary Fund (IMF) saying that Saudi Arabia's official reserve holdings had plunged significantly and that the estimate was that the reserve holdings had plummeted from $32 billion at the end on 1977 to $17 billion in September 1979. Lewis also quoted another anonymous—possibly Western—government source describing the situation as "the tip of an iceberg."[67] He noted that "in the past the Saudis disguised the true size of their dollar and gold holdings, not only to avoid upsetting financial markets, but also because the government's money got mixed up with the private wealth of the large royal family."[68] In accordance, Peter Edgley of the Bank of England commented the press reports and iterated that "it is perfectly true that Saudi reserves have fallen from $30 billion in December 1977 to $16 billion in October 1979."[69] His report explained that instead of decreasing, the Saudi government reserves should have been growing around $1 billion per month due to the oil price increases during 1979. Edgley's report gave three plausible explanations. First, that there had been military imports and political grants and aid abroad. Second, that there had been backlog in financial payments to various international contractors. Third, and the most plausible explanation, that there had been substantial capital outflows since the Islamic Revolution in Iran, which "could have been exacerbated by the growing tension in the region, and, latterly, the domestic disturbances in the kingdom itself."[70] Regarding the rumored embezzlement of Saudi government funds, Edgley wrote, perhaps a bit naively, that he did not

[66] It was alleged, that following the attack on the Grand Mosque in Mecca in November 1979, several Saudi princes had entered SAMA's gold vaults, taken tons of gold and fled the country in fear of a revolution. This was claimed by "The Young Revolutionaries"; see: "Undated letter" attached to "Letter" (confidential), Craig to Tatham, March 23, 1980, no. 41, *FCO 8/3734*; "Khalid Flees August Coup D'état".

[67] Lewis has not specified the origin of his anonymous source. It is likely, however, that he had consulted Western financial sources. See: Lewis, "Saudis' Money Reserves Decline, Puzzling West."

[68] Lewis, "Saudis' Money Reserves Decline, Puzzling West."

[69] "Saudi Arabia: Reserves," January 2, 1980; "Stability of the Middle East" (letter), David Peretz (Deputy Director, International Finance, H.M. Treasury, London) to Hannay, October 25, 1979, no. 32, *FCO 8/3414*.

[70] Ibid.

184   S. E. WILLNER

believe the Western officials running the day-to-day management at SAMA could have been involved in covering up such a large-scale operation.[71] Edgley argued that "even if short-lived, a fraud of this kind would be difficult to conceal." Christopher McMahon, the Executive Director of the Bank of England, questioned such a conclusion, and added a two-word handwritten comment in Edgley's report saying: "*I wonder?*"[72]

It would seem that one way by which the Saudis managed to conduct substantial financial transfers without the detection of the foreign financial institutions, was to sell oil on the spot markets, where commodities are traded for immediate delivery. For instance, the royal family could have sold oil at the spot market for $40 per barrel, which the panicky buyers were willing to pay in the aftermath of the Islamic Revolution, while officially the sale was being recorded at the standard of $18 per barrel, which was the price the Saudis were committed to selling their oil in accordance with long-term contracts. The Bank of England calculated that such scheme of daily exports of 900,000 barrels of oil sold in the free markets— which the rumors alleged—would have resulted in a windfall of a $20 million per day or $600 million per month or $7.2 billion per year.

In addition, there had been rumors circulating among anonymous Western diplomats in Jeddah that several Saudi princes had been accused of "stealing some $18 billion from SAMA over a period of several years."[73] However, it would seem less likely that royal princes had been stealing massive amounts of money. Rather, it would seem more likely that the whole money transfer operation was part of a more systematic coordination, in which the Saudis were 'laundering' their oil money through private, lower-ranking Saudi officials to minimize public exposure. Although

[71] Peter Edgley also wrote in his report that "I found SAMA in some disarray, as an institution ... but this seemed largely attributable to the move [of its offices] from Jeddah [to Riyadh] and the damage this caused to morale and efficiency [of its operation]." Foreign advisors and professionals were primarily in charge of the operational responsibility for day-to-day management of the Saudi reserves, of which Edgley mentioned the investment banks of the Barings, Merrill Lynch, and White Weld. He added that they were "by a long way the most efficient part of SAMA." See: Untitled letter, Edgley to Peretz, October 31, 1979, no. 35, *FCO 8/3414.*

[72] The comment was handwritten in the margin. "Saudi Reserves" (secret letter), Edgley to Myers, January 23, 1980, no. 2, enclosed in: "Saudi Arabia: Reserves" (secret report), Edgley to Christopher McMahon (Executive Director, Bank of England, London), January 2, 1980, *FCO 8/3759;* "Saudi Reserves" (confidential report), Segar to Miers, March 13, 1980, no. 6, *FCO 8/3759.*

[73] Lewis, "Saudis' Money Reserves Decline, Puzzling West."

the SAMA and other Saudi government authorities had denied any such reports,[74] and although some of the financial figures might not have been completely accurate, it would appear reasonable to assume that the government and corporate sources, which the Western news reports had quoted, were reliable. Nonetheless, the Saudi decision to transfer large sums of money away from the kingdom seems to indicate that the royal family wanted to play it safe and was preparing potential safe heavens outside the kingdom. In other words, their aim was to have these assets ready for use had the royal family been forced to leave the kingdom, as had happened to the Shah of Iran.[75]

[74] Ibid; The Ministry of Finance and National Economy released a statement to the official Saudi SNA on December 18, 1979. See: "Reported fall in foreign currency reserves denied," FBIS, December 19, 1979, C4.

[75] "Saudi Billions" (confidential report), Segar to Grey, June 15, 1981, FCO 8/4236. See also: Michael Field, The Merchants: The Big Business Families of Saudi Arabia and the Gulf States, New York, NY: The Overlook Press, 1985, 335.

CHAPTER 13

Saudi, CIA Messages to President Carter: A US Policy Change Toward the Saudis Is Necessary

SAUDI RESPONSE TO CIA 'WARNING' OF A POSSIBLE REGIME COLLAPSE

The Saudi decision to acquire significant gold holdings—and the consequent transfer of billions of dollars outside of the kingdom—indicates that the royal family expected the geopolitical situation to worsen around Saudi Arabia. As the dramatic political events of 1978–1979 unfolded in Iran, the Carter Administration had lost much of its credibility in the Saudi eyes. Indeed, the deep rift between the Saudis and the Carter Administration over the President's Middle East policy is well-documented. However, it appears that there was also increasing anger within the CIA toward President Carter's way of not taking the advice of his intelligence community. Undoubtedly, Saudi Arabia was the world's most important oil exporter, and, as such, the collapse of its pro-Western monarchy would have been detrimental not only to the United States but also to the whole Western world. In an attempt to wake up President Carter—so that he would change his policy toward the Saudis—the CIA seemed to have run series of psychological operations around January 1980.

In the beginning of February 1980, just a week after the Carter Doctrine had been declared (January 23, 1980), National Security Advisor Brzezinski departed on a tour to Pakistan and Saudi Arabia. His aim, according to the news reports, had been to "draw the line in Southwest Asia against the Soviet Union" and to rally the United States' allies in

© The Author(s), under exclusive license to Springer Nature Switzerland AG 2023
S. E. Willner, *Preserving the Saudi Monarchy*,
https://doi.org/10.1007/978-3-031-30006-6_13

187

188 S. E. WILLNER

Pakistan and Saudi Arabia around the Carter Doctrine.[1] It would seem that while in Riyadh, the Saudi Government had told Brzezinski that it was ready to assist with the defense of the Persian Gulf by financing military assistance to Pakistan and by helping the Americans to "obtain air and naval facilities elsewhere in the region."[2] According to Brzezinski, the Saudis had "particularly stressed" the growing threat from the communist military presence in South Yemen (PDRY).[3] Despite these earlier negotiations with the US representatives, on March 7, 1980, one month after Brzezinski's trip, the Pakistanis communicated that they were not interested in the American assistance.[4] It is possible that the Saudis had advised the Pakistanis do so.

This sudden Pakistani change of mind coincided with an article published in the *Newsweek* on March 3, 1980. The article cited a CIA briefing and a secret report assessing that "[the Saudi monarchy's] survival could not be assured beyond the next two years."[5] The *Newsweek* also quoted anonymous American diplomatic sources saying that, following the Mecca rebellion in November 1979, "the Saudis [had been] dead scared" while the Soviet invasion of Afghanistan had "given them nightmares about the territorial integrity of the Persian Gulf states."[6] The article also claimed that a serious rift had developed within the royal family threatening to split it. Furthermore, the anonymous CIA sources had assessed that the developments of the Mecca rebellion had closed the Saudi ranks. Interestingly, it would also appear that the CIA had suggested in the

---

[1] Don Oberdorfer, "Pakistan 'Package' Unravels; New Blow to US Diplomacy," *The Washington Post*, March 8, 1980, A21; Angus Deming et al. "The Mideast: The Doctrine's Acid Test," *Newsweek*, February 18, 1980, 53.

[2] Deming, "The Mideast: The Doctrine's Acid Test."

[3] Zbigniew Brzezinski, *Power and Principle: Memoirs of the National Security Adviser 1977-1981*, London: Weidenfield and Nicolson, 1983, 450.

[4] As stated by Hodding Carter III, the Spokesman for the Department of State: Oberdorfer, "Pakistan 'Package' Unravels; New Blow to U.S. Diplomacy"; Brzezinski, *Power and Principle*, 448.

[5] It was also revealed that the CIA had given a detailed background briefing to two American journalists: Roberta Hornig of the *Washington Star* and Jane Whitmore of *Newsweek*. See: David Leigh, "CIA Redfaced over Its Gaffe on Saudis," *The Washington Post*, July 22, 1980, A8. It was also mentioned by Barry Rubin that Kermit Roosevelt, a former CIA agent (1943–1958), had "tried to explain the [Shah's] shortcomings to the Carter Administration, but his advice fell on deaf ears." Barry Rubin, *Paved with Good Intentions*, 204.

[6] John Nielsen et al. "Saudi Arabia: A Shaky Pillar of Security," *Newsweek*, March 3, 1980, 34.

briefing that it was time for Crown Prince Fahd to abdicate and instead, Prince Abd Allah should replace him.[7] There are no declassified records available that could reveal why the CIA had briefed the reporters concerning Fahd and Abd Allah. However, it is possible that CIA had blamed, at least partly, the Saudi weakness on Fahd who, at the time, was one of the most powerful princes in Saudi Arabia.

Although there is no direct evidence, the timing of the CIA briefing could indicate that the spy agency had attempted similar approach of psychological warfare through the British newspapers as well. Coinciding with the publishing of the *Newsweek* article, the London-based newspaper *Financial Times* had received a 13-page undated letter from an alleged group of Saudis calling themselves "The Young Revolutionaries." The letter, which had arrived in the *Financial Times* in early March 1980, was a critical manifestation of the many faults of the Saudi monarchy. It revealed details of alleged corruption within the royal family and exposed several other unflattering details about some of its members. Perhaps most interestingly, the "Revolutionaries" claimed that the reason why they wanted their letter to be published was to make the world know "what has happened and what is happening in the kingdom" and to make sure that "[Saudi Arabia would not] become another Iran."[8] This was probably made in reference to the subversive activity within and near the kingdom, which had increased following the revolution in Iran.

Instead of publishing the letter, the *Financial Times* decided to hand it over to the FCO in London, which forwarded the letter to the British Embassy in Jeddah. On March 23, 1980, Ambassador Craig commented on the contents of the letter by writing that it was "manifestly written by someone who knows Saudi Arabia: he has all the names [possibly in reference to the Saudi royals mentioned in the letter] and he is familiar with all the rumors."[9] Craig's analysis indicates (and confirms) that whoever had been behind the letter was definitely someone who had access to sensitive information concerning senior Saudi decision-makers. In turn, David

[7] Leigh, "CIA Redfaced over Its Gaffe on Saudis."

[8] A copy of "The Young Revolutionaries"-letter, which was sent to the *Financial Times*, was attached to a letter sent from the FCO to the British Embassy in Jeddah; see: "Saudi Internal: Dissidents" (confidential letter), Tim Hollaway (MED, FCO, London) to British Embassy (Jeddah), March 16, 1980, *FCO 8/3734*.

[9] Untitled (confidential letter), Craig to Tatham, March 23, 1980, no. 41, *FCO 8/3734*.

190   S. E. WILLNER

Tatham, a staff member at the FCO, wrote that "some of this [letter] may be inaccurate, but, *alas*, it is all credible."[10]

Although the letter from the "Revolutionaries" ended up not being published, the *Newsweek* article had already infuriated the Saudis. In April 1980, in an apparent response to the above-mentioned press reports in the American media, Defense Minister Sultan iterated—although quite vaguely—that such "venomous campaigns" are characterized by "rancor and jealousy."[11] Furthermore, on May 26, 1980, two and a half months after the publishing of the *Newsweek* article, Meg Greenfield of *The Washington Post* reported from Riyadh writing that the Saudi sentiment toward the United States was filled with "volcanic resentment, even rage, at what [was] regarded as a malevolent misunderstanding and misinterpretation of the Saudis' own situation and purposes."[12] These Saudi statements signified that the relations between Riyadh and Washington had reached a new low-point.

To understand the potential reasons behind such a CIA press campaign, which seemed to have been against the Saudis, it is very important to put the whole issue into proper historic context and to address the possible CIA role behind such an operation. Since there does not seem to be real justification for the claims presented in the CIA-sourced press reports, it was most likely not a serious message. Had there been a real danger against the Saudis, the CIA would not have published such information. Instead, the press campaign was reflecting CIA's fears, and not that the Saudi monarchy would have been facing an imminent collapse. Although the CIA campaign highlighted the monarchy's weaknesses, and although it might have also shown criticism toward the royal family, the most plausible explanation for such an approach might have been to point out the apparent frailty of President Carter's Middle East policy. As it seems, the purpose of such a campaign was to convince President Carter that he should be more attentive to the Saudis especially after the downfall of the Shah's monarchy in Iran.

---

[10] Ibid.

[11] Prince Sultan's statement was published by the *SPA* in Arabic on April 16, 1980. It was also published in the Saudi newspaper *Al-Bilad* on the same day. "Prince Sultan Confident of Gulf Security," *FBIS*, April 18, 1980, C3.

[12] Meg Greenfield, "Saudi Arabia: Paradox in the Desert," *The Washington Post*, May 26, 1980, A15.

THE SOVIET MILITARY EXERCISE TO INVADE IRAN AND THE SAUDI APPEAL FOR CHANGE OF THE US ADMINISTRATION (AUGUST–SEPTEMBER 1980)

In August 1980, the Soviet Union conducted an ambitious military exercise to simulate its ability to invade Iran. According to a top-secret Pentagon assessment[13]—which was quoted by Michael Gordon of *The New York Times*—the military exercise took place near Soviet Union's border with Iran.[14] In reference to the same intelligence report, National Security Adviser Brzezinski wrote in his memoirs that, by late August 1980 the United States "had mounting intelligence that the Soviets were deploying forces on the Iranian frontier in a mode suited for intervention in Iran."[15] The Iranians had also observed unusual concentration of Soviet troops near USSR's border with Iran.[16] An important question to address here is what might have triggered the Soviet Union to conduct such a military exercise?

Anonymous American military officials had assessed that the exercise was intended to improve Soviet military capabilities due to the increasing instability near its southern borders.[17] However, it seems that the exercise was meant, perhaps most significantly, to enhance the Soviet military readiness against the threat that the Islamic revolution posed to its Muslim majority Soviet states in the Caucasus (including the Soviet Azerbaijan) and in the region of Transcaspia in the east of the Caspian Sea (Turkmenistan, Kazakhstan, and Uzbekistan), also constituting a large Shi'a population. Therefore, the simulation of Soviet invasion might have been a message to the theocratic regime in Tehran saying that it should

---

[13] As a historic point of interest, the timing of the CIA leak (November–December 1986) coincides with the exposure of the 'Iran-Contra Affair', which was a political scandal taking place during 1985–1987. Through this covert operation the Reagan Administration secretly assisted the sale of weapons to Iran, while the proceedings of the sale were used to fund the rebel Contras fighting the socialist government in Nicaragua. Several books have been written about the affair. See, for instance: William LeoGrande, *Our Own Backyard: The United States in Central America, 1977–1992,* Chapel Hill, NC: University of North Carolina Press, 1998, 388–393.

[14] Michael Gordon, "1980 Soviet Test: How to Invade Iran," *The New York Times,* December 15, 1986, 12.

[15] Brzezinski, *Power and Principle,* 451.

[16] Abol Hassal Bani-Sadr, *My Turn to Speak: Iran, the Revolution and Secret Deals with the U.S.* Washington, D.C.: Brassey's, 1991, 94.

[17] Gordon, "1980 Soviet Test: How to Invade Iran."

192 S. E. WILLNER

not attempt to export its Islamic revolution to the southern communist states lest Moscow should implement the implied threat and invade Iran. The Russians probably wanted to convey to the Iranians that, if there would be a danger from Iran to Russia, or to its allies, it could invade Iran under the pretense of the 1921 Persia–Russia Treaty of Friendship.[18]

Possibly triggered by the Soviet military exercise, and in an apparent response to President Carter's consistently "weak and indecisive" foreign policy, the Saudis seemed to have sponsored an article in the Virginia-based monthly magazine *Armed Forces Journal* in early September 1980. After assessing the article, a British diplomatic report described it as a "comprehensive and accurate account" of the "main Saudi concerns and anxieties about US policy."[19] In mid-September 1980, about two weeks after its publication, Roger Merrick, the Deputy Director of Arabian Peninsula Affairs at the Department of State, revealed to the British diplomats in Washington that he had circumstantial evidence that Prince Turki al-Faysal, the Head of the Saudi General Intelligence, had had a copy of the article on his desk one day before it was published.[20] Several intriguing unanswered questions arise: Who was this person that had seen the article on Turki al-Faysal's desk, and had the article been left on his desk unintentionally, or would it be possible that it was left on purpose to make sure that the Americans would get the Saudi message? Nevertheless, such fascinating detail of intelligence points out that the Saudis probably were behind the article.[21]

---

[18] The agreement prohibited "the formation or presence within their respective territories of any organizations or groups of persons … whose object [was] to engage in acts of hostility against Persia or Russia, or against allies of Russia." Furthermore, according to the agreement, "If a third party should attempt to carry out a policy of usurpation by means of armed intervention in Persia, or if such power should desire to use Persian territory as a base of operations against Russia … Russia shall have the right to advance her troops into the Persian interior for the purpose of carrying out the military operations necessary for its defense." J.C. Hurewitz, *Diplomacy in the Near and Middle East: A Documentary Record: 1914–1956 Volume II*, New York, NY: Octagon Books, 1972, 90–91.

[19] Abdul Kasim Mansur, "The American Threat to Saudi Arabia," *Armed Forces Journal*, September 1980, 47–56. See also an assessment of the article: "US/Saudi Arabia: Article from the September Edition of the *Armed Forces Journal*" (confidential report), Fortescue to Henry Pakenham (FCO, London), September 17, 1980, *FCO 8/3744*.

[20] "US/Saudi Arabia: Article from the September Edition of the *Armed Forces Journal*," September 17, 1980.

[21] Another less likely possibility is that the CIA had authored the article to send another message to President Carter. If this were the case, then it would not have been true that someone had seen the article on Turki al-Faysal's desk.

Through the *Armed Forces Journal* article, the Saudis expressed their deep dissatisfaction toward the American unwillingness and inability to understand Saudi Arabia's security needs and sensibilities. The article claimed that the Saudi royal family felt that its reliance on US military assistance had become a liability. It explained that the Saudis were casting doubt whether the United States was willing to intervene to a threat anything less than the most overt attack. Furthermore, it accused that Carter's foreign policy had increased the attempts of various insurgent groups to undermine Saudi Arabia.[22] My earlier analysis indicates that the Saudis were convinced that the weak US Middle East policy had emboldened its enemies, such as Muammar Qadhafi, and thus, the perceived weakness of the US policy had encouraged the enemies of the Saudi monarchy to make more attempts to overthrow it.

Despite Carter Administration's attempts to improve the security situation, and despite its consequent decision to establish the Rapid Deployment Force (RDF) in March 1980 (mainly in response to the Soviet invasion of Afghanistan in December 1979), the article claimed that the force had "done nothing to help the [security] situation." Instead, the Saudis suspected that the actual purpose of the RDF was to be on standby, and if needed, to take over the kingdom's oil fields in case the Saudi monarchy was overthrown (and therefore, not to intervene and protect its regime, as in the case of the Shah). In an apparent reference to the earlier CIA psychological operations to publicly expose the Saudi vulnerabilities, the article stated that the constant American questioning of Saudi Arabia's internal stability and its monarchy's ability to rule cohesively was threatening the kingdom. Accordingly, the Saudis were "firmly convinced" that the US Embassy in Jeddah—and particularly its CIA station—was "responsible for a steady stream of reports indicating that Saudi Arabia [was] on the edge of collapse." Thus, the CIA's attempts to awaken the Carter Administration to be more actively supporting the Saudis were weakening the position of the royal family. That is to say, the royal family was angry, because of the American "lack of discretion" in such delicate issues.[23]

The article in the *Armed Forces Journal* highlighted the Iranian threat against Saudi Arabia and claimed that the Saudis were not happy about the way Washington was handling Tehran's export of Islamic revolution to

---

[22] Mansur, "The American Threat to Saudi Arabia."
[23] Ibid.

Saudi Arabia.[24] It even hinted that in a crisis the Saudis might be willing to accept the long-term risk of Soviet penetration to the Persian Gulf region.[25] This was made in reference to the earlier Soviet military exercise. The Saudis probably expected the United States to act according to the practical needs of the given circumstances and factors (the *realpolitik*-approach to foreign policy) and not according to ideology and moral or ethical ideas. Therefore, the Saudis wanted the US to resolutely confront the threat posed by Iran's export of Islamic revolution (and if necessary, by military means). Such a Saudi statement was likely meant as a message to wake up the Americans by saying that maybe the Russians were able to deal with the Islamic revolutionary threat more effectively, because the revolution was also threatening Moscow's interests in the Caucasus. In other words, although, in response to the Soviet invasion of Afghanistan (December 1979), the Saudis had expressed their concern that the Soviets desired to have access to the Persian Gulf and, therefore, to control the oil production areas there, they had probably realized that the Soviets faced the same revolutionary threat from Iran as they did.[26]

In conclusion, the most urgent message the Saudis wanted to communicate to Washington—in a reference to the upcoming November 1980 US Presidential Elections—was that "unless American policy changes significantly over the next six months, it is time to put a substantial distance between Saudi Arabia and the United States," that the preservation of the pro-Western Saudi policy depended on a change in the US foreign policy. The article's concluding remarks said that "the November [1980] election must be a comprehensive US reappraisal of its relations with Saudi Arabia."[27] These Saudi remarks are clear and strong, and one can draw at least two important conclusions concerning the Saudi–US relations. On the one hand, it is possible that the Saudis didn't want to openly promote the idea of inviting the US troops to Saudi Arabia or elsewhere in the region because they were concerned about the political implication had they done so. On the other hand, the Saudis might have calculated that

---

[24] As discussed in Chap. 12, during the Qatif uprising (November 1979) in the Eastern Province, the Shi'a demonstrators had been carrying posters of Ayatollah Khomeini and had demanded that Saudi Arabia should halt its oil exports to the United States and that the Saudis should support the Islamic Revolution in Iran. The Saudis were convinced that Iranian instigators had been behind the uprising.

[25] Mansur, "The American Threat to Saudi Arabia."

[26] "Yamani: USSR Invasion of Oilfields would Cause War."

[27] Ibid.

because of Carter's foreign policy orientation, the US military presence in the region would not have made that much of a difference. Therefore, instead of asking Carter to send forces to the Middle East, the Saudis were strongly suggesting that the Americans would need to elect a new president who would return to the *realpolitik*-approach in foreign policy. Only a meaningful change in the US foreign policy would make a difference. Interestingly, on September 22, 1980, just few weeks after the article had been published in the *Armed Forces Journal*, the Iran–Iraq War broke out.

THE START OF THE IRAN–IRAQ WAR (SEPTEMBER 1980)

The 1980–1988 Iran–Iraq War began on September 22, 1980, when Iraqi forces invaded Iranian territory. The eight-year-long war grew out of a mixture of ancient and modern enmity between the two nations. Accordingly, the roots of the conflict can be traced to several contributing factors. The immediate reasons were the disputes over boundaries and control over most of the Shatt al-Arab waterway, which has been Iraq's crucial transit point to the Persian Gulf. Another immediate cause was the profound influence Khomeini had over Iraq's Shi'a majority and his call to them to topple the secular Baath regime in Iraq. There was also the issue of Khomeini's personal animosity toward Saddam Husayn who, upon the request of the Shah, banished him from Najaf, where he had been a political refugee. To all that, one may add: the perennial Arab-Persian rivalry; and the struggle between Iraq's secularist Ba'ath ideology and Iran's Shi'i Islamic fundamentalism. President Husayn seemed to have reasoned that he could take advantage of the political turmoil in Iran following the Islamic Revolution, and thus seize Iran's oil-production areas in the southwest province of Khuzestan (or Arabistan, as he referred to it).[28]

President Jimmy Carter's foreign policy had been a colossal disappointment to the Saudis. Therefore, in the light of the American weakness following the revolution in Iran, and with Iraq neighboring and rivaling Iran,

---

[28] Baram, *Saddam Husayn and Islam*, 144–145. See also: Anthony and Abraham Wagner, *The Iran-Iraq War*, Boulder, CO. Westview Press, 1990; Tareq Ismael, *Iraq and Iran: Roots of Conflict*, Syracuse, NY: Syracuse University Press, 1982; Anthony Cordesman and Abraham Wagner, *The Iran-Iraq War*, Boulder, CO. Westview Press, 1990; Shirin Tahir-Kheli, ed. *The Iran-Iraq War: New Weapons, Old Conflicts*, New York, NY: Praeger, 1983; Efraim Karsh, ed. *The Iran-Iraq War: Impact and Implications*, New York, NY: St. Martin's Press, 1989; and Pesach Malovany, *Wars of Modern Babylon: A History of the Iraqi Army from 1921–2003*, Lexington, KY: The University Press of Kentucky, 2017.

196   S. E. WILLNER

the Saudis had calculated that Saddam Husayn was the only foreign leader who could check Iranian exporting its revolution, and who was willing and capable to confront Iran in an open military campaign, especially after the purges in the high-ranking officers in the Iranian military and air force. The Saudi decision to side with the Iraqis was not based on any pan-Arab ideology or even so much from fear of revolutionary Arabs, but on Saudi pragmatism and cold calculation. The Saudis needed to build a coalition against the theocratic regime in Tehran.

As it seems, the Iraqi attack on Iran was no sudden decision. In fact, it is quite possible that ever since Ayatollah Khomeini's return to Iran in February 1979,[29] the Saudis had been slowly grooming Saddam Husayn to challenge the Iranian threat, and it might have even encouraged him to go to war against the Islamic Republic by promising substantial financial aid. In support of such assessment, Amatzia Baram has quoted a memo prepared by Alexander Haig, the US Secretary of State (1981–1982), which asserted that Crown Prince Fahd had told Saddam Husayn sometime before the war that "President Carter gave the Iraqis a green light to launch the war against Iran." On the contrary, however, Baram doubts that Carter would have asked Fahd to convey to Saddam that the United States would support an Iraqi offensive. Baram continues to say that "there is no record of it, but Fahd may have invented the American support in order to push Saddam to war."[30] One should also add that if there was a record, it is unlikely that any scholar was able to trace it. Moreover, considering the highly calculative and shrewd traits of Saudi decision-making dynamics, and considering the threat that Iran posed to both Riyadh and Baghdad, it would make sense that Fahd had approached Saddam in such an attempt, as suggested by Baram. The Saudis understood that prior to the 1975 border agreement between Iran and Iraq, there had been many border skirmishes between the two states, and that the Iranians had been supporting the Iraqi Kurds to fight against the Iraqi government forces. In this respect, it could be that the Saudis had calculated that Saddam Husayn was the only political leader they thought that would be willing to militarily confront the Iranians. Nevertheless, without having any substantial

---

[29] Ayatollah Khomeini came officially to power through the establishment of the Islamic Republic in April 1979.

[30] Baram, *Saddam Husayn*, 152. Baram quoted: "Talking points" (top secret memo), Alexander Haig (Secretary of State, Washington), ca. April 1981, *National Security Archives*, George Washington University, Washington, D.C.

evidence, it is hard to conclude what could have been the ultimate turning point in Saddam Husayn's decision-making to go to war against Iran. However, Baram's remarks support the conclusion that the Saudis played a role in that process.

If the above-mentioned assessment is accurate, it could indicate that the Saudi policy concerning the conflict between Iran and Iraq had been deeply pragmatic. However, the main problem for the royal family was that, at the time, both Baghdad and Tehran were committed to revolutionary activity in Saudi Arabia. Therefore, the Saudi policy was based on its strategic calculation that both the Iranian and the Iraqi threat needed to be confronted and hopefully weakened. In addition, if neither country could gain an overwhelming victory and become a regional superpower, there were also many other countries (like Israel) that benefited from the Iran–Iraq clashing against each other. As highlighted by Mordechai Abir, the Saudi policy was "influenced by the fortunes of the war and their effect on Saudi interests."[31] That being said, for the Saudis, "the fortunes of war" meant that both Iran and Iraq would continue to exhaust one another's offensive military capabilities, which had posed a major threat to the Saudis.

The following remarks made by a senior Saudi Foreign Ministry official support Abir's assessment. In early October 1980, Ismail Shura, the Director of Arab Affairs at the Saudi Foreign Ministry, expressed "his personal view" to the British diplomats in Jeddah about the Iran–Iraq War. He said that the best outcome for the Saudis "would be a long indecisive war confined to the present opponents." The worst outcome, he said, "would be for either side to win a resounding victory; the victor would be unbearable." He continued that the only danger in a sustaining conflict was the possibility that either the United States or the Soviet Union would get drawn in. Shura also thought that it was likely that Moscow would end up supporting Iran because it was fed up with the evolution of Iraqi policy and would wish to maintain good relations with Syria.[32] Shura concluded—although the British reported that he had said it "only halfjokingly"—that conflicts of inter-Arab politics were perhaps "the best defense that Arab states had against domination by a single [Arab]

---

[31] Abir, Saudi Arabia: *Government, Society*, 129.
[32] Syria was against Iraq.

198   S. E. WILLNER

superpower."[33] In other words, the militarily weak Saudi Arabia was better off when its enemies were busy fighting and weakening each other.[34]

At first, these above-mentioned Saudi messages of the preferred outcome of the war might seem provocative and perplexing. Interestingly, Shura's comments of the Saudi preference for "a long indecisive war" seem intricate, considering that: his comments were made less than two weeks after the start of the war; that Iraq at the time was a much lesser threat to Saudi Arabia than Iran; and that Iran was the only state that had proclaimed Saudi Arabia as its main enemy.[35] Instead, Shura's comments could indicate that the Saudis were trying to hide, or at least play down, the possibility that it had played a role in grooming Saddam Husayn to go to war against Iran by promising financial support, and by misleading the Iraqis by saying that Washington had okayed its war plans. In other words, although in the early stage of the war the Saudis had tried to avoid making public statements about taking sides in the conflict, behind the scenes the Saudi monarchy supported Iraq without reservations. Because of Saudi Arabia's significant financial support[36] for Iraq's war efforts against Iran, and because Saudi Arabia had kept its petroleum production high to accommodate the international oil markets, the Iranian enmity against the Saudis intensified. Finally, while the Saudis had openly called for an American military assistance to secure their oil facilities and transit routes,

[33] "Iran/Iraq" (confidential report), Grey to Segar, October 6, 1980, no. 145, *FCO 8/3746*; Yodfat, *The Soviet Union and the Arabian Peninsula*, 61, 86, 98.

[34] However, when at the end of 1981 it began to look as if Baghdad was losing following Iran's successful counteroffensives, the Saudis became increasingly worried about a situation where there would have been a "regime established in Iraq susceptible to Iranian influence" and which would have given Iran much greater ability to threaten Saudi Arabia's strategic interests. "POP: Political Paper" (confidential telegram), P.F.M. Wogan (MED, FCO, London) to Haley (FCO, London), August 6, 1982, no. 45, *FCO 8/4804*.

[35] Prince Turki al-Faysal's interview on PBS Frontline. See: "Bitter Rivals: Iran and Saudi Arabia," *PBS Frontline*, Season 2018, Episode 17, video, 26:40–26:50, https://www.pbs.org/wgbh/frontline/film/bitter-rivals-iran-and-saudi-arabia

[36] The Saudis lent the Iraqis billions of dollars to support Baghdad's war efforts against Iran. Although the funds were presented as loans, interesting questions emerge, such as: How much of that money the Saudis were expecting to get back from the Iraqis, and were they perhaps willing to accept financial losses had the Iraqis been unable to pay back their billion-dollar loans? It is quite likely that the Saudis expected that the Iraqis would eventually be unable to pay back some of the loans but were willing to forgo them because they thought supporting Iraq's war efforts against Iran was a contribution worth making. However, Kuwait defined its support strictly as loan and refused to forget the debt, which was one of the reasons for the 1990–1991 Gulf War during which Iraq invaded Kuwait.

RONALD REAGAN STARTS IN THE WHITE HOUSE

the Saudis knew that, under the prevailing circumstances, Saddam Husayn was their best bet to counter the Iranian threat, and therefore, to prolong their monarchy's survival.

RONALD REAGAN STARTS IN THE WHITE HOUSE

The dramatic 444-day-long hostage crisis and its aftermath—which started on November 4, 1979, when 66 Americans were taken as hostage at the US Embassy in Tehran—was a turning point that eventually led President Carter's defeat in his reelection campaign at the 1980 presidential elections. Therefore, Ronald Reagan was elected as the 40th President of the United States (1981–1988) in November 1980.[37] At this point it is useful to note that President Reagan's foreign policy approach was very different in comparison to what President Carter had advocated during his term in the White House. Concerning Saudi Arabia, however, President Reagan's foreign policy was most significantly pragmatic with the aim of confronting the Soviet Union and winning the Cold War.

The Reagan Administration's anti-communist strategy to defeat the global influence of the Soviet Union came to be known as the 'Reagan Doctrine' and it was the highlight of US foreign policy from the start of Reagan's term in the White House until the collapse of the Soviet Union and the end of the Cold War in 1991. Under the Reagan Doctrine, the United States supplied overt and covert aid to anti-communist resistance movements and mercenaries in effort to curtail Soviet-sponsored pro-communist governments in Africa, Asia, and Latin America. Since Saudi monarchy considered Soviet-sponsored revolution as one of the main threats to its survival, its royal family welcomed Reagan's foreign policy, which was more in line with the Saudi strategic interests. In other words, the primary reason, which contributed to the changed Saudi position

---

[37] Two embarrassing implications emerge from the American policy regarding the hostage crisis. First is Carter Administration's blatant failure to bring the hostages home because of a botched rescue operation in April 1980, which greatly increased the tension in the oil market. Second is the alleged deal between the Reagan's presidential campaign and the Tehran regime to delay the release of the American hostages—first to ensure Carter's defeat in his reelection and second to continue delaying the release of the hostages until Reagan's inaugural ceremony in January 1981. In return, the Iranians were admitted spare parts and resupplies for their American-made weapons, which the Iranians needed in the battle against the Iraqi forces. Gary Sick, *October Surprise*, 144; Gary Sick, "The Election Story of the Decade," *The New York Times*, April 15, 1991, 17. See also: Bani-Sadr, *My turn to Speak*, 21–39.

200   S. E. WILLNER

toward the American foreign policy, was that the Reagan Administration had returned to *realpolitik*, which was a major contrast to Carter's earlier human rights-focused foreign policy. In February 1981, one month after President Reagan had assumed office, Deputy Prime Minister Fahd stated that "[Reagan's] statements are strong and they place opinions in specific and clear frameworks and this is something which is required of the United States."[38] From the Saudi point of view, the difference between Carter's and Reagan's foreign policies was quite significant.

As noted by Paul Wolfowitz, the Director of the Policy Planning Staff at the Department of State (1981–1982), in September 1981, "the United States had taken the plunge and given the Saudis what they really wanted," which was "a guarantee that the US would safeguard the dynasty."[39] According to Wolfowitz, this was a major reversal in the American foreign policy. He said that following the Vietnam War there had been a popular conviction in the United States that it should never again engage in "comparable foreign adventures and must not tie itself to unstable or dictatorial regimes." Wolfowitz indicated that such an ideology had influenced Carter's foreign policy toward the Shah of Iran and had been a factor in his downfall. To highlight the difference in the new American foreign policy, Wolfowitz manifested that "the new administration had, however, decided to change course and to accept a commitment to the Saudi regime."[40] In other words, as President Reagan had pointed out in his memoirs, "[he did not] want Saudi Arabia to become another Iran."[41]

Finally, it is useful to point out that Saudi Arabia became a major financial contributor to the Reagan Doctrine. Rachel Bronson, an American political scientist, quoted an anonymous CIA operative who said that "the Saudis had independent motives to fund anti-Communists anywhere they were in need."[42] In accordance with such policy, the Saudis secretly

---

[38] Crown Prince Fahd made his remarks during a press conference on February 22, 1981, following the visit of King Carl Gustav of Sweden: "Interview Granted by Crown Prince Fahd ibn Abd al-Aziz to Swedish newsmen accompanying visiting King Carl Gustav of Sweden on February 22 in Riyadh," *SPA*, February 22, 1981; "Prince Fahd Discusses Domestic, Foreign Policy," *FBIS*, February 23, 1981, C1-C4.

[39] "US/Saudi Relations" (secret report), John Fretwell (Minister, British Embassy, Washington) to Moberly, September 24, 1981, no. 152, *FCO 8/4772.*

[40] Ibid.

[41] Ronald W. Reagan, *An American Life: The Autobiography*, New York, NY: Simon Schuster, 1990, 410.

[42] Bronson, *Thicker than Oil*, 155.

financed billions of dollars to movements and governments, such as the Contras in Nicaragua, to support anti-Marxist interests. Although Marxism was an inevitable enemy of the Saudi monarchy, its logic of operation suggests that the royal family had been supporting anti-Marxist forces, such as the Contras, because they wanted something in return from the Americans. The Saudis were not fighting communism for ideological reasons, but rather because they had calculated that by agreeing to CIA's request to finance its covert (warfare) operations in Nicaragua (and in Afghanistan), it would help them to negotiate better weapons from the United States. For instance, in the 1980s the Saudis transferred millions of dollars to the Nicaraguan Contras.[43]

In conclusion, the secret Saudi–US understanding in terms of sending Saudi funds to the CIA- supported anti-Marxist forces outside the Middle East region, and Saudi Arabia's financial support to Iraq to fund its war efforts against Iran, were hugely important decisions for the monarchy. This is because the Saudis were able to lobby the White House to support Saudi Arabia's weapons purchases by agreeing to financially support the anti-communist Reagan Doctrine. Furthermore, by supporting Iraq, the Saudis were able to keep the Iranian revolutionary threat in control as Iran was busy fighting Iraq.

---

[43] LeoGrande, *Our Own Backyard*, 388–393; Steven Roberts, "Prop for U.S. Policy: Secret Saudi Funds," *The New York Times*, June 21, 1987, 1.

Conclusion of Part IV The Survival of the Saudi Monarchy During the Carter Administration (1977–1981)

CONCLUSIONS

President Jimmy Carter's term (1977–1981) in the White House was not an easy period for the Saudi monarchy. In fact, throughout Carter's presidency, the Saudis had witnessed several disturbing characteristics in his Middle East policy. First, the Saudis blamed that Carter's *naïve* worldview and his unwillingness to help the Shah of Iran had led to the Pahlavi-dynasty's downfall. Second, in response to the Islamic Revolution, the royal family indicated both privately and publicly that President Carter's ineffectiveness in his Iran policy was one of the primary reasons that had enabled the religious, anti-Saudi, anti-American regime taking over in Tehran. Third, the Saudis accused that Carter's weak foreign policy had emboldened Saudi Arabia's enemies, who, in turn, had increased their attempts to undermine the Saudi monarchy. Finally, the royal family accused that the United States was more interested in Saudi oil reserves than preserving its monarchy. In response to these emerging challenges, the Saudis decided to revise their foreign policy.

Part of the Saudi strategy to prepare for the changing political situation was to restructure the composition of its financial assets. Throughout President Carter's tenure, the Saudis invested billions of dollars in gold reserves. In addition to these gold acquisitions, at the height of the political instability caused by the Islamic Revolution, the royal family made also substantial money transfers from the kingdom to foreign banking institutions. The billion-dollar gold purchases and massive money transfers after Jimmy Carter won the 1976 US Presidential Elections, and particularly following the 1978–1979 Islamic Revolution in Iran, indicate that the royal family made these moves in anticipation of the situation getting worse. These transfers were to ensure that in case there was a revolution in Saudi Arabia, the royal family would have its wealth securely deposited outside the kingdom.

Throughout Carter's presidency, Saudi foreign policy was consistently pragmatic. The royal family was often secretive and shrewd. Due to the underlying circumstances during Carter Administration, utmost secrecy was central to Saudi political maneuvering. Accordingly, Riyadh bought multi-billion-dollar weapon systems, supported its allies, and attempted to buy its enemies. It used various backchannels to convey sensitive messages and it manipulated political events for its benefit. It is paramount to understand that Riyadh's decision to side with Baghdad to publicly condemn the Egypt–Israel Peace Treaty was not based on any pan-Arab ideology or even so much from fear of revolutionary Arabs, but rather on Saudi pragmatism and cold calculation.

Essentially, the Saudis needed to build a coalition against Tehran. Siding with Baghdad and grooming Saddam Husayn to act militarily against the Iranians was a natural option since both Riyadh and Baghdad shared similar concerns about Khomeini's ideological threat. The Saudi fears of Iranian involvement in stirring insurgency in the kingdom were further justified following the Sunni-led rebellion in Mecca and the Shi'a-inspired uprising in the city of Qatif, the Eastern Province, both of which emerged in November 1979.

Usually, the Saudis would first present the less concerning issues, perhaps even overemphasizing their importance, and only in the sidelines would they present the most important issues. By acting this way, the Saudis wanted to avoid any sign of weakness. When they wanted to make a point, the Saudis often tended to show concern for other nations' problems, while indicating that they were worried about the survival of the Saudi monarchy. The Saudis chose either private or public channels to convey messages, based on which option served their interests better. For instance, if for one reason or another its private channel messages were not properly received or understood by the intended government, the Saudis turned into using public outlets such as the foreign press. Although the Saudis had made several attempts to appeal to President Carter so that he would change his foreign policy approach, the Saudis must have realized that no matter how hard they would try to convince the US president, he would still not do enough to secure Saudi interests.

Eventually, in November 1980, President Carter failed to secure enough votes for his reelection and consequently, the Democratic Carter Administration was replaced by the Republican Reagan Administration, which was more willing to accommodate the Saudi security needs. In return, the Saudis supported anti-Communist movements when and wherever it served their interests. The Saudis were not fighting communism for ideological reasons, but rather because they had calculated that by agreeing to finance CIA's covert operations, it would help them negotiate better weapons from the United States. In conclusion, for the Saudis, their own security and survival has always come first and ideological preferences second.

CHAPTER 14

Final Conclusions

The decision-making mechanism of the Saudi monarchy is fundamentally based on group cohesion, according to which the king or the heir apparent is expected to build coalitions and shape the family consensus through consultation. Within such a decision-making framework, the king is the ultimate decision-maker, but he is still expected to make decisions together with the royal family based on the interests of the monarchy. Accordingly, the most fundamental interest of the Saudi monarchy is to maintain its survival. Based on such logic of operation, everything else is secondary. Therefore, instead of ideological purity, the Saudis have been highly pragmatic when formulating their decisions, and that the survival of their monarchy always went beyond the survival of individuals. In addition to being highly pragmatic, the royal family has also been very secretive, calculative, and manipulative, and its decision-making has been often influenced by conspiratorial thinking. Basically, to be conspiratorial, one needs to be very secretive. As the Saudi case indicates, the fact that something is conspiratorial does not necessarily mean it is not true. In accordance with such characteristics, perhaps one of the most fundamental mistakes a foreign observer can make concerning Saudi Arabia is to misinterpret its monarchy's strategic interests. I am convinced that Saudi policymaking is more organized than what has been reported in the diplomatic communications and what is thought by some scholars. Behind its veil of secrecy, the Saudi interests are based on clear objectives.

© The Author(s), under exclusive license to Springer Nature   207
Switzerland AG 2023
S. E. Willner, *Preserving the Saudi Monarchy*,
https://doi.org/10.1007/978-3-031-30006-6_14

THE REPERCUSSIONS OF KING FAYSAL'S DECISION TO JOIN THE OIL EMBARGO

When in October 1973 King Faysal made his historic decision to join the Arab oil embargo, it had become obvious to many foreign observers that the Saudis held the keys to decisions that—as being the world's largest petroleum exporter—were shaping the lives of hundreds of millions of people around the globe. However, because of Saudi Arabia's weak military, but growing financial power, the radical Arab regimes considered the Saudi royal family an attractive target for political blackmail. To achieve this, these regimes used subversive activity against the Saudis. Central to their anti-Saudi campaign was to sponsor Palestinian guerrilla organizations to sabotage and terrorize the kingdom so that these organizations could extort financial gain from the monarchy. By doing so, the radical Arab regimes wanted to alter the pragmatic pro-Western Saudi foreign policy, of which oil played a key role. In response to this radical Arab threat, the Saudis began to explore the spectrum of available foreign policy options.

The fact that there was initially no clear Saudi position concerning the possible use of oil weapon *vis-à-vis* the 1973 Arab–Israeli War could indicate that the Saudis wanted to play time and avoid openly taking sides in such a politically dangerous conflict. Such a conduct is consistent with the Saudi preference of leaving all options open and thus avoiding hazardous political alliances. However, as several diplomatic communications point out, during King Faysal's rule there were notable differences within the royal family concerning the policy of how the Saudi monarchy's survival should be achieved.

Around the time when King Faysal decided to join the oil embargo, some of the senior princes had a major concern regarding the wisdom of such a decision. As it seems, the king had disregarded their warnings about the dangers of the embargo to their monarchy. It remains unknown whether the royal family had been unanimously against Faysal's decision to join the oil embargo. However, based on the available evidence, it is obvious that there had been serious objections to the embargo.

King Faysal's decision not to follow the advice of his senior brothers could indicate that he had a stubborn mindset, but also that he had decided to join the oil embargo under great pressure from the radical Arab regimes. It is also possible that Faysal had made his decision based on emotions. Nevertheless, concerning the Saudi foreign policy decision-making process, the senior members of the royal family formulate major foreign policy guidelines. Following a thorough consultation process, the king either approves or disapproves the position represented by the family consensus. Furthermore, the king has the final word if the royal family is split about a certain foreign policy decision. However, if most of the royal family had opposed the oil embargo, and if Faysal still decided to go against such a family consensus, it would indicate that his decision had been against the principles of pragmatic Saudi policy.

A detailed assessment of Saudi decision-making around the oil embargo, and its aftermath until the murder of King Faysal (March 1975), highlights that the fundamental schism within the royal family was about King Faysal's handling of the whole decision-making process. Perhaps most importantly, the senior members of the Saudi monarchy were upset about what they called the king's inflexibility and his flawed understanding of the changing world. Possibly because of his old age, and perhaps also because of his religious extremism, King Faysal was increasingly preoccupied with his embarrassing anti-Semitic conspiracy theories, which caused him to believe that communism was a product of Zionism. In fact, this was one of Faysal's favorite topics on which he liked having long monologues, often taking his entire meeting time with foreign leaders. Such a state of mind left several senior princes to conclude that King Faysal was arrogant and disrespectful, and because his rigidity, he was also unwilling to follow the principles of consultation and consensus when he was making important decisions. Faysal's behavior was fundamentally against the principal concepts of the Saudi pragmatism.

One can always speculate about King Faysal's state of mind and his ultimate motivation when he decided to join the Arab oil embargo, which he made despite the swarm of objections presented by his senior brothers. Because of such a blatant disregard of the fundamental principles of the royal family, Faysal placed himself on a direct collision course with some of his senior family members. Although some members of the royal family had disagreed with Faysal about the usefulness of the oil embargo (and, foremost, they had addressed the king that the embargo endangered their survival), the royal family had stayed behind the king out of respect and to avoid embarrassment had the disagreements on such a delicate issue been published. Whereas the oil embargo was finally terminated in March 1974, Faysal decided to continue his confrontational statements of a possible reimposition of the oil embargo if his political demands were not met. Such a conduct was not in line with pragmatism. Accordingly, the royal

210   S. E. WILLNER

family did not want to risk its own survival and be involved in other people's conflicts, unless there were direct security implications to its survival as the ruling family of Saudi Arabia.

The confrontation with Washington was not in the strategic interests of Riyadh. The United States supplied the Saudis modern weapon systems, while within the framework of the 'Twin Pillars' strategy, the United States expected Saudi Arabia and Iran to keep the region from the advance of Soviet influence. From the Saudi point of view, the king's rigidity became dangerous, as it prevented him from listening to the other members of the royal family, and furthermore, because it prevented him from evaluating risks. Thus, Faysal's decisions had seriously threatened the interests of the Saudi royal family. It is very possible that Faysal's stubbornness blinded him from seeing, firstly, what the consensus of strategic interests really was inside the royal family and, secondly, how most of the senior princes might have opposed him on the way that such interests should be achieved. Thereupon, it appears that King Faysal's inability to comprehend the importance of the Saudi–US relationship in the aftermath of the oil embargo turned him into a major liability for some of the powerful Saudi princes. In a possible indication of such eventuality, in the spring of 1974 anonymous senior princes revealed to US Ambassador Akins that they had started to deliberate the next royal succession. However, it took another year until March 1975 that the succession eventually took place following Faysal's assassination. In fact, political pragmatism was so important for the royal family that alteration from such a precept could have fateful repercussions for the king. In such a case where the king repeatedly decides against the interests of the majority, the majority within the royal family could initiate a process to replace the king.

The chain of events that led to the assassination of King Faysal in March 1975 was a major turning point for the Saudis. Although the analysis lacks direct proof, the available reports and diplomatic correspondence point out that there were powerful princes who wanted King Faysal deposed and might have even been involved in manipulating Prince Faysal al-Musaid to commit the murder. It is possible that the murder, and the succession process that followed, were carefully prepared by the royal family. When King Khalid was given the oath of allegiance [*ba'yah*] shortly after, it had become evident that the new Saudi leadership had emerged considerably less confrontational *vis-à-vis* the United States—and most importantly, in terms of its oil policy. Since the Saudis had many times in the past proven to be pragmatic—while following the patterns of tribalism in such processes, which emphasize the importance of putting the monarchy's survival first—it would not be meaningful to credit this change as a repercussion of a major revival within the royal family, but rather because stubborn and confrontational King Faysal was gone.

The Importance of Understanding Saudi Foreign Policy Interests

In accordance with the Saudi strategic interests, the United States has been a major partner for Saudi Arabia since World War II. Nevertheless, the pragmatic Saudi approach to purchase arms from the United States indicates that the Saudis have, primarily, appreciated their relationship with the United States because of the very advanced American military industry. Furthermore, based on the Saudi experience with the Americans, the Saudis often suspected Washington's willingness to support them politically and militarily—especially during President Jimmy Carter's White House years.

In mid-1976, the Saudis decided to use the 'Soviet card' to put pressure on the Ford Administration so that it would provide better weapons for their armed forces. However, the declassified diplomatic communications and intelligence reports suggest that the Saudis were not serious about establishing diplomatic relations with Moscow or about buying Soviet-made weapons. In fact, the Saudis had expressed their concern that the Soviets were only eyeing their oil and that a presence of a possible Soviet military training mission would have further encouraged radical Arab activity against their monarchy. In this respect the royal family had a challenge: how to establish such a convincing disinformation campaign that the American intelligence services would believe its authenticity, or at least that they could not just disregard the Saudi attempt as deceptive.

Saudi foreign policy is largely based on personal relations. Also, keeping secrets is an essential part of their political system. To succeed in this high-level deception operation, the Saudis used the most secure and top-level personal channel. Accordingly, the royal family sent King Khalid's full-brother Muhammad to convey the Finnish government that its intention was to explore the possibility of establishing diplomatic relations with Moscow. Furthermore, to make the message even more believable, the Saudis were spreading disinformation among the diplomatic community in Jeddah that the royal family was having a trivial disagreement. Indeed, the rumored argument was so trivial that it should have alarmed an intelligence officer to conclude that perhaps the royal family had disagreed on something more serious; namely, about buying Soviet-made weapons. The successful implementation of such a deceptive approach confirms that the royal family and its inner circle of advisers truly are a very close-knit group. The royal advisors are highly loyal to the monarchy, while its members are a cohesive group the primary aim of which is to prolong their mutual survival. Moreover, such an approach also indicates that what the royal family conveys to foreign diplomats is usually carefully articulated and coordinated from its senior ranks. Therefore, to decipher these Saudi communications, and to understand their true meaning, one would need, first, to study very carefully Saudi decision-making dynamics and, second, to understand its interests before making any hasty conclusions.

SAUDI POLITICAL PRAGMATISM IN BUILDING A COALITION AGAINST IRAN

Almost every aspect of Saudi political thinking is ruled by a deep sense of pragmatism. This can be reviewed by assessing the Saudi response to President Carter's foreign policy. The Saudis claimed that the Americans only cared for the Saudi oil and that in his naivety President Carter had enabled the Shah's overthrow in January 1979—just to be replaced by an anti-American, anti-Saudi Islamic regime. The Saudis had concluded that since the Americans did not help the Shah when he was in trouble, then the Americans might do the same had their monarchy been threatened.

The Saudis have avoided risky foreign policy and military ventures in order not to jeopardize their financial assets and monarchy's survival. In accordance with the principal concepts of Saudi policymaking, the royal family has repeatedly used deception in foreign policy formulation. In light of the American weakness following the revolution in Iran, the Saudis had calculated that Saddam Husayn's government in Baghdad might turn out to be the only one willing to confront Tehran in an open military campaign. However, to gain Saddam Husayn's favor, the Saudis decided to endorse the Iraqi government's proposal to boycott Egypt after it had signed a historic peace agreement with Israel (March 1979) in spite of the fact that Egypt had been an important partner of Saudi Arabia. At the time, it was more important for the Saudis to build a coalition against Iran. The declassified documents suggest that to groom Saddam Husayn

14 FINAL CONCLUSIONS 213

to confront Iran militarily, the Saudis promised financial support and used disinformation saying that President Carter had approved the Iraqi war-plans against Iran (September 1980). Such a coalition building-process against Iran demonstrates that the Saudis were persistent about their foreign policy objectives.

The Saudis have repeatedly avoided taking unnecessary risks. However, they have still been ready to take calculated risks if they have determined that such a policy was in accordance with their monarchy's survival. Saudi Arabia's communications concerning President Carter's foreign policy provide an interesting case study. The Saudis were frustrated that President Carter had at numerous times disregarded their concerns about the Iranian threat. To convey messages to Carter, the Saudis used various methods, some of which seemed quite risky. An example of calculated risk taking can be traced to November 1979, when the armed militants seized the Grand Mosque in Mecca. If it is true that the Saudis allowed the seizure to commence despite having allegedly known about the attackers' intentions months prior, it could indicate that, following careful deliberations, the royal family had come to a conclusion that such a calculated risk was in its best interests. Perhaps most importantly, the Saudis had reckoned that by allowing the Mecca rebellion to take place, they wanted to message President Carter that Ayatollah Khomeini was not only preaching his revolution but that the Iranian revolutionary activity was seriously undermining their monarchy. As I have argued earlier, primarily, the royal family has been traumatized by the fear that they could lose the grip on their people, and by the threat of revolutions, which could overthrow the royal family, as had happened when the monarchies were overthrown in Egypt (1952), Iraq (1958), Yemen (1962), Libya (1969), and Iran (1979).

For the benefit of the Saudis, the Democratic Jimmy Carter was defeated by Republican Ronald Reagan in the November 1980 US Presidential Elections. From the Saudi point of view, the Reagan Administration's commitment to safeguard Saudi Arabia was a major reversal in the American policy compared to Carter's foreign policy. Reagan was considerably more willing to listen and accommodate Saudi needs in comparison to Carter. In return, Saudi Arabia became a major financial contributor to the Reagan Doctrine. Although Marxism was an inevitable enemy, the Saudis were not fighting communism for ideological reasons, but rather because they had calculated that agreeing to finance CIA's covert operations would help them negotiate better arms deals from the United States.

Finally, it is useful to return to the two key questions that have guided my analysis in this concluding chapter, namely—are there certain principal concepts (logic of operation) in Saudi foreign policymaking, and have the Saudis been persistent in following such principals? One can distinguish several repeating patterns in Saudi decision-making processes. For most part, the rationale of Saudi foreign policy is based on pragmatism. While operating within the framework of *badawī* tribal processes and highly personalized means of decision-making, the Saudis have consistently followed the above-discussed principal foreign policy concepts. Accordingly, the Saudis deal with each foreign policy issue based on what course best preserves their monarchy.

Appendix

Main Historic Events

Table A.1 The chronology from 1967 to 1981

1967	June	Arab–Israeli War
1967	December	Egyptian military presence ends in Yemen
1968	January	Organization of the Arab Petroleum Exporting Countries (OAPEC) founded
1969	July	Nixon Doctrine put forth; 'Twin Pillar' strategy promoted
1969	September	King Idris of Libya deposed; Colonel Muammar Qadhafi assumes power
1970	September	Abd al-Nasir died, and Anwar al-Sadat becomes the President of Egypt
1970	September	Events of the 'Black September' take place
1971	December	British withdraws military forces from the Persian Gulf
1973	March	Saudi Embassy in Khartoum attacked: hostages taken
1973	September	Saudi Embassy in Paris attacked; hostages taken
1973	October	October 1973 War starts (aka. Yom Kippur War)
1973	October	Oil embargo declared
1974	March	Oil embargo terminated by the Saudis
1974	November	International Energy Agency (IEA) established
1975	March	OPEC Summit in Algiers; Iran–Iraq border treaty signed
1975	March	King Faysal is murdered; Khalid becomes king
1975	April	Civil War in Lebanon starts

(*continued*)

© The Author(s), under exclusive license to Springer Nature Switzerland AG 2023
S. E. Willner, *Preserving the Saudi Monarchy*,
https://doi.org/10.1007/978-3-031-30006-6

216 APPENDIX

Table A.1 (continued)

1976	July–August	The Saudis make an approach to the Soviets
1976	November	Jimmy Carter wins the 1976 US Presidential Elections
1977	January	Jimmy Carter becomes the US President
1977	February	Marxist military government takes over Ethiopia
1977	May	Sabotage in the Abqaiq oil fields
1977	October	Demonstrations against the Shah begin
1977	July–August	Failed coup attempts against the Saudi monarchy
1978	April	Communist coup in Afghanistan
1978	November	Violent demonstrations against the Shah
1979	January–February	Victory of the Islamic Revolution in Iran
1979	February–March	Yemenite War
1979	March	Egypt–Israel Peace Treaty signed
1979	August	Failed military coup against the Saudi monarchy
1979	November	Mecca Rebellion
1979	November	Qatif uprising
1979	November	Iranian hostage crisis starts
1979	December	Soviet Union invades Afghanistan
1980	February	Carter Doctrine is declared
1980	April	The failed attempt to rescue the American hostages
1980	August	Soviet military exercise near the Soviet–Iran border
1980	September	Iran–Iraq War starts
1980	November	Ronald Reagan wins the 1980 US Presidential Elections
1981	January	Ronald Reagan becomes the US President

APPENDIX 217

AL SAUD'S FAMILY TREES

Table A.2 The sons of Abd al Aziz ibn Abd al-Rahman (ca. 1880–1953)

Seniority	Name of the prince	Mother's tribe	Mother	Seniority	Name of the prince	Mother's tribe	Mother
1.	Turki (1900-1919)	Banu Khalid	(A) Wadhah	21.	Nawwaf (1932-2015)	Armenian concubine	(J) Munaiyir
2.	Saud (1902-1969)	Banu Khalid	(A) Wadhah	22.	Nayif (1934-2012)	Sudayri	(F) Hassa
3.	Faysal (1906-1975)	Al-Shaikh	(B) Tarfa	23.	Turki (1934-2016)	Sudayri	(F) Hassa
4.	Muhammad (1910-1988)	Jalwi	(C) Jawhara	24.	Fawwaz (1934-2008)	Moroccan concubine	(D) Bazza
5.	Khalid (1913-1982)	Jalwi	(C) Jawhara	25.	Salman (1935-)	Sudayri	(F) Hassa
6.	Nasir (1919-1984)	Moroccan concubine	(D) Bazza	26.	Thamir (1937-1958)	Ruwwalah	(N) Nouf
7.	Saad (1919-1993)	Sudayri	(E) Jawhara	27.	Majid (1938-2003)	Armenian concubine	(M) Mudhi
8.	Fahd (1921-2005)	Sudayri	(F) Hassa	28.	Abd al-Ilah (1939-)	Sudayri	(L) Halya
9.	Mansur (1921-1951)	Armenian concubine	(G) Shahida	29.	Sattam (1941-2013)	Armenian concubine	(M) Muhdi
10.	Abd Allah (1924-2015)	Shammar	(H) Fahda	30.	Mamduh (1941-2013)	Ruwwalah	(N) Nouf
11.	Bandar (1923-2019)	Moroccan concubine	(D) Bazza	31.	Ahmad (1942-)	Sudayri	(E) Hassa
12.	Musaid (1923-2013)	Sudayri	(E) Jawhara	32.	Hadhlul (1942-2012)	Yemenite concubine	(O) Baraka
13.	Abd-al-Muhsin (1925-1985)	Sudayri	(E) Jawhara	33.	Mashhur (1942-)	Ruwwalah	(N) Nouf
14.	Abd al-Rahman (1926-2017)	Sudayri	(F) Hassa	34.	Abd al-Majid (1942-2007)	Sudayri	(L) Halya
15.	Sultan (1924-2011)	Sudayri	(F) Hassa	35.	Miqrin (1945-)	Yemenite concubine	(O) Baraka
16.	Mishal (1926-2017)	Armenian concubine	(I) Shahida	36.	Hamud (1947-1994)	Yemenite concubine	(P) Futaima
17.	Mitaab (1931-2000)	Armenian concubine	(I) Shahida				
18.	Talal (1931-2018)	Armenian concubine	(J) Munaiyir				
19.	Mishari (1932-2000)	origin unknown	(K) Bushra				
20.	Badr (1932-2013)	Sudayri	(L) Halya				

Note for the reader: Due to conflicting source information, the birthdates of the royal princes should, in general, be considered with an accuracy of around ±2 years. Source: Bligh, *From Prince to King*, 109

Table A.3 The most important branches of the sons of Al Saud

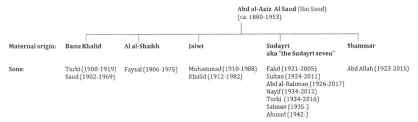

Maternal origin:	Banu Khalid	Al al-Shaikh	Jalwi	Sudayri aka "the Sudayri seven"	Shammar
Sons:	Turki (1900-1919) Saud (1902-1969)	Faysal (1906-1975)	Muhammad (1910-1988) Khalid (1912-1982)	Fahd (1921-2005) Sultan (1924-2011) Abd al-Rahman (1926-2017) Nayif (1934-2012) Turki (1934-2016) Salman (1935-) Ahmad (1942-)	Abd Allah (1923-2015)

Table A.4 The Saudi kings and heir apparents

King:	Reign:	Heir Apparent:	Period of regency:
Abd al-Aziz	1932-1953	Faysal	1953-1964
Saud	1953-1964	Khalid	1964-1975
Faysal	1964-1975	Fahd	1975-1982
Khalid	1975-1982	Abd Allah	1982-2005
Fahd	1982-2005	Sultan	2005-2011
Abd Allah	2005-2015	Nayif	2011-2012
Salman	2015-	Salman	2012-2015
		Muhammad ibn Nayif	2015-2017
		Muhammad ibn Salman	2017-

Oil Price and Production Charts

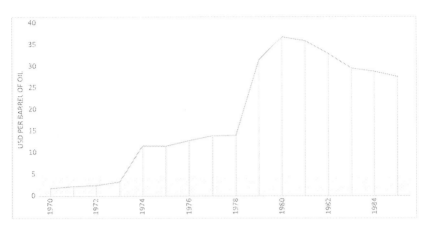

Chart A.1 Oil Prices (1970–1985), money of the day. Data source: "Annual Statistical Bulletin," OPEC

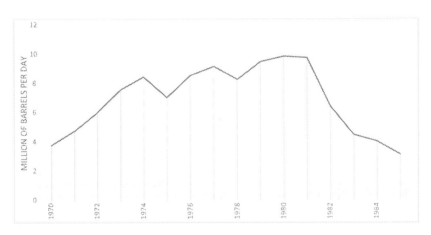

Chart A.2 Crude oil production in Saudi Arabia (1970–1985). Data source: "Annual Statistical Bulletin," OPEC

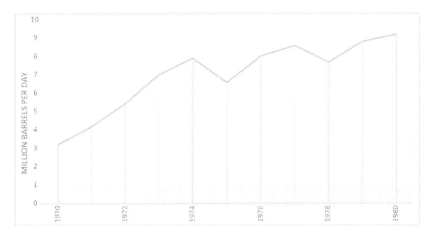

Chart A.3 Crude oil exports from Saudi Arabia (1970–1980). Data source: "Annual Statistical Bulletin," OPEC

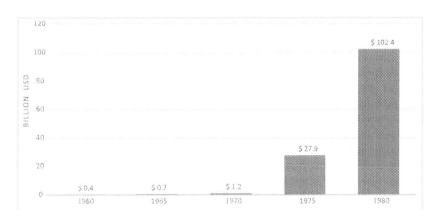

Chart A.4 Oil revenues of Saudi Arabia (1960–1980), money of the day. Data source: "Annual Statistical Bulletin," OPEC

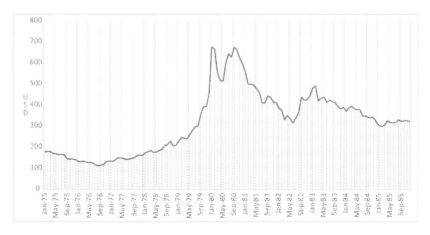

Chart A.5 Gold prices (1975–1985). Data source: "Historical Gold Charts and Data," Kitco, accessed January 15, 2020, https://www.kitco.com/charts/historicalgold.html

SELECTED BIBLIOGRAPHY

PRIMARY SOURCES

NATIONAL ARCHIVES

Ministry for Foreign Affairs, Helsinki
The United Kingdom National Archives, Kew, London
British Foreign and Commonwealth Office
Ministry of Defense
Bank of England
H.M. Treasury
Library of US Congress, Washington D.C.
Congressional Research Service
United States National Archives, Washington D.C.
Central Intelligence Agency (CIA)
Department of Defense
Department of State
National Security Council
The White House

© The Author(s), under exclusive license to Springer Nature
Switzerland AG 2023
S. E. Willner, *Preserving the Saudi Monarchy*,
https://doi.org/10.1007/978-3-031-30006-6

221

222 SELECTED BIBLIOGRAPHY

ORGANIZATION ARCHIVES

Dayan Center Arabic Press Archives (Tel Aviv)
Oral History of the Department of State (National Foreign Affairs Training
Center/Foreign Service Institute, Arlington VA)
National Security Archive (George Washington University, Washington D.C.)
WikiLeaks (https://wikileaks.org/)

PUBLISHED OFFICIAL DOCUMENTS

ENGLISH

Annual Reports of the Saudi Arabian Monetary Agency
Foreign Broadcasting Information Service (FBIS, *English*)
Foreign Relations of the United States (FRUS, *English*)
OPEC. *OPEC Solemn Declarations: 1974 Algiers, 2000 Caracas and 2007* Riyadh,
Vienna: OPEC, March 2009.

NEWSPAPERS, JOURNALS, AND PERIODICALS

ARABIC

Al-Anwar (Beirut, Lebanon)
Al-Bilad (Jeddah, Saudi Arabia)
Al-Hawadith (Beirut, Lebanon)
Al-Jazirah (Riyadh, Saudi Arabia)
Al-Jumhuriyah (Cairo, Egypt)
Al-Madinah (Jeddah, Saudi Arabia)
Al-Madinah al-Munawwarah (Medina, Saudi Arabia)
Al-Muharrir (Beirut, Lebanon)
Al-Musawwar (Cairo, Egypt)
Ar-Ray al-Am (Kuwait City, Kuwait)
Al-Safir (Beirut, Lebanon)
Asharq al-Awsat (London, UK)
Al-Siyasah (Kuwait City, Kuwait)
Al-Thawrah (Sana, Yemen Arab Republic)
Ukaz (Jeddah, Saudi Arabia)

English

Adelphi Papers (London, UK)
Arab Oil and Gas (Beirut, Lebanon)
Arab Report and Record (Ann Arbor, MI)
Business Week (New York, NY)
Financial Times (London, UK)
The Guardian (London, UK)
Gulf News (Dubai, UAE)
Harper's Magazine (New York, NY)
Kansas City Star (Kansas City, MO)
Middle East Contemporary Survey (*MECS*) (Boulder, CO)
Middle East Economic Digest (*MEED*) (London, UK)
Middle East Economic Survey (*MEES*) (Beirut, Lebanon)
Middle East Journal (Washington D.C.)
Middle East Record (Tel Aviv, Israel)
Middle East Report (New York, NY)
Mother Jones (San Francisco, CA)
New York Times (*NYT*) (New York, NY)
Newsweek (New York, NY)
Petroleum Intelligence Weekly (*PIW*) (New York, NY)
Platt's Oilgram (New York, NY)
The Sunday Times (London, UK)
Time (New York, NY)
The Washington Post (Washington D.C.)
Washington Star (Washington D.C.)

Italian

L'Europeo (Milano, Italy)

Persian

Ittilaat (Tehran, Iran)

224 SELECTED BIBLIOGRAPHY

DATA SOURCES

Economist Intelligence Unit (London, UK) (https://www.eiu.com)
International Energy Agency (IEA) (https://www.iea.org)
Kitco Metals Inc. (https://www.kitco.com/)
Organization for Arab Petroleum Exporting Countries (OAPEC) (https://www.oapec.org)
Organization for Petroleum Exporting Countries (OPEC) (https://www.opec.org)
World Bank (https://www.worldbank.org)

SECONDARY SOURCES

BOOKS

ARABIC

Al-Da'ajānī, Ahmad bin Zaid bin Ghāzī. *Khalid bin 'Abd al-'Azīz Sīrat malik wa-nahḍat mamlakah* [*Khalid ibn Abd al-Aziz: Biography of the king and the growth of the kingdom*]. Riyadh: Al-Dīwān Al-Malikī [The Royal Court], 2017.

Al-Kabbah, 'Abd Allah. *Al-sīyāsah al-khārijiah al-Sa'ūdīyyah* [The Foreign Policy of Saudi Arabia]. Riyadh: Al-Farazdaq Commercial Press, 1986.

Al-Sarḥān, Tāj. *Al-Sīyāsah al-khārijiyyah fī 'ahd al-Malik Faysal ibn 'Abd al-'Azīz Al Saud* [Foreign Policy under the Reign of King Faysal ibn Abd al-Aziz Al Saud]. Beirut: The Arab House for Encyclopedias, 2007.

Al-Tahawī, Abdel-Hakim. *Al-Malik al-Faysal wa-al-'alaqāt al-khārijiah al-Sa'ūdīyyah* [King Faisal and the Saudi Foreign Relations]. Elharm: Ein for Human and Social Studies, 2002.

Ibn Khaldūn, *Muqaddimat Ibn Khaldūn*. Beirut: Al-Maṭba'a Al-Adbīyyah, 1900.

Kurd 'Ali, Muhammad, ed. *Rasā'il al-Bulaghā* [Letters of Communication]. Cairo: Muṣṭafa Al-Bābī Al-Ḥalabī, 1913.

Kutbī, Hasan M. *Sīyāsatanā wa-ahdāfinā* [Our Aims and Our Policies]. Jeddah: Dar al-Shroweq Publication, 1981.

Shahrī, 'Ali, Muhammad, 'Ahmad. *Al-'alāqāt al- Sa'ūdīyyah al-Sūfiatīyyah wa-al-Sa'ūdīyyah al-Rūsīyah, 1926 -1997* [The Saudi-Soviet and the Saudi-Russian Relations, 1926-1997]. Riyadh: Dar Ashbīlīyah, 2001.

ENGLISH

Abir, Mordechai. *Oil, Power and Politics: Conflict in Arabia, the Red Sea and the Gulf.* London: Frank Cass and Company, 1974.

Abir Mordechai. *Saudi Arabia in the Oil Era: Regime and Elites: Conflict and Collaboration.* London: Croom Helm, 1988.

SELECTED BIBLIOGRAPHY 225

Abir, Mordechai. *Saudi Arabia: Government, Society and the Gulf Crisis*. London: Routledge, 1993.

Aburish, Said K. *The Rise, Corruption and Coming Fall of the House of Saud*. New York, NY: St. Martin's Griffin, 1996.

Adelman, Morris. *The Genie Out of the Bottle*, Cambridge, MA: The MIT Press, 1996.

Ahmad, Zaid. *The Epistemology of Ibn Khaldun*. London: Routledge Curzon, 2003.

Ahrari, Mohammed E. *OPEC: The Failing Giant*. Lexington, KY: The University Press of Kentucky, 1986.

Algosaibi, Ghazi, A. *Yes. (Saudi) Minister: A Life in Administration*. London: London Centre of Arab Studies, 1999.

Allen, Robert, ed., *Chambers Encyclopedic English Dictionary*. Edinburgh: Chambers, 1994.

Amuzegar, Jahangir. *Managing the Oil Wealth: OPEC's Windfalls and Pitfalls*. New York, NY: I.B. Tauris & Co, 1999.

Arjomand, Said. *The Turban for the Crown: The Islamic Revolution in Iran*. New York, NY: Oxford University Press, 1988.

Arkless, David C. *The Secret War: Dhofar, 1971-1972*, London: W. Kimber, 1988.

Badeeb, Saeed. *The Saudi-Egyptian Conflict over North Yemen, 1962-1970*. Boulder, CO: Westview Press, 1986.

Badeeb, Saeed. *Saudi-Iranian Relations, 1932-1982*. London: Centre for Arab and Iranian Studies, 1993.

Baer, Robert, *Sleeping with the Devil: How Washington Sold Our Soul for Saudi Crude*. New York, NY: Three Rivers Press, 2003.

Bailey, Clinton. *A Culture of Desert Survival: Bedouin Proverbs from Sinai and the Negev*. New Haven, CT: Yale University Press, 2004.

Bakhash, Shaul. *The Politics of Oil and Revolution in Iran*. Washington, D.C.: The Brookings Institute, 1982.

Bakhash, Shaul. *The Reign of the Ayatollahs: Iran and the Islamic Revolution*. New York, NY: Basic Books, 1984.

Bani-Sadr, Abol Hassal. *My Turn to Speak: Iran, the Revolution and Secret Deals with the U.S.* Washington, D.C.: Brassey's, 1991.

Bar-Joseph, Uri. *The Watchman Fell Asleep: The Surprise of Yom Kippur and its Sources*. Albany, NY: State University of New York Press, 2005.

Baram, Amatzia. *Culture, History and Ideology in the Formation of Bathist Iraq, 1968-1991*. New York, NY: St. Martin's Press, 1991.

Baram, Amatzia. *Saddam Husayn and Islam, 1968-2003: Ba'thi Iraq from Secularism to Faith*. Washington, D.C.: Woodrow Wilson Center Press, 2014.

Barnett, Michael. *Dialogues in Arab Politics*. New York, NY: Columbia University Press, 1998.

Ben-Dor, Gabriel and David B. Dewitt eds. *Conflict Management in the Middle East*. Lexington, MA: Lexington Books, 1987.

226 SELECTED BIBLIOGRAPHY

Binah, Shulamit. *United States-Iraq Bilateral Relations: Confusion and Misperception from 1967 to 1979.* London: Vallentine Mitchell, 2018.

Bligh, Alexander. *From Prince to King: Royal Succession in the House of Saud in the Twentieth Century.* New York, NY: New York University Press, 1984.

Bronson, Rachel. *Thicker Than Oil: America's Uneasy Partnership with Saudi Arabia.* Oxford: Oxford University Press, 2006.

Brzezinski, Zbigniew. *Power and Principle: Memoirs of the National Security Advisor 1977-1981.* New York, NY: Farrar, Strauss, and Giroux, 1983.

Burr, J. Millard and Robert O. Collins. *Africa's Thirty Years War: Libya, Chad and the Sudan 1963-1993.* Boulder, CO: Westview Press, 1999.

Carter, Jimmy. *Keeping Faith: Memoirs of a President.* New York, NY: Bantam Books, 1995.

Chalabi, Fadhil, J. *Oil Policies and Myths: Analysis and Memoir of an OPEC Insider.* New York, NY: I.B. Tauris & Co, 2010.

Chubin, Shahram and Sepehr Zabih. *The Foreign Relations of Iran: A Developing State in a Zone of Great-Power Conflict.* Berkeley, CA: University of California Press, 1974.

Citino, Nathan, J. *From Arab Nationalism to OPEC: Eisenhower, King Saud, and the Making of U.S.-Saudi Relations.* Bloomington, IN: Indiana University Press, 2002.

Claes, Dag Harald. *The Politics of Oil-Producer Cooperation.* Boulder, CO: Westview Press, 2001.

Cobban, Helena. *The Palestinian Liberation Organization: People, Power and Politics.* New York, NY: Cambridge University Press, 1984.

Collier, David. *Democracy and the Nature of American Influence in Iran, 1941-1979.* Syracuse, NY: Syracuse University Press, 2017.

Cordesman, Anthony and Abraham Wagner. *The Iran-Iraq War.* Boulder, CO: Westview Press, 1990.

Cottrell, Alfred J. *The Persian Gulf States: A General Survey.* Baltimore, MD: The Johns Hopkins University Press, 1980.

Cooper, Andrew Scott. *The Oil Kings: How the US, Iran and Saudi-Arabia Changed the Balance of Power in the Middle East.* London: OneWorld Publications, 2012.

Crone, Patricia. *God's Rule: Government and Islam.* New York, NY: Columbia University Press, 2004.

Deeb, Mary Jane. *Libya's Foreign Policy in North Africa.* Boulder, CO: Westview Press, 1991.

Edmonds, Robin. *Soviet Foreign Policy: The Brezhnev Years.* Oxford: Oxford University Press, 1984.

Emerson, Steven. *The American House of Saud: The Secret Petrodollar Connection.* New York, NY: F. Watts, 1985.

SELECTED BIBLIOGRAPHY   227

Evans, John and Gavin Brown. *OPEC and the World Energy Market: A Comprehensive Reference Guide*. Essex: Longman, 1993.

Fawcett, Louise L'Estrange. *Iran and the Cold War: the Azerbaijan Crisis of 1946*. Cambridge: Cambridge University Press, 1992.

Field, Michael. *The Merchants: The Big Business Families of Saudi Arabia and the Gulf States*. New York, NY: The Overlook Press, 1985.

Gasiorowski, Mark and Malcolm Byrne, eds. *Mohammad Mosaddeq and the 1953 Coup in Iran*. Syracuse, NY: Syracuse University Press, 2004.

Gaury De, Gerald. *Faisal: King of Saudi Arabia*. London: Arthur Barker, 1966.

Gause, F. Gregory III. *Saud-Yemeni Relations: Domestic Structures and Foreign Influence*. New York, NY: Columbia University Press, 1990.

Gause, F. Gregory III. *Oil Monarchies: Domestic and Security Challenges in the Arab Gulf States*. New York, NY: Council on Foreign Relations, 1994.

Gause, F. Gregory III. *Saudi Arabia in the Middle East*. New York, NY: Council on Foreign Relations, 2011.

Ghanim, Shukri. *OPEC: The Rise and Fall of an Exclusive Club*. London: Routledge & Kegan Paul, 1986.

Gilbar, Gad G. *The Middle East Oil Decade and Beyond: Essays in Political Economy*. London: Frank Cass & Co, 1997.

Gold, Dore. *Hatred's Kingdom: How Saudi Arabia Supports the New Global Terrorism*. Washington, D.C.: Regnery Publishers, 2003.

Goldberg, Jacob. *The Foreign Policy of Saudi Arabia: The Formative Years, 1902-1918*. Cambridge, MA: Harvard University Press, 1986.

Goldstein, Judith and Robert O. Keohane, eds. *Ideas and Foreign Policy: Beliefs, Institutions, and Political Change*. Ithaca, NY: Cornell University Press, 1993.

Golub, David. *When Oil and Politics Mix Saudi Oil Policy, 1973-1985*. Cambridge, MA: Center for Middle East Studies, Harvard University, 1985.

Goodin, Robert E. *The Oxford Handbook of International Relations*. Oxford: Oxford University Press, 2010.

Griffin, James M. and David J. Teece, eds. *OPEC Behavior and World Oil Prices*. London: George Allen & Unvin, 1982.

Halliday, Fred. *Arabia without Sultans: A Political Survey of Instability in the Arab World*. New York, NY: Vantage Books, 1975.

Hart, Parker, T. *Saudi Arabia and the United States: Birth of a Security Partnership*. Bloomington, IN: Indiana University Press, 1998.

Haydock, Michael D. *City under Siege: The Berlin Blockade and Airlift, 1948-1949*. Washington, D.C.: Brassey's, 2000.

Hegghammer, Thomas and Stephanie Lacroix. *The Meccan Rebellion: The Story of Juhaiman al Utaibi Revisited*. Bristol: Amal Press, 2011.

Helms, Christine Moss. *The Cohesion of Saudi Arabia: Evolution of Saudi Arabia*. Baltimore, MD: The Johns Hopkins University, 1981.

228 SELECTED BIBLIOGRAPHY

Herb, Michael. *All in the Family: Absolutism, Revolution, and Democracy in the Middle Eastern Monarchies.* Albany, NY: State University of New York Press, 1999.

Hertog, Steffen. *Princes, Brokers and Bureaucrats: Oil and the State in Saudi Arabia.* Ithaca, NY: Cornell University Press, 2010.

Hobday, Peter. *Saudi Arabia Today.* New York, NY: St. Martin's Press, 1978.

Holden, David and Richard Johns. *The House of Saud.* London: Sidgwick & Jackson, 1981.

Holden, David. *Inside the Kingdom: Kings, Clerics, Modernists, Terrorists, and the Struggle for Saudi Arabia.* London: Penguin Books, 2010.

House, Karen Elliott. *On Saudi Arabia: Its People, Past, Religion Fault-Lines and Future.* New York, NY: Vantage Books, 2013.

Hudson, Michael C. *Arab Politics: The Search for Legitimacy.* New Haven, CT: Yale University Press, 1980.

Hurewitz, Jacob Coleman. *Diplomacy in the Near and Middle East: A Documentary Record: 1914-1956 Volume II.* New York, NY: Octagon Books, 1972.

Ibn Khaldoun. *The Muqaddimah: An Introduction to History.* Transl. Franz Rosenthal. Princeton, NJ: Princeton University Press, 1967.

Ismael, Tareq. *Iraq and Iran: Roots of Conflict.* Syracuse, NY: Syracuse University Press, 1982.

Jeapes, Tony. *SAS: Secret War.* London: Harper Collins, 1996.

Johany, Ali D. *The Myth of the OPEC Cartel: The Role of Saudi Arabia.* New York, NY: John Wiley, 1982.

Jones, Toby Craig. *Desert Kingdom: How Oil and Water Forged Modern Saudi Arabia.* Cambridge, MA: Harvard University Press, 2010.

Kaplan, Robert D. *The Arabists: The Romance of an American Elite.* New York, NY: Free Press, 1993.

Karmon, Eli. *Coalitions between Terrorist Organizations: Revolutionaries, Nationalists and Islamists.* Leiden: Martinus Nijhoff Publisher, 2005.

Karsh, Efraim ed. *The Iran-Iraq War: Impact and Implications.* New York, NY: St. Martin's Press, 1989.

Katz, Mark N. *Russia and Arabia: Soviet Foreign Policy toward the Arabian Peninsula.* Baltimore, MA: The Johns Hopkins University Press, 1986.

Katzenstein, Peter J. ed. *The Culture of National Security: Norms and Identity in World Politics.* New York, NY: Columbia University Press, 1996.

Kechichian, Joseph A. *Oman and the World: The Emergence of Independent Foreign Policy.* Santa Monica, CA: Rand, 1995.

Kechichian, Joseph A. *Succession in Saudi Arabia.* New York, NY: Palgrave, 2001.

Kechichian, Joseph A. *Power and Succession in Arab Monarchies: A Reference Guide.* Boulder, CO: Lynne Rienner Publishers, 2008.

Kechichian, Joseph A. *Iffat al Thunayan: An Arabian Queen,* Sussex: Sussex Academic Press, 2014.

SELECTED BIBLIOGRAPHY   229

Keddie, Nikki. *Modern Iran: Roots and Results of Revolution*. New Haven, CT: Yale University Press, 2003.

Khoury, Philip S. and Joseph Kostiner, eds. *Tribe and State Formation in the Middle East*. London: I.B. Tauris, 1990.

Khuri, Fuad, I. *Tribe and State in Bahrain. The Transformation of Social and Political Authority in an Arab State*. Chicago, IL: University of Chicago Press, 1980.

Kimche, David. *The Last Option: After Nasser, Arafat, & Saddam Hussein: The Quest for Peace in the Middle East*. New York, NY: Charles Scribner's Sons, 1991.

Kinzer, Stephen. *All the Shah's Men: An American Coup and the Roots of Middle East Terror*. Hoboken, NJ: John Wiley & Sons, 2008.

Kissinger, Henry. *White House Years*. Boston, MA: Little Brown, 1979.

Kissinger, Henry. *Years of Upheaval*. Boston, MA: Little Brown, 1982.

Kissinger, Henry. Years of Renewal. New York, NY: Touchstone, 2000.

Korn, David. *Assassination in Khartoum*. Bloomington, IN: Indiana University Press, 1993.

Kostiner, Joseph. *The Struggle for South Yemen*. London: Croom Helm, 1984.

Kostiner, Joseph. *South Yemen's Revolutionary Strategy, 1970-1985: From Insurgency to Bloc Politics*. Boulder, CO: Westview Press, 1990.

Kostiner, Joseph. *The Making of Saudi Arabia 1916-1936: From Chieftaincy to Monarchical State*. New York, NY: Oxford University Press, 1993.

Lacey, Robert. *The Kingdom*. New York, NY: Harcourt Brace Jovanovich, Publishers, 1982.

Lacey, Robert. *Inside the Kingdom: Kings, Clerics, Modernists, Terrorists, and the Struggle for Saudi Arabia*. New York, NY: Penguin Books, 2009.

LeoGrande, William. *Our Own Backyard: The United States in Central America, 1977-1992*. Chapel Hill, NC: University of North Carolina Press, 1998.

Lieber, Robert J. *The Oil Decade: Conflict and Cooperation in the West*. Lanham, MD: University Press of America, 1986.

Lippman, Thomas. *Inside the Mirage: America's Fragile Partnership with Saudi Arabia*. Boulder, CO: Westview Press, 2004.

Lippman, Thomas. *Saudi Arabia on the Edge: The Uncertain Future of an American Ally*. Washington, D.C.: Potomac Books, 2012.

Long, David. *Kingdom of Saudi Arabia*. Gainesville, FL: University Press of Florida, 1997.

Lorenz, Joseph, P. *Egypt and the Arabs: Foreign Policy and the Search for National Identity*. Boulder, CO: Westview Press, 1990.

Louer, Laurence. *Transnational Shia Politics: Religious and Political Networks in the Gulf*. New York, NY: Columbia University Press, 2008.

Mackey, Sandra. *The Saudis: Inside the Desert Kingdom*. Boston, MA: Houghton Mifflin, 1987.

230 SELECTED BIBLIOGRAPHY

El Mallakh, Ragaei. ed. *OPEC: Twenty Years and Beyond*. Boulder, CO: Westview Press, 1982.

Malovany, Pesach. *Wars of Modern Babylon: A History of the Iraqi Army from 1921-2003*. Lexington, KY: The University Press of Kentucky, 2017.

Maoz, Moshe. *Syria Under Hafiz al-Assad: New Domestic and Foreign Policies*. Jerusalem: Hebrew University of Jerusalem, 1975.

Maoz, Moshe and Avner Yaniv. *Syria under Assad: Domestic Constraints and Regional Risks*. London: Croom Helms, 1986.

Maoz, Moshe. *The Sphinx of Damascus: A Political Biography*. London: Weidenfeld and Nicolson, 1988.

Mason, Robert. *Foreign Policy in Iran and Saudi Arabia: Economics and Diplomacy in the Middle East*. London: I.B. Tauris, 2014.

Menoret Pascal. *The Saudi Enigma: A History*. London: Zed Books, 2005.

OPEC. *Official Resolutions and Press Releases, 1960-1980*. Oxford: Pergamon Press, 1980.

Page, Stephen. *The Soviet Union and the Yemens: Influence on Asymmetrical Relationships*. New York, NY: Praeger, 1985.

Partrick, Neil, ed. *Saudi Arabian Foreign Policy: Conflict and Cooperation*. London: I.B. Tauris & Co., 2016.

Pennar, Jaan. *The U.S.S.R. and the Arabs: The Ideological Dimension*. New York, NY: Crane, Russak, 1973.

Peterson, Eric R. *The Gulf Cooperation Council: Search for Unity in a Dynamic Region*. Boulder, CO: Westview Press, 1988.

Peterson, J.E. *Saudi Arabia and the Illusion of Security*. New York, NY: Oxford University Press, 2002.

Podeh, Elie. *The Decline of Arab Unity: The Rise and Fall of the United Arabic Republic*. Brighton: Sussex Academic Press, 1999.

Posner, Gerald. *Secrets of the Kingdom: The Inside Story of the Saudi-U.S. Connection*. New York, NY: Random House, 2005.

Primakov, Yevgeny. *Russia and the Arabs: Behind the Scenes in the Middle East from the Cold War to the Present*. Transl. Paul Gould. New York, NY: Basic Books, 2009.

Quandt, William B. *Saudi Arabia in the 1980s: Foreign Policy, Security, and Oil*. Washington, D.C.: Brookings Institution, 1981.

Quandt, William B. *Saudi Arabia's Oil Policy*. Washington, D.C.: Brookings Institution Press, 1982.

Ramazani, Rouhollah, K. *The Gulf Cooperation Council: Record and Analysis*. Charlottesville, VA: University Press of Virginia, 1988.

Al-Rasheed, Madawi, ed. *Salman's Legacy: The Dilemmas of a New Era in Saudi Arabia*. New York, NY: Oxford University Press, 2018.

Al-Rasheed, Madawi. *The Son King: Reform and Repression in Saudi Arabia*. Oxford, Oxford University Press, 2021.

SELECTED BIBLIOGRAPHY 231

Reagan, Ronald. *An American Life: The Autobiography.* New York, NY: Simon Schuster, 1990.

Rieger, Rene. *Saudi Arabian Foreign Relations: Diplomacy and Mediation in Conflict Resolution.* New York, NY: Routledge, 2017.

Robinson, Jeffrey. *Yamani the Inside Story.* New York, NY: The Atlantic Monthly Press, 1989.

Ronen, Yehudit. *Qadhafi's Libya in World Politics.* Boulder, CO: Lynne Rienner Publishers, 2008.

Rubin Barry. *Paved with Good Intentions: The American Experience and Iran.* New York, NY: Oxford University Press, 1980.

Rubin, Barry. *Revolution until Victory: The Politics and History of the PLO.* Cambridge, MA: Harvard University Press, 1994.

Rugh, Andrea B. *The Political Culture of Leadership in the United Arab Emirates.* New York, NY: Palgrave Macmillan, 2007.

Rustow Dankwart A. and John F. Mugno. *OPEC: Success and Prospects.* London: Martin Robertson & Company, 1976.

Rustow, Dankwart A. *Oil and Turmoil: America Faces OPEC and the Middle East.* New York, NY: Norton, 1982.

Safran, Nadav. *Saudi Arabia: The Ceaseless Quest for Security.* Cambridge, MA: The Belknap Press of Harvard University Press, 1985.

Al-Semmari, Fahd. *A History of the Arabian Peninsula.* Transl. Salma K. Jayyusi. New York, NY: I.B. Tauris, 2010.

Seymour, Ian. *OPEC: Instrument of Change.* London: Palgrave Macmillan, 1980.

Shawcross, William. *The Shah's Last Ride: The Fate of an Ally.* New York, NY: Simon and Schuster, 1988.

Shlaim, Avi. *The United States and the Berlin Blockade, 1948-1949: A Study in Crisis Decision-Making.* Berkeley, CA: University of California Press, 1983.

Shwadran, Benjamin. *The Middle East, Oil, and the Great Powers.* Jerusalem: Israel Universities Press, 1973.

Shwadran, Benjamin. *The Growth and Power of the Middle Eastern Oil Producing Countries.* Tel-Aviv: The Shiloah Center for Middle Eastern and African Studies, Tel-Aviv University, 1974.

Shwadran, Benjamin. *Middle East Oil Crisis since 1973.* Boulder, CO: Westview Press, 1986.

Sick, Gary. *All Fall Down: America's Tragic Encounter with Iran.* New York, NY: Random House, 1985.

Sick, Gary. *October Surprise: America's Hostages in Iran and the Election of Ronald Reagan.* London: I.B. Tauris, 1991.

Skeet, Ian. *OPEC: Twenty-Five Years of Prices and Politics.* Cambridge: Cambridge University Press, 1988.

St John, Ronald Bruce. *Qadhafi's World Design: Libyan Foreign Policy, 1969-1987.* London: Saqi Books, 1987.

232 SELECTED BIBLIOGRAPHY

Taheri, Amir. *The Persian Night: Iran under the Khomeinist Revolution.* New York, NY: Encounter Books, 2010.

Tahir-Kheli, Shirin, ed. *The Iran-Iraq War: New Weapons, Old Conflicts.* New York, NY: Praeger, 1983.

Terzian, Pierre. *OPEC: The Inside Story.* London: Zed Books Ltd, 1985.

Townsend, John. *Oman: The Making of a Modern State.* London: Croom Helm, 1977.

Vanderwalle, Dirk. *A history of Modern Libya.* Cambridge: Cambridge University Press, 2006.

Vassiliev, Alexei. *Russian Policy in the Middle East: From Messianism to Pragmatism.* Reading: Ithaca Press, 1993.

Wendt, Alexander. *Social Theory of International Politics,* Cambridge: Cambridge University Press, 1999.

U.S. Congressional Research Service. *Oil Fields as Military Objective: A Feasibility Study.* Washington, D.C.: U.S. Government Printing Office, 1975.

Walt, Stephen M. *The Origins of Alliances.* Ithaca, NY: Cornell University Press, 1987.

Waltz, Kenneth H. *Man, the State, and War: A Theoretical Analysis.* New York, NY: Columbia University Press, 1959.

Wehr, Hans. *A Dictionary of Modern Written Arabic.* Wiesbaden: Otto Harrassowitz, 1966.

Wilson, Peter W., and Douglas W. Graham. *Saudi Arabia: The Coming Storm.* Armonk, NY: M.E. Sharpe, 1994.

Wright, John. Libya: *A Modern History.* Baltimore, MD: Johns Hopkins University Press, 1983.

Yapp, Malcolm E. *The Near East since the First World War.* New York, NY: Longman, 1991.

Yergin, Daniel. *The Prize: The Epic Quest for Oil, Money & Power.* London: Simon & Schuster, 2012.

Yizraeli Sarah. *The Remaking of Saudi Arabia: The Struggle Between King Sa'ud and Crown Prince Faysal, 1953-1962.* Tel Aviv: Moshe Dayan Center for Middle Eastern and African Studies, 1998.

Yodfat Aryeh and Mordechai Abir. *In the Direction of the Persian Gulf: The Soviet Union and the Persian Gulf.* London: Frank Cass and Company, 1977.

Yodfat, Aryeh and Yuval Arnon-Ohanna. *PLO: Strategy and Tactics.* New York, NY: St. Martin's Press, 1981.

Yodfat, Aryeh. *The Soviet Union and the Arabian Peninsula.* Kent: Croom Helm, 1983.

Yodfat, Aryeh. *The Soviet Union and Revolutionary Iran.* Kent: Croom Helms, 1984.

Zonis, Marvin. *Majestic Failure: The Fall of the Shah.* Chicago, IL: University of Chicago Press, 1991.

Journal Articles

English

Akins, James E "The Oil Crisis: This time the wolf is here." *Foreign Affairs*. 51, 3 (1973): 462-490.

Arom, Eli. "Saudi Arabia's Oil Policy." *The Jerusalem Quarterly* 28, (1983):125-144.

Baran, Amatzia. "Saddam Hussein: A Political Profile." *The Jerusalem Quarterly*, 17 (1980): 115-144.

Baran, Amatzia. "Qawmiyya and Wataniyya in Ba'thi Iraq: The Search for a New Balance." *Middle Eastern Studies*, 19, 2 (1983): 188-200.

Bligh, Alexander. "The Saudi Religious Elite (Ulama) as Participant in the Political System of the Kingdom," *International Journal of Middle East Studies*, 17, 1, (1985): 37-50.

Bligh, Alexander. "Changes in the Domestic-Foreign Policies Relationship in the Saudi Context in the Wake of the Change of the Guard," *The Journal of the Middle East and Africa* 9, 1 (2018): 93-116.

Dawisha, Adeed. "Internal Values and External Threats: The Making of Saudi Foreign Policy." *Orbis* 23, 1 (1979a): 129.

Dawisha, Adeed. "Saudi Arabia's Search for Security." *Adelphi Papers* 158 (1979b): 1-36.

Dietl, Gulshan, "Foreign Policy of Saudi Arabia: Internal and External Contexts." *India Quarterly*, 4, 3-4, (1985): 363-375.

Kanovsky, Eliyahu. "Saudi Arabia in the Red." *The Jerusalem Quarterly* 16 (1980): 137-144.

Kanovsky, Eliyahu. "Rise and Fall of Arab Oil Power." *Middle East Review*. 18, 1 (1985): 5-10.

Kostiner, Joseph. "Saudi Arabia and the Arab-Israeli Peace Process: The Fluctuation of Regional Cooperation." *British Journal of Middle Eastern Studies* 36, 3 (2009): 417-429.

Longva, Anh Nga. "Nationalism is Pre-Modern Guise: The Discourse in Hadhar and Badu in Kuwait." *International Journal of Middle Eastern Studies* 38 (2006): 171-187.

Roosevelt, Archie Jr. "The Kurdish Republic of Mahabad." *Middle East Journal*, 1, 3 (1947): 247-269.

French

Mouline, Nabil. "Pouvoir et Transition Générationnelle En Arabie Saoudite." *Critique Internationale*, 46, (2010): 125–146.

234 SELECTED BIBLIOGRAPHY

UNPUBLISHED PhD DISSERTATIONS

Samore, Gary. *Royal Family Politics in Saudi Arabia*, 1953-1982, Unpublished PhD dissertation, Harvard University, 1984.

Willner, Samuel. *Tribal Solidarity, Pragmatism and Family Survival: Al Saud and the Enigma of Its Decision-Making during 1973-1980*. Unpublished PhD Dissertation, University of Haifa, 2020.

INDEX[1]

A

Abd al-Aziz ibn Abd al-Rahman, King of Saudi Arabia, 17, 111
Abd al-Karim, Tayeh, 123
Abd al-Nasir, Jamal, 35–38, 47
Abd-Allah ibn Abd al-Aziz, Commander of the Saudi National Guard, 17, 43, 62, 92, 189
Abir, Mordechai, 38, 144, 197
Abqaiq oilfields, 52, 143, 144
Abu Daud, 50, 50n61, 51
Abu Dhabi, 40, 45, 170
Aden, South Yemen (PDRY), 26, 35, 37n12
Adham, Kamal, 18, 18n33, 89, 90, 117, 155, 172
Afghanistan
    communist coup of April 1978, 145, 146, 148, 182
    Soviet invasion of 1979, 176–180, 182, 193, 194

Afro-Asian Affairs, 167, 182
Agreement of Friendship, Cooperation, and Mutual Assistance, 130
Ahmad ibn Abd al-Aziz, 17, 62
Ahram, al-, 113
Akhwāl, 18, 111
Akins, James, 64n30, 82, 83, 85, 87–90, 87n39, 101, 105, 105n8, 109, 114–118, 136, 210
Algeria, 40
Algiers Agreement of 1975, 122n62
Ali, Anwar, 81
Ameen, Mike, 143
Anti-Western liberation movements, 47
Anwar, al-, 98
Arabism of Jerusalem, 78
Arab-Israeli conflict, 44, 55, 57, 58
Arab-Israel War of 1973, 4, 33–71, 37n12, 87, 106, 145n12, 208
Arab-Israel War of 1967, 39n17, 121

---

[1] Note: Page numbers followed by 'n' refer to notes.

© The Author(s), under exclusive license to Springer Nature Switzerland AG 2023
S. E. Willner, *Preserving the Saudi Monarchy*,
https://Doi.org/10.1007/978-3-031-30006-6

235

236 INDEX

Arabistan, *see* Khuzestan
Arab oil, politicization of, 35–52
Araif, 18
Aramco, 24, 42, 51, 56, 76, 83,
83n26, 143
Arjomand, Said Amir, 149
Armed Forces Journal, 192, 193, 195
Asad, Hafiz al-, 24n5, 92, 93
Azerbaijan, 191
Aziz, Tariq, 124

B
Ba'athists, Saudi, 38
Badawī, 1, 9, 11, 21, 171, 214
Baghdad, Iraq, 19n36, 26, 29, 35, 38,
41, 42, 123, 124, 165, 196, 197,
198n36, 204, 212
Bahrain, 40
Bailey, Clinton, 10, 11, 28, 158
Bank of England, 183, 184
Baram, Amatzia, 122n61, 123,
196, 197
Baring, Rowland, 86
Bar-Joseph, Uri, 67, 129
Behrooz, Maziar, 150
Beirut, Lebanon, 48
Berlin Blockade of 1948, 76
Bishara Sirhan, Sirhan, 48
Black September of 1970, 41–44,
42n29, 49, 166
Black September Organization, 48,
48n47, 48n50, 49, 166, 166n2
Bligh, Alexander, 15
Brezhnev, Leonid, 145n12
British withdrawal from the Persian
Gulf, 53
Bronson, Rachel, 68, 200
Brzezinski, Zbigniew, 153, 163, 187,
188, 191
Tour to Pakistan and Saudi Arabia
of January 1980, 187

Bumedien, Hawwari, 93
Buraimi oasis dispute, 45
Burr, Millard and Robert Collins, 46
Business Week, 100, 101

C
Cairo, Egypt, 29, 35, 38, 50, 78,
107, 113
Camp David accords, 159
Canada, 66
Carrington, Peter, 59, 60
Carter Administration,
139–205, 199n37
Carter Doctrine, 179, 187
Carter, Jimmy, 4, 6, 139–205, 142n1,
155n23, 156n29, 182n65,
192n21, 211–213
Central Intelligence Agency (CIA), 5,
33–135, 100n14, 107n14,
113n36, 133n21, 142, 144, 154,
155, 155n21, 157, 163, 163n63,
167, 168, 182n65, 187–201,
188n5, 191n13, 192n21,
205, 213
Chapra, Umer, 181, 182
China, 177
CIA, *see* Central Intelligence Agency
Citibank, 182
Civil war in Lebanon, 122
Close, Raymond, 68, 95
Cold War, 1, 27, 53, 59n16, 76, 83,
142, 150, 199
Collegial responsibility, 13
Communism, 43, 108n15, 125, 132,
144, 146, 148n25, 201, 205,
209, 213
Constellation, US aircraft carrier, 162
Contras in Nicaragua, 201
Cooper, Andrew Scott, 109
Craig, James, 24n4, 174, 189
Cuba, 47n45, 144

INDEX 237

D
Danish Television, 79, 80, 107n13
Dawisha, Adeed, 144
Deception operations, 129
Denial policy, 76, 77
Dhahran, 52, 60
Dhofar
revolt, 37
War in the province of, 91
Diego Garcia, 92
Drexel, Burnham, Lambert Inc., 181
Dubai, 40

E
Eastern Province, 43n32, 175, 176,
180, 182, 194n24, 204
East Germany, 76, 144
Edgley, Peter, 183, 184, 184n71
Egypt, 4, 5, 24n5, 33–71, 36n6,
38n13, 78, 92, 95, 116, 121,
127, 128, 145n12, 159, 212, 213
Financial assistance from Saudi
Arabia, 33–71
monarchy overthrown, 28
Egypt-Israel Peace Agreement of
March 1979, 160, 204
Eid, Guy, 48
Ethiopia, 144, 144n10

F
Fahd ibn Abd al-Aziz, 12, 17, 19n36,
59, 59n17, 60, 62–64, 66–68,
81, 84, 89, 95–99, 109, 116,
118–120, 129–131, 136n1, 143,
152–155, 158–161, 171, 177,
189, 196, 200, 200n38
Fawzan, Muhammad al, 51
Faysal al-Musaid ibn Abd al-Aziz, 110,
112, 113, 118, 210

Faysal ibn Abd al-Aziz, King of Saudi
Arabia, 4–6, 17, 23, 26, 33–137,
167, 208–211
murder of, 74–136, 209
Faysal II of Iraq, 36
Financial Times, 43, 189, 189n8
Ford, Gerald, 109, 127, 128, 132,
133, 142, 211
Fortune magazine, 178
Fox, James, 120
Fulbright, J. William, 59–61,
59n16, 96, 97

G
Giscard d'Estaing, Valery, 145
Golan Heights, 66, 121
Gold, Saudi purchases, 168, 203
Gordon, Michael, 191
Grand Mosque in Mecca, 169,
170n16, 172, 174, 183n66, 213
Grand Mufti of Russia, 90, 129
Greenfield, Meg, 190

H
Haig, Alexander, 196
Hannay, David, 167
Harper's Magazine, 103, 105, 106,
109, 136
Hart, Parker, 114
Hawadith, al-, 58, 98
Hegghammer, Thomas, 170, 171
Helaissi, Abd al-Rahman, 59–61, 92,
121, 122
Helsinki, Finland, 92, 130, 131
Herdman, Mark, 120
Hoagland, Jim, 154n17, 158n39,
159, 159n43
Holden and Johns, 114
Hollaway, Tim, 182

238 INDEX

Horan, Hume A., 65
Horn of Africa, 145
Husayn, Saddam, King of Jordan, 24,
  36, 49, 122, 123, 127, 128,
  139–204, 212
  Official visit to Moscow, June
  1976, 127

I
Ibn Khaldun, 9, 9n1
Ibn Saud, *see* Abd al-Aziz ibn Abd
  al-Rahman, King of Saudi Arabia
Idris, King of Libya, 36, 39, 84
IEA, *see* International Energy Agency
Ignotus, Miles, 105–110
Imamate of Yemen, 36
IMF, *see* International Monetary Fund
Indian Ocean, 91, 92n57, 176
International Energy Agency
  (IEA), 123
International Monetary Fund
  (IMF), 183
International Oil and Aid
  Organization, 108
Intifadah of Muharram 1400, *see* Qatif
  uprising of November 1979
Iqab, al-, 50
Iran, 6, 40, 42, 47n46, 53, 69, 76,
  122, 125, 139–204, 150n2,
  155n23, 210, 212–214
  hostage crisis of November
  1979, 199
  monarchy overthrown, 28
Iran-Contra Affair, 191n13
Iran, Coup of August 1953, 150
  Operation TP-AJAX, 151
Iranian Azerbaijan, 76
Iranian Kurdistan, 76
Iran-Iraq War
  Start of, 195–199
Iraq, Ba'athist, 39, 126
Iraq, monarchy overthrown, 28

Islamic Republic of Iran, 149
Islamic Revolution in Iran, 6,
  139–204, 149n1, 151n7, 180n55
Israel, 33–71, 78, 87, 121, 167
Israeli military withdrawal, 78
Ives, British Defense Attache, 67

J
*Jabhah al-Sha'biyah li-Tahrir
  al-Filastin, al-*, 171
Jakobson, Max, 65
Jalwi, 17
*Jama'a Al-Salafiyah Al-Muhtasibah,
  al-*, 171
Japan, 63, 66
Jiluwi, Abd al-Muhsin ibn Abd-Allah
  al-, 175
Jordan-Soviet Relations
  Soviet card, pressuring the US, 128
Jumhuriyah, al-, 78

K
Kabul, Afghanistan, 176
Kekkonen, Urho, 131, 132
KGB, *see* Komitet Gosudarstvennoy
  Bezopasnosti
Khalid al-Musaid ibn Abd al-Aziz, 112
Khalid ibn Abd al-Aziz, King of Saudi
  Arabia, Deputy Prime Minister, 17,
  81, 82, 110, 117–120, 131, 132,
  136, 145–148, 159, 210, 211
  Official visit to Paris in May
  1978, 145
Kharj, 167
Khartoum, the attack against the Saudi
  Embassy, 46–52, 48n48,
  49n54, 166n2
Khawarij, al-, 170
Khomeini, Ruhollah, Ayatullah, 149,
  152–154, 157, 161, 175, 176,
  195, 196, 204, 213

INDEX 239

Khuzestan, 195
Kimche, David, 75, 167
Kimche, Jon, 167
Kissinger, Henry, 57, 58, 64n30,
    78, 79, 82–89, 87n39, 88n43,
    93, 94, 96, 96n3, 100,
    101, 105–110, 105n8,
    118, 136
Komitet Gosudarstvennoy
    Bezopasnosti (KGB), 65, 132
Kompromat, 65
Kuwait, 50

L
Lacroix, Stephane, 170, 171
Lamb, Robin D., 167, 168
Lassila, Carolus, 22, 65, 79, 92,
    97–99, 115, 116, 130, 131
Levy, Walter, 100, 100n14
Lewis, Paul, 183, 183n67
Libya, monarchy overthrown, 28
Libyan intelligence, 52, 144, 166
Lindsay, Robert (aka Lord Balniel), 43
Lippman, Thomas, 2, 65
Lord Balniel, *see* Lindsay, Robert
Louer, Laurence, 176

M
Machiavellian, 105
Madinah, al-, 96
Malhuq, Abd-Allah al, 48
Mansur ibn Abd al-Aziz, 111
Mansuri, Sayid Abd al-Rahman, 45
Marxist revolutionary
    movements, 27, 145
Massud, Muhammad Ibrahim, 65
McMahon, Christopher, 184
Mecca rebellion of November 1979,
    169–175, 182, 188, 213
Merrick, Roger, 192

Middle East Economic Survey, 148
Military intervention,
    hypothetical US, 55
Monte Carlo, 98
Moore, George, 48
Morris, Willie, 23, 45, 69
Moss, Robert, 171
Mossad, 167
Mu'assah an-Naqd al-'Arabī al-Sa'udī,
    see Saudi Arabian Monetary
    Authority (SAMA)
Muhammad ibn Abd al-Aziz, 17, 117,
    120, 131, 132
Muharrir, al-, 52
Muir, Richard, 160
Munazzamat al-Aqtār al-'Arabiyyah
    al-Musaddirah lil-Naft, see
    Organization of the Arab Oil
    Exporting Countries (OAPEC)
Munazzamat at-Tahrīr
    al-Filastīniyyah, see Palestine
    Liberation Organization (PLO)
Munazzamat Aylūl al-Aswad, see Black
    September Organization
Muqaddimah, 9
Musaddiq, Muhammad, 150, 153
Musaid ibn Abd al-Aziz, 17
Muslim world, 177

N
Nasir ibn Abd al-Aziz, 111
Nasserism, 39
NATO, 85
Nayif ibn Abd al-Aziz, 17, 43, 62
Netherlands, 66
Newsweek, 98, 100, 116, 188, 190
New York Times, 100, 143, 154, 162,
    171, 191
Nixon, Richard, 5, 43, 53, 61, 66,
    73–135, 142
Noel, Cleo, 48

240 INDEX

North Korea, 47n45, 144
North Yemen (YAR), 36–38,
36n7, 91, 161
Nuclear bombardment, 77
Numan, Ahmad Muhammad, 114

O

OAPEC, see Organization of the Arab
Oil Exporting Countries
Oil crisis, 139–203
Oil embargo, 4, 5, 33–136, 40n19,
47n46, 88n43, 93n62, 179,
180, 208–211
Oil weapon, 5, 33–71, 79, 81, 86, 87,
95, 120–122, 208
OPEC, see Organization for Petroleum
Exporting Countries
Organization for Petroleum Exporting
Countries (OPEC), 88, 104, 106
Organization of the Arab Oil
Exporting Countries (OAPEC),
55, 69, 100
Ottaway, David B., 145, 146

P

Pahlavi, Muhammad Riza Shah,
88n43, 91, 91n54, 108n15, 119,
128, 139–203, 150n2, 156n29,
181n60, 212
Palestine Liberation Organization
(PLO), 15n24, 44, 46, 48n47
Palestine-problem, the threat posed
by, 44–46
Palestinian guerrillas, 43, 47, 107
Palestinian sabotage teams, 42
Pan-Arabism, 35–52, 35n2
Paris, the attack against the Saudi
Embassy, 33–72, 50n59, 146–148
Patrice Lumumba University in
Moscow, 172

PDRY, see People's Democratic
Republic of Yemen
People's Democratic Republic of
Yemen (PDRY), 124, 126, 133,
144, 161, 188
Persia-Russia Treaty of Friendship of
1921, 192
Petroleum Intelligence Weekly, 139–203
Pharaon, Rashad, 23
Phillips, Alan, 122
PLO, see Palestine Liberation
Organization
Popular Front for the Liberation of
Palestine, 171
Portugal, 66
Posner, Gerald, 86
The Protocols of the Elders of Zion, 65
Psychological warfare, 59,
73–136, 193

Q

Qadhafi, Muammar, 39, 40, 46–49,
58, 84, 123, 145, 146, 165,
166, 193
Qahtani, Muhammad ibn Abd-Allah
al-, 169
Qatar, 40
Qatif uprising of November 1979,
175–176, 194n24
Qazimi, Abd al-Mutalib al-, 110, 112
Quandt, William, 3, 14, 46, 57,
58, 93
Quddus, Ihsan Abd al-, 113

R

Radical Arabism, 33–71
Radiological weapons, 77
Rapid Deployment Force, 193
Ras Tanura, 42
Reagan Administration, 205

INDEX 241

Reagan Doctrine, 199
Reagan, Ronald, 199
Republicanism, 36
Revolutionary Arab regimes, 26,
  33–71, 49n52, 85, 91, 123, 125
Rhodesia, 66
Ri'āsat al-Istiḥbārāt al-'Āmah, see
  Saudi General Intelligence
  Directorate
Riyadh, al-, 27
Riza, Ali, 91, 174, 174n35
Rösiö, Bengt, 131
Rothnie, Alan K., 57, 66, 67, 82, 83,
  83n27, 119
Rumaih, Shaikh, 170

S
Sadat, Anwar al-, 38, 56, 58,
  92, 93, 159
Sahari Palace, 43
St. John Armitage, Henry, 42n24, 56
Sakharov, Vladimir N., 132
Salafi doctrines, 169
Salman ibn Abd al-Aziz, 62
SAMA, *see* Saudi Arabian Monetary
  Authority
Samson Option, 80
Saqqaf, Umar, 41, 41n20, 42, 55–57,
  63, 64, 87–90, 93, 94
Saud al Faysal ibn Abd al Aziz, 56,
  115, 120, 151, 178
Saud ibn Abd al-Aziz, King of Saudi
  Arabia, 111
Saudi Arabian Monetary Authority
  (SAMA), 127, 179, 181, 182,
  183n66, 184, 184n71, 185
Saudi General Intelligence
  Directorate, 18
Saudi National Guard, 133
Saudi Press Agency, 105
Saudi revolutionaries, 37

Saudi-Soviet relations, 130, 131
  Prior to the Second World War, 126
  Secretive Saudi disinformation
    campaign, 125
  Withdrawal of Soviet diplomatic
    mission, 126
Saudi-US relations, 58, 63,
  73–135, 194
  American military intervention, 79
  Deteriorating relationship, 79
  Henry Kissinger's visit to Saudi
    Arabia on December 14,
    1973, 87
  Saudi capacity to destroy its oil
    installations, 80
Schlesinger, James R., 83, 84, 86, 87
Second World War, 1, 76, 126, 211
Shaibani, 92, 97, 116
Shaikh, Al al-, 17
Shammar, 17
Sharon, Andre, 181
Sharqa, 167
Shatt al-Arab, 122, 195
Shawwaf, Ziyad, 42, 131, 132
Shura, Ismail, 197, 198
Sick, Gary, 152, 160
Silāḥ al-nafṭ, see Oil weapon
Silent foreign policy, 23–25
Simon, William, 96
Sinai Peninsula, 66
Skeet, Ian, 119, 179
South Africa, 66
Soviet military exercise to invade
  Iran, 191–195
Soviet Union, 27, 47n45, 53, 62, 65,
  75, 76, 83, 85, 90, 91, 99,
  99n13, 107, 108n15, 121,
  125–133, 126n2, 130n12,
  144–148, 145n12, 150, 152,
  153, 172, 176–178, 177n48,
  187, 188, 191–194, 197,
  199, 210–212

INDEX

Stalin, Joseph, 150
Stockholm, Sweden, 131, 132
Subversive activity, radical Arab states-sponsored, 33–71, 189, 208
Sudayri, Turki al-, 17, 18, 19n36, 27, 28, 62, 116, 120
Suez Canal, 38, 66, 121
Sultan ibn Abd al-Aziz, 17, 59, 59n17, 60, 62–64, 66, 81, 120, 162, 190
Sun Tzu, 105
Syria, 128

T

Taipei, Taiwan, 156
TAP, *see* Trans-Arabian Pipeline
Tatham, David, 81, 159, 160, 173n29, 189–190
Tehran, Iran, 139–203
Terror groups, 44, 47
Thacher, Nicolas, 49
Thawrah, al-, 129
Thunayan, Iffat Al, 51
Time, 100, 113
  King Faysal the "Man of the Year", 100
Tiran and Sanafir, Saudi islands of, 45
Trans-Arabian Pipeline (TAP), 43, 43n32
Transcaspia, region of, 191
Tribal politics, 14
Tripoli. Libya, 26, 35, 38, 41, 48, 48n50, 123, 166
Truman, Harry S.
  Truman Administration, 76
Tudeh party of Iran, communist, 150
Turki al-Faysal ibn Abd al-Aziz, 166, 177, 192

Turki ibn Abd al-Aziz, 17
Turki, Abd al-Aziz al-, 143
Twin Pillars policy, 53, 54, 61, 125, 210

U

Udeh, Muhammad Daud, 50
Ukaz, 136n1, 152, 153
United Arab Republic, 36
US Presidential Elections
  of 1976, 179, 203
  of 1980, 194
Utaibi, Juhaiman al-, 169n15, 170–172, 174

Y

The Young Revolutionaries, 189

V

Vance, Cyrus, 153, 154, 158
Vassiliev, Alexei, 177
Venezuela, 69
Vietnam War, 53, 77n7, 108, 147n19, 200

W

Walker, Harold B., 58
Washington, 57
Washington Post, 114, 145, 147, 159, 190
Watergate scandal, 73–135
Western Europe, 63
Wilton, John, 156–158
Wolfowitz, Paul, 200
Wright, Patrick, 59–61, 92

Y

Yamani, Abdu, 168
Yamani, Ahmad Zaki, 26, 54, 57, 63, 64, 79–81, 84, 90, 95, 96, 101, 113, 121, 143, 148, 177, 178
YAR, *see* Yemen Arab Republic
Yassa, Fuad, 49n52
Yemen Arab Republic (YAR), 163

Yemen, monarchy overthrown, 28
Yizraeli, Sarah, 68
Yom Kippur War, *see* Arab-Israel War of 1973

Z

Zumwalt, Elmo Russell, Admiral, 83, 83n25, 92n57